Windows 2 ... Security Fo...

MW00719782

Super Security Snap-Ins

Snap-in	Use
Security Templates	Create templates of security options, which can be applied to group policy and/or individual workstations (via group policy)
Security Configuration and Analysis	Compare security settings in force on a workstation to those stored in security template
Certificates	Manage certificate issued to you, a computer, or service
Certificates Service	Manage the certificate services for the domain
Event Viewer	Review details of events captured, including logon/logoff events and access to audited objects
Group Policy	Configure computer configuration and user options, as well as security settings
IP Security Policy Management	Create IP Security policies, rules, and filters.

Advanced Permissions Granted by Basic Permissions for Files and Folder

	Full Control	Modify	Read/Execute	Read	Write
Traverse Folder/ Execute File	Yes	Yes	Yes	No	No
List Folder/Read Data	Yes	Yes	Yes	Yes	No
Read Attributes	Yes	Yes	Yes	Yes	No
Read Extended Attributes	Yes	Yes	Yes	Yes	
Create Files/Write Data	Yes	Yes	No	No	Yes
Create Folders/ Append Data	Yes	Yes	No	No	Yes
Write Attributes	Yes	Yes	No	No	Yes
Write Extended Attributes	Yes	Yes	No	No	Yes
Delete Subfolders and Files	Yes		No	No	No
Delete	Yes	Yes	No	No	No
Read Permissions	Yes	Yes	Yes	Yes	Yes
Change Permissions	Yes	No	No	No	No
Take Ownership	Yes	No	No	No	No

For Dummies®: Bestselling Book Series for Beginners

Windows® 2000 Server Security For Dummies®

Cheat Sheet

Command Line Security Configuration

Command	Use
SECEDIT /refreshpolicy machine_policy / configure	Forces security settings in Computer Configuration Node of group policy to be refreshed to all objects affected by the policy
SECEDIT /refreshpolicy user_policy/configure	Forces security settings in User Configuration Node of group policy to be refreshed to all objects affected by the policy
SECEDIT /validate filename	Checks the security template specified by filename for errors
SECEDIT /configure /db db_filename / cfg templ_filename	Applies a security template, specified by templ_filename, to the security database, specified by db_filename, and then applies security in the database to local computer policy

Super Security Web Sites

The following sites have particularly useful information about security.

Site	Description
www.Microsoft.com/security	Microsoft's security resources
www.cert.org	Computer Emergency Response Team
www.w3.org	World Wide Web consortium
www.verisign	Home page of a digital certificate and public key company

Built-in Groups Created in the Active Directory

The following is the list of groups that are created automatically in the Active Directory:

- Account Operators
- Administrators
- Backup Operators
- Guests
- Print Operators
- Replicator
- Server Operators
- Users

For Dummies®: Bestselling Book Series for Beginners

Windows® 2000 Server Security

FOR

DUMMIES®

Windows® 2000 Server Security FOR DUMMIES®

by Paul Sanna

IDG BOOKS WORLDWIDE®

IDG Books Worldwide, Inc.
An International Data Group Company

Foster City, CA ◆ Chicago, IL ◆ Indianapolis, IN ◆ New York, NY

Windows® 2000 Server Security For Dummies®

Published by
IDG Books Worldwide, Inc.
An International Data Group Company
919 E. Hillsdale Blvd.
Suite 400
Foster City, CA 94404
www.idgbooks.com (IDG Books Worldwide Web site)
www.dummies.com (Dummies Press Web site)

Library of Congress Catalog Card No.: 99-66704

ISBN: 0-7645-0470-3

Printed in the United States of America

10 9 8 7 6 5 4 3 2 1

1B/RU/RS/ZZ/IN

Distributed in the United States by IDG Books Worldwide, Inc.

Distributed by CDG Books Canada Inc. for Canada; by Transworld Publishers Limited in the United Kingdom; by IDG Norge Books for Norway; by IDG Sweden Books for Sweden; by IDG Books Australia Publishing Corporation Pty. Ltd. for Australia and New Zealand; by TransQuest Publishers Pte Ltd. for Singapore, Malaysia, Thailand, Indonesia, and Hong Kong; by Gotop Information Inc. for Taiwan; by ICG Muse, Inc. for Japan; by Intersoft for South Africa; by Eyrolles for France; by International Thomson Publishing for Germany, Austria and Switzerland; by Distribuidora Cuspide for Argentina; by LR International for Brazil; by Galileo Libros for Chile; by Ediciones ZETA S.C.R. Ltda. for Peru; by WS Computer Publishing Corporation, Inc., for the Philippines; by Contemporanea de Ediciones for Venezuela; by Express Computer Distributors for the Caribbean and West Indies; by Micronesia Media Distributor, Inc. for Micronesia; by Chips Computadoras S.A. de C.V. for Mexico; by Editorial Norma de Panama S.A. for Panama; by American Bookshops for Finland.

For general information on IDG Books Worldwide's books in the U.S., please call our Consumer Customer Service department at 800-762-2974. For reseller information, including discounts and premium sales, please call our Reseller Customer Service department at 800-434-3422.

For information on where to purchase IDG Books Worldwide's books outside the U.S., please contact our International Sales department at 317-596-5530 or fax 317-596-5692.

For consumer information on foreign language translations, please contact our Customer Service department at 1-800-434-3422, fax 317-596-5692, or e-mail rights@idgbooks.com.

For information on licensing foreign or domestic rights, please phone +1-650-655-3109.

For sales inquiries and special prices for bulk quantities, please contact our Sales department at 650-655-3200 or write to the address above.

For information on using IDG Books Worldwide's books in the classroom or for ordering examination copies, please contact our Educational Sales department at 800-434-2086 or fax 317-596-5499.

For press review copies, author interviews, or other publicity information, please contact our Public Relations department at 650-655-3000 or fax 650-655-3299.

For authorization to photocopy items for corporate, personal, or educational use, please contact Copyright Clearance Center, 222 Rosewood Drive, Danvers, MA 01923, or fax 978-750-4470.

is a registered trademark under exclusive license to IDG Books Worldwide, Inc. from International Data Group, Inc.

About the Author

Paul Sanna is an independent computer consultant/author. Paul's background is varied but is grounded in software. He has sweated development schedules as a programmer, quality assurance engineer, and a product development manager. In addition, Paul has carried a bag in the field as a technical pre-sales rep selling software. Paul has also managed a team responsible for IT and sales force automation.

Paul has written books on Windows NT, Windows 2000, Windows 95, Visual Basic for Applications, and Visual Basic. In addition, he has contributed to Windows 98, Internet Explorer, and QuickBooks projects. Paul also has been known to write a magazine article or two, including covering ActiveX controls and the Microsoft Outlook programming model.

Paul lives in what he considers to be the greatest place in the world, Charlotte, North Carolina, with his wife and their three daughters — no pets now, maybe fish one day. Besides his family, his golf game and his Fender Stratocaster keep him happy during his free time.

ABOUT IDG BOOKS WORLDWIDE

Welcome to the world of IDG Books Worldwide.

IDG Books Worldwide, Inc., is a subsidiary of International Data Group, the world's largest publisher of computer-related information and the leading global provider of information services on information technology. IDG was founded more than 30 years ago by Patrick J. McGovern and now employs more than 9,000 people worldwide. IDG publishes more than 290 computer publications in over 75 countries. More than 90 million people read one or more IDG publications each month.

Launched in 1990, IDG Books Worldwide is today the #1 publisher of best-selling computer books in the United States. We are proud to have received eight awards from the Computer Press Association in recognition of editorial excellence and three from Computer Currents' First Annual Readers' Choice Awards. Our best-selling ...For Dummies® series has more than 50 million copies in print with translations in 31 languages. IDG Books Worldwide, through a joint venture with IDG's Hi-Tech Beijing, became the first U.S. publisher to publish a computer book in the People's Republic of China. In record time, IDG Books Worldwide has become the first choice for millions of readers around the world who want to learn how to better manage their businesses.

Our mission is simple: Every one of our books is designed to bring extra value and skill-building instructions to the reader. Our books are written by experts who understand and care about our readers. The knowledge base of our editorial staff comes from years of experience in publishing, education, and journalism — experience we use to produce books to carry us into the new millennium. In short, we care about books, so we attract the best people. We devote special attention to details such as audience, interior design, use of icons, and illustrations. And because we use an efficient process of authoring, editing, and desktop publishing our books electronically, we can spend more time ensuring superior content and less time on the technicalities of making books.

You can count on our commitment to deliver high-quality books at competitive prices on topics you want to read about. At IDG Books Worldwide, we continue in the IDG tradition of delivering quality for more than 30 years. You'll find no better book on a subject than one from IDG Books Worldwide.

John Kilcullen
Chairman and CEO
IDG Books Worldwide, Inc.

Steven Berkowitz
President and Publisher
IDG Books Worldwide, Inc.

Eighth Annual Computer Press Awards ≥ 1992

Ninth Annual Computer Press Awards ≥ 1993

Tenth Annual Computer Press Awards ≥ 1994

Eleventh Annual Computer Press Awards ≥ 1995

IDG is the world's leading IT media, research and exposition company. Founded in 1964, IDG had 1997 revenues of $2.05 billion and has more than 9,000 employees worldwide. IDG offers the widest range of media options that reach IT buyers in 75 countries representing 95% of worldwide IT spending. IDG's diverse product and services portfolio spans six key areas including print publishing, online publishing, expositions and conferences, market research, education and training, and global marketing services. More than 90 million people read one or more of IDG's 290 magazines and newspapers, including IDG's leading global brands — Computerworld, PC World, Network World, Macworld and the Channel World family of publications. IDG Books Worldwide is one of the fastest-growing computer book publishers in the world, with more than 700 titles in 36 languages. The "...For Dummies®" series alone has more than 50 million copies in print. IDG offers online users the largest network of technology-specific Web sites around the world through IDG.net (http://www.idg.net), which comprises more than 225 targeted Web sites in 55 countries worldwide. International Data Corporation (IDC) is the world's largest provider of information technology data, analysis and consulting, with research centers in over 41 countries and more than 400 research analysts worldwide. IDG World Expo is a leading producer of more than 168 globally branded conferences and expositions in 35 countries including E3 (Electronic Entertainment Expo), Macworld Expo, ComNet, Windows World Expo, ICE (Internet Commerce Expo), Agenda, DEMO, and Spotlight. IDG's training subsidiary, ExecuTrain, is the world's largest computer training company, with more than 230 locations worldwide and 785 training courses. IDG Marketing Services helps industry-leading IT companies build international brand recognition by developing global integrated marketing programs via IDG's print, online and exposition products worldwide. Further information about the company can be found at www.idg.com.   1/24/99

Dedication

For my girls, Victoria, Allison, Andrea, and Rachel.

Author's Acknowledgments

Like a TV awards show, there's so many people to acknowledge. Let's get started before the "get off the stage" music starts. Firstly, the author would like to acknowledge Joyce Pepple and thank her for the steady diet of motivation, leadership, guidance . . . and discipline ;-). Thanks also to Jill Pisoni for having the confidence to sign me up.

Kelly Ewing, thanks for the steady and calm project management and the great suggestions. Thanks for being so patient ("yup, you'll have that chapter right away"). Thanks also to Kyle Looper for firing me up and getting this project rolling. Thanks also to Mr. Looper for the 3-hour "Dummies 101" phone call and the copy of *Guitar For Dummies*.

Lisa Swayne, my agent, is awesome. I'll write it again, she's awesome — what a great coach and sounding board.

Thanks to Allen Wyatt for my keeping the 1s and 0s from becoming 0s and 1s. Thanks to GemPlus for the smart card kit and thanks to Jeff Ciraulo at Envoy Data Corporation for being so smart about smart cards.

I should acknowledge Coffee Works in the Arboretum. I don't know the name of the folks who work there, but those double lattés are the writers' rocket fuel!

Thanks also to our friends who baby-sat for my family on a few occasions.

And lastly, special thanks to my four girls for the regular delivery to my office of cookies, coffee, and kisses while I worked!

Publisher's Acknowledgments

We're proud of this book; please register your comments through our IDG Books Worldwide Online Registration Form located at http://my2cents.dummies.com.

Some of the people who helped bring this book to market include the following:

Acquisitions, Editorial, and Media Development

Project Editor: Kelly Ewing

Acquisitions Editor: Joyce Pepple

Technical Editor: Allen L. Wyatt

Media Development Editor: Marita Ellixson

Associate Media Development Editor: Megan Decraene

Editorial Director: Kristin A. Cocks

Editorial Administrator: Michelle Hacker

Production

Project Coordinator: Regina Snyder

Layout and Graphics: Amy M. Adrian, Kate Jenkins, Tracy Oliver, Jill Piscitelli, Michael A. Sullivan, Brian Torwelle, Mary Jo Weis, Dan Whetstine

Proofreaders: Laura Albert, Laura Bowman, John Greenough, Christine Pingleton, Marianne Santy

Indexer: Sherry Massey

Special Help: Kyle Looper, Sanders Group

General and Administrative

IDG Books Worldwide, Inc.: John Kilcullen, CEO; Steven Berkowitz, President and Publisher

IDG Books Technology Publishing Group: Richard Swadley, Senior Vice President and Publisher; Walter Bruce III, Vice President and Associate Publisher; Joseph Wikert, Associate Publisher; Mary Bednarek, Branded Product Development Director; Mary Corder, Editorial Director; Barry Pruett, Publishing Manager; Michelle Baxter, Publishing Manager

IDG Books Consumer Publishing Group: Roland Elgey, Senior Vice President and Publisher; Kathleen A. Welton, Vice President and Publisher; Kevin Thornton, Acquisitions Manager; Kristin A. Cocks, Editorial Director

IDG Books Internet Publishing Group: Brenda McLaughlin, Senior Vice President and Publisher; Diane Graves Steele, Vice President and Associate Publisher; Sofia Marchant, Online Marketing Manager

IDG Books Production for Dummies Press: Debbie Stailey, Associate Director of Production; Cindy L. Phipps, Manager of Project Coordination, Production Proofreading, and Indexing; Tony Augsburger, Manager of Prepress, Reprints, and Systems; Laura Carpenter, Production Control Manager; Shelley Lea, Supervisor of Graphics and Design; Debbie J. Gates, Production Systems Specialist; Robert Springer, Supervisor of Proofreading; Kathie Schutte, Production Supervisor

Dummies Packaging and Book Design: Patty Page, Manager, Promotions Marketing

◆

The publisher would like to give special thanks to Patrick J. McGovern, without whom this book would not have been possible.

◆

Contents at a Glance

Cartoons at a Glance

By Rich Tennant

page 9

"I guess you could say this is the hub of our network."

page 153

"They were selling contraband online. We broke through the door just as they were trying to flush the hard drive down the toilet."

page 61

"I'm sure there will be a good job market when I graduate. I created a virus that will go off that year."

page 213

"If it works, it works. I've just never seen network cabling connected with Chinese handcuffs before."

page 299

Fax: 978-546-7747
E-mail: richtennant@the5thwave.com
World Wide Web: www.the5thwave.com

Table of Contents

Introduction

· ·

*T*here's such a wide-ranging level of understanding when it comes to computer security, even among Windows 2000 users. The mental picture some persons draw when they think of security and computers is of a jean-wearing slacker (the author wears jeans and got good grades) pounding away at a keyboard (the author is hard on keyboards) in a caffeine-fuel fury (the author is crazy about espresso) attempting to break into some computer somewhere (the author does not break the law). Other people know full well that the person sitting in the cube next to them could be hacking away at a competitor's site when everyone else thinks they should be answering Help desk calls.

Some experienced users have no idea of the risk involved in sending data over the Internet, less obviously so of how data flows over the Internet. Still others see no big deal in giving someone their password or entering a credit card number when asked. Contrast that with plain old users like you and me who know to use the Windows network monitor to see whether the header on an HTTP packet includes a clear text user ID!

In fact, it's unbelievable how much everyone's understanding of security differs, even when he (or she) is close to the action. My wife told a bunch of people that the author was writing about Windows 2000 *securities*. So, lots of the author's friends wondered about the tie-in between Microsoft and the stock market. Oh, well — so much for knowledge transfer through osmosis.

So, in this increasingly security-sensitive landscape, along comes Windows 2000, with its gaggle of security enhancements. What a coincidence, or what great marketing and planning. It would seem, then, that there should be a book to help people understand how security and Windows 2000 fit together. So, when they asked who was going to describe how to implement Windows 2000 Server securely in a networked environment without boring persons to tears, this author stood up and said, "Sign me up for that duty, sir. I'll start as soon as I change out of these jeans and pour out my coffee cup."

About This Book

This book is mainly about Windows 2000 Server and then about securing it. Because Server is the brand of Windows 2000 used to service Windows 2000 networks, the book pays most of its attention to network issues. The book also pays attention to the other services Windows 2000 Server provides, like web server services. Hey, no offense meant, I like Windows 2000 Professional, and I was the person who gave Bill Gates the idea for Windows 2000 Professional's predecessor, Windows NT Workstation (only kidding). At the same time, Windows 2000 Professional is only considered in this book as a possible node on a Windows 2000 network and as a product that is extremely similar to Windows 2000 Server — most of the computer-specific things you can do on Server you can do on Professional, too, like file permissions, password control, auditing, and registry.

Security is serious, but this book doesn't take itself too seriously. You'll leave this book knowing what you must secure and how in Windows 2000 Server. You'll also leave the book with a smile on your face. I make fun of me, very little fun of you, a medium amount of fun of the software, a bit less fun of the folks who made Windows 2000, and a ton of fun of the people who hack into networks, intercept packets, deface Web sites, and masquerade as others on the Internet (they deserve it!).

I avoid using lots of the techno-jargon that would otherwise have caused you to think things like, "Yeah, but what does an IP filter packet-sniffer do?" Where I have to, I use those cyber-stumping terms and acronyms, but they're explained in as friendly terms as possible. If I need to give you step-by-step instructions, I don't gloss over any of the steps, even the obvious ones, assuming that you already know how to do parts of the procedure in the first place.

Also, don't confuse this book with *Every Window, Dialog Box, Option, Feature, Fact (Including Mundane History), And Anecdote Related to Windows 2000 Server Security For Dummies.* This book provides all the important stuff and almost none of the nonimportant stuff. If you can do some task 15 ways in Windows 2000, you'll find only one of the ways described here — usually the easiest one, but always the one that gets the job done right.

How to Use This Book

This book was built to be a reference about software security issues related to Windows 2000 Server. Because it's a reference, you shouldn't have to move from chapter to chapter to figure stuff out. You won't miss anything (like any running jokes or secret messages) if you don't read from cover to cover.

Actually, you might miss a few things if you read from the back cover to the front cover, but I think you get the right idea. You should be able to get into a chapter, get the info you want, and then get out.

Wanna find out how to encrypt file stuff on your hard drive so that the files become useless if someone steals them? Bam! Turn to Chapter 5. Are you planning on putting up a web server and would like to make sure that you cover your security tracks? Bam! Try Chapter 12. That's the way the book works.

As for each of the chapters, there's a little of everything — whatever is needed to do the job. You might find just a short description of some feature in Windows 2000. Maybe you'll find a blurb on some function in Windows 2000 and then the steps to get the function running.

What You're Not to Read

I want you to read every piece of text in this book from the front cover to the back cover. You know those tiny numbers that appear under the bar code on the back cover of this book? Yup, read those numbers, too. Actually, you can skip a few things — and you certainly aren't expected to read this book cover to cover!

Whenever you see one of these icons, you know there's technical information in the neighborhood. This information is added to make you smarter. You won't miss anything important if you skip it, except for the opportunity to get smarter.

Also, you'll find sidebars sprinkled throughout the book. You can tell a sidebar by the gray background. You can skip these if you want — you won't miss anything critical to your understanding of the topic the chapter covers. They're added to enhance your secure-reading pleasure.

Foolish Assumptions

I assume that you're bright, capable, attractive, and always well intentioned. Hopefully, those compliments will make you recommend this book to someone else. Enough of the personal stuff, though. Here's what I assume about you in terms of your Windows 2000, networking, and security know-how:

> ✔ I assume that you have used Windows. Specifically, I write as if you have used Windows 95, Windows 98, or Windows NT 4 before. Still not sure? If you know where the Start menu is, then the assumption is correct (even if a bit foolish).

✔ I assume that you have some sort of responsibility (or at least share it) for the network in your organization. You may be what everyone in your organization calls The Administrator, or you might be on the team of network geniuses, or maybe you're just the computer go-to person in your organization. Either way, I think you know something about taking care of a bunch of users. With this assumption, it's a pretty good guess that you know what a network is, too.

Here's a quick caveat to the last assumption. If you're not an administrator, it's okay — you can still read this book. However, in order to do lots of configuring described in this book, you need to have the rights to do so. Hey, you can read the book, but you might not be able to follow along with the software.

✔ I assume that you have a basic understanding of networking concepts, especially those in Windows 2000. Remember, the book title does have the word *Server* in it, so the focus will be on network issues. At the same time, Chapter 2 might get you over the hump if you're confused or unsure about Windows 2000 networking know-how.

How This Book Is Organized

Yes, there is organization to this book. It wasn't easy, but someone did bother to figure out what should come first. Here are some of the tough questions that had to be answered when it came to organizing this book:

✔ Should firewalls come before the encrypting file system?

✔ Should browser security go in the Internet Server chapter?

✔ Was that Elvis I saw buying a smart card reader?

Anyway, the following sections tell you what to expect in each part of the book.

Part I: Windows 2000 Server Security Basic Training

Part I is the table-setter of the book. Even if you know nothing about Windows 2000 (before reading the book, not after!), you'll be able to put the advice and instruction in this book to use, compliments of the chapters in this part. Same for security. Do you really know how cyber-intruders try to hack into your network? Are you clear on the risk involved in letting users in your organization browse the open waters of the Internet? If the answer is no, then Part I is for you.

Part II: Starting with a Good Defense

Strong security starts at home, and building a foundation of properly secured files, folders, printers, and everything else is covered at the start of this part. Later on, you see how you can secure a file or folder so that the file or folder can't be viewed if someone copies the files to a floppy or even steals the entire drive. Yikes. The part wraps up with two large chapters where you find out how to set the hundreds (yes, hundreds) of different security options (called settings and policy) available in Windows 2000. You also see how to roll these configurations out to everybody on the network in about six mouse-clicks, max!

Part III: A Few More Ounces of Protection

When you have created secure user accounts, figured out who should have access to what, and created security templates making it easy to roll out security, you're still not done! In fact, you're not even close. Part III is designed to raise the security bar even higher on your network. The Registry is one of the most attractive targets, so you can certainly read how to defend it in this part. Will any of your users be accessing your network from the field, maybe by tunneling in using the Internet? If the answer's yes, then Part III should be on your must-read list.

Part IV: Just When You Think You're Safe

Have you heard about IP Security? Windows 2000 provides the support you need to secure all Internet Protocol (part of TCP/IP) traffic in and out of the devices on your network. IP Security does this by examining the guts of each piece of data that hits your network, either heading in or out. Part IV covers this newest-really-cool thing.

What about that fancy web browser that ships with Windows 2000? Don't forget a browser needs secure configuring. A browsing organization might also be a browsed organization, so if you use Windows 2000 to serve up Internet content, take a look at this part.

Lastly, just building the walls isn't enough. You've got to check your defenses, monitor for breaches, see what the troops are thinking and doing, and more. This part includes a chapter that helps you monitor and audit activity on your network and presumably secured workstations.

Part V: The Part of Tens

You know it, you love it, it's The Part of Tens! Every *For Dummies* book has one, and this book is no different. This version of The Part of Tens has four chapters. Each of these chapters has ten something-or-others. For example, you can read ten pieces of advice to keep secrets secret when your users hit the road (actually, there's a lot more than ten pieces of advice). Are you thinking of kicking firewall tires? If so, The Part of Tens has a chapter with at least ten things you should know about firewalls.

Icons Used in This Book

I try not to repeat too many things in the book. Something, though, that you'll find on just about every page in this book is one of those familiar *For Dummies* icons. Here's what those icons mean:

When you see this icon, take your hands off the keyboard, move the children to a safe location, read the text next to the icon, and then read it again. You find this icon wherever there's a chance of some misfortune befalling you or your network because of something you're doing to Windows 2000.

The idea of a tip in this book is that you can skip reading it and not be deprived of anything you really must know. At the same time, if you skip reading a tip, you miss out on a great tidbit, timesaver, work-avoider, or shortcut.

Attention all MCSEs, CNAs, MCPs, CCNAs, CCNPs, CCIEs, MCTs, A+-ers, ABCs, TCP/IPs, MICKEYMOUSEs, and anyone else, certified or otherwise, known-by-acronym or not, who likes the under-hood details. This icon points out any geeky details.

There might be a few nuggets of information I want you to store in the front part of your brain (or whatever part remembers things). Watch for items with this icon. You might be asked to recall them later.

Where to Go From Here

If you're new to Windows 2000, especially Windows 2000 networking, certainly take a peak at the introduction to Windows 2000 in Chapter 2.

If you're interested in an overview of the security issues this book is worried about, as well as what you can do about security threats, then Chapter 1 is a good place to start.

Lastly, if you know Windows 2000 well and you understand security, then you're probably ready to start securing the different areas of your Windows 2000 network. Lots of the security features in Windows 2000 require you to pick which users can and can't do certain things. If you haven't added user accounts and groups to the network yet, Chapter 3 can help you do this securely. If you already have users crawling all over the network, then check that chapter to see whether there is anything you can do to ratchet-up the security around the accounts.

If you're ready to get your hands dirty, then look over the Table of Contents and pick a place to start. You really can't go wrong wherever you choose.

Part I

Windows 2000 Server Security Basic Training

The 5th Wave   By Rich Tennant

CYBERSIZERS

Thigh-Master Laptop

Nordic-Server

Abdominizer Keyboard

In this part . . .

Welcome to security in Windows 2000! If you had preferred that Microsoft trotted out Windows 1999 first so that you could warm up, then you'll appreciate chapters in this part. Also, if you're really insecure, then you might become even more insecure when you read about all the threats out there against your network. So, what's the point? The point is to give you an overview of Windows 2000 networking, including all the most basic concepts, like what's a window.

The point is also to help you understand security, but not just threats, but the defense, too. Wanna get your hands dirty early in the game, too? You're in the right part of the stadium. The last part of your warmup in this part is to configure a little security on some of the basics, like domains, groups, and users. Hey, if you don't have users, then what's the point of networking?

Chapter 1

Overcoming Your Insecurity about Security

In This Chapter

▶ Needlessly confirming that you should be concerned about security

▶ Blaming technology for most of your security woes

▶ Rounding up the usual security-risk suspects

▶ Taking inventory of your security defenses

*I*n this new, interconnected world, you're surrounded by security threats. You, your network, your computers, your family PC, and even your family dog's computer-programmed invisible fence receiver are all at risk. Okay, maybe it's unlikely that anyone would hack ol' Spot out into the neighborhood, but almost any computer is at risk. Bad folks want to steal information from your network; disable your network; acquire your users' credit cards, passwords, social security numbers, and waist sizes; and generally ruin your day. And some of these folks may already be employed at your organization! What about the outside world that wants to hack their way into your network?

But I don't need to waste time telling you what's obvious. You're looking at this book, so you don't need me to coerce or convince you about the importance of network security. All you need to know is where to look for leaks in your security plumbing and how to plug 'em up. In this chapter, I fill you in on the different types of risks to your network and give you a sampling of the defenses you can construct.

Knowing Why You Should Worry

You may be better off sweating your network security details *before* your manager's forefinger is repeatedly stabbing four inches into your chest cavity and your ears are ringing from the question, *"How did the entire sales organization get access to my salary planning model!?!"* The following list contains reasons why computer security is an important issue today:

✔ **Bad people do bad things.** *Hackers* are people outside your organization who target your corporate systems for violation, threat, and other offenses. *Crackers* try to circumvent your security measures and rifle through your sensitive documents. Keep in mind, however, that all the threats to your network don't necessarily come from outside your organization. Although resume screening, reference calls, and personal interviews can reveal much about candidates, these techniques are not foolproof. And even one-time happy campers can become disgruntled and dishonest as promotions, raises, choice projects, and good office locations go to others. You have to plan your security as carefully for threats from within your company as for threats from outside it.

✔ **The information on your network is valuable and sensitive.** Even information that's otherwise harmless, such as a user ID, a name, or information about your network infrastructure, can be a valuable aid in later attempts to break into your systems. And just because you think the information on a particular server or workstation isn't valuable doesn't make it less of a target. Much of the thrill for hackers and crackers is getting into places where they don't belong, whether the data they find is sensitive or not.

Don't forget that the same amount of damage can be done by the accidental release of private information such as salary planning, a reorganization plan, or personnel records into your organization as by an attack by your closest competitor. A simple mistake in assigning drive and server permissions can allow the release of information that was never meant for mass consumption.

✔ **Today's corporate network infrastructure is as insecure as a kitten at the rocking chair factory.** As technologies have advanced, security issues have become more challenging. The following list highlights technological advances that have become indispensable to communication and productivity (and so are probably here to stay), but are conversely security nightmares:

- *WANs.* When networks were small local area networks (LANs), it wasn't hard to figure out who was logged on to the network and who had access to certain resources by just walking around the office and taking a census of the LAN users. With the application of network bridges, however, LANs have grown into wide area networks (WANS), in which users in many different physical locations all over the world can share network resources and information. The challenge of WANs is to secure many servers in many locations, sometimes running disparate network operating systems and different classes of hardware.

- *Remote Access.* Dial-up access enables companies to grow from static, stoic, physically anchored entities to virtual organizations where a corporate office node can be born wherever a remote connection can be created. This faceless, nameless, and anonymous aspect of network access, though, is more a reason for gray hair on the heads of network and security administrators than anything else. The bank of modems that support the gaggle of remote users is often times too strong an attraction for the dark side. Remote access allows anonymous attack. By allowing remote access to your network resources, you allow a hacker to work at leisure from his or her spacious home in the hills attempting to break into your system.

- *Mobile computing.* The only good thing about mobile computing is that it allows users to compute when they're on the road. Everything else is bad. In particular, laptops are easily and often stolen. Also, data you type into a computer 35,000 feet over the Atlantic Ocean can be stolen by the wandering eyes of the passenger sitting next to you.

- *The Internet and TCP/IP.* If the struggle between technological advancement and security was civil just a few years ago, both combatants have dropped their gloves now that the Internet and TCP/IP have become important parts of network computing. A TCP/IP network, like the Internet, is actually a communal network of many connected computers, each helping to send information to its targeted destination. With this system, it is possible for a hacker to examine these packets of information as they move across the Internet as long as he knows the route.

New initiatives and technology raise the stakes even higher. Companies are integrating vendors, suppliers, and partners into their networks via *extranets* using *PPTP (point-to-point tunneling protocol)* applications. These technologies allow outsiders to become insiders on your networks by taking advantage of the biggest network infrastructure of all: the Internet.

Wait, you say you really don't know much about TCP/IP? Well, now is absolutely the time to learn. Chapter 2 can provide a baseline. To find out all the ins and outs, consider *TCP/IP For Dummies,* 3rd Edition, by Candace Leiden and Marshall Wilensky (IDG Books Worldwide, Inc.).

So What's the Worst Thing That Can Happen?

You may think that the worst thing that can happen to your network from a security-breach perspective is that someone slips in to your network and grabs a bunch of records from your AP system. Or perhaps you believe the worst that can happen is that someone logs on to another person's workstation and reads her e-mail. While each of these events should be considered serious, you probably should consider yourself lucky if these incidents were the most serious that occurred in your organization. Security breaches can range from nuisances to full-fledged disasters.

Denial-of-service nuisances

A *denial-of-service attack* does not directly damage your systems or steal information. Rather, these attacks disrupt the normal operation of your organization by denying some sort of required service. What a nuisance!

A denial-of-service attack hits your organization in one of two fashions:

- ✔ A denial-of-service attack stops one or more of your corporate systems from working, including networks or subsystems (for example, the accounts payable system or the Intranet).
- ✔ A denial-of-service attack prevents your users from receiving the services provided by your network and other systems.

An example of a denial-of-service attack at your home might be one in which your neighbor, who is really mad at you about the new shrubbery you planted, tells the garbage service that you moved. They tell the garbage service that the garbage truck should no longer stop at your home. This attack really is not damaging, it's just a nuisance. Until you figure what your neighbor did to you, your garbage will pile up, and your other neighbors will become mad at you because of the stink emanating from your home. What a nuisance!

Real life denial-of-service attacks are targeted at systems using TCP/IP. In this scenario, a large number of connection requests are made against your server. These requests have an invalid IP address as their source. Depending on how your server is configured, it will make repeated attempts to reply to the request for service. Naturally, its attempts will be unsuccessful because the source IP address is garbage. Eventually, as your server fields more and more of these invalid requests, performance on the server will degrade from hare to turtle speed.

Now, for some of your users, an inaccessible network, or a downed general ledger, may be a welcome respite from the drudgery of work (even though these users *do get paid* for the drudgery). The reality, though, of a denial of service to any of your corporate systems is a serious issue. The time your systems are down costs time, and, stated here for the first time ever, time is money.

Illegal access

One of the most benign yet still sinister types of attacks is categorized as *illegal access*. The goal of this attack is to simply outwit any network protection in place in order simply to gain access. Theft usually isn't the motive, nor is denial of service, nor acquisition of sensitive information. Some people out there get no greater thrill than being somewhere that they aren't allowed, and that somewhere is your corporate network. Probably the greatest percentage of hackers fall into this category of those who like to go where no hacker has gone before. Persons in this category aren't limited to those who don't work for your organization. This intruder may be working in your organization and doing the same sort of thing. Rather than completing work, there are those who waste time by trying to access various servers and volumes on your network to which they seemingly have no access.

Theft and disclosure

An extremely damaging threat is one posed to the value of information. What would happen if either someone were to steal valuable information owned by your organization or if sensitive information were accessed by either outsiders or by persons in your organization? Imagine the ruckus in the coffee room if someone had accessed your organization's payroll system and posted a list of everyone's name and their salary. Theft and disclosure probably are the two biggest risks persons think of when it comes to network and computer security.

You're not my session, you're an imposter!

What if someone appeared at your door claiming to be the town tax adjuster and requested all your financial and personal records? Well, if the person presented what seemed to be proper credentials, you might just hand over the documents that person asked for. Ding! Bad idea, McFly! You find out later that you handed the information to an imposter, and who knows what she will do with all the information you gave up.

This same type of attack is relevant in the computer world. It is possible, but not easy to accomplish, that someone can masquerade as the entity you expect on the other end of a network connection. When you think you are sending an order to buy zillions of dollars' worth of stock in the author's new company, you are instead sending bank account information and other details to Mr. Inscrutable.

A related cousin to the imposter type of attack is the data modification attack. In the data modification scenario, data you send or receive has been modified. For example, that order to buy stock might turn into an order for stock of another issue. Another scenario sees a hacker finding his or her way into an organization's network and then changing the content of a Web site.

Data destruction and corruption

Quick! How bad do you feel at that moment when you first realize you probably deleted a critical file? Worse — how bad would you feel (or did you feel) at that moment when you first realized your hard drive went South for the winter and decided not to come back? Imagine that same feeling tenfold if someone or something were able to break into your network and delete or corrupt data off of the servers. This type of attack falls under the data destruction and corruption category. In this attack scenario, the objective isn't to steal data or to simply prove your network can be hacked; the objective here is much simpler. The guilty parties are interested in just destroying your property. This threat can come from the outside from an external enemy or rogue individual looking to making your life absolutely miserable, or it can easily come from within your doors from an employee who is clearly having a bad day. There are only two methods used to launch this type of attack:

- ✔ **Press the Delete Key.** Hmmm. What methods might be used to destroy or corrupt data? How about . . . press the Delete key! With this method of data destruction and corruption, the target data is accessed directly, such as by gaining access to its location on the network, and then someone simply presses the Delete key.

- ✔ **A virus or other destructive program.** Once a virus infects your computer or network, it's up to the intentions of the person who developed the virus as to how much damage, if any, will be done. Some viruses do nothing more than sit around and periodically let you know they're there. Others corrupt data, such as the boot sector of a machine, making it unstartable. Other viruses chew up available disk space and memory until none of either are left and your system is nearly unusable. It's the latter form of viruses that fall into the data destruction and corruption category. Without a sound virus protection scheme, you are at serious risk.

Making Life Miserable for Cybersnoops and Thieves

The world of electronic information is dangerous, but that world isn't without protection and safeguards. A wide range of techniques and technologies protect your networks and data from the menu of security risks, hacks, cheats, and cyberthieves. Some of these techniques, such as encryption, have been around as long as there has been a need for secrecy and privacy. (Didn't primitive man need to exchange private messages with primitive woman?) Other techniques reflect the latest that the technically motivated world provides, such as *smart cards* that produce new passwords on a credit card-sized device every minute. The following sections describe the types of defenses you can raise to oppose the threats against your network and the not-so-nice elements on the Internet.

Cryptography for nonspymasters

Cryptography is the one of the most important elements to computer and network security. Cryptography is not hard to understand, but it's a bit more sophisticated than using lemon juice as ink in order to make the words you write on a page invisible. Cryptography is the technique of scrambling information into an unreadable form so that information is kept private. What kind of information might be encrypted in order to be kept secret? Here are some examples:

✔ Important, sensitive information stored on a computer, such as salary information, an organization's ledger, or even everyone's passwords

✔ Contents of e-mail messages sent over the network at an organization or even over the Internet

✔ Information exchanged between browsers and Web sites

Cryptography was at its most glamorous during World War I when United States forces worked feverishly to break German codes, and vice versa. Cryptography has lost some its glamour today as the need for secure messages and protected data has become more a peacetime necessity than a life-during-wartime requirement. Any data that is protected in one form or another, such as a password or a secured e-mail, is done so with cryptography.

Becoming enlightened on encryption

Cryptography is not random. A number of standard techniques encrypt information. This doesn't mean that if you know the technique used to encrypt a message that you can automatically decrypt it. These encryption schemes produce unique keys each time they are used. The key is the component that encrypts the message.

Here is a rundown of the encryption, algorithm, and other things in the cryptography realm you might encounter in this book:

✔ **DES:** DES stands for Data Encryption Standard. DES, an encryption algorithm, was developed originally by IBM with help from the U.S. government. DES is a 56-bit key.

✔ **Tripe-DES, or 3DES:** 3DES is a variant of DES in which the input data is encrypted three times.

✔ **hash:** A hash is a numeric representation of some data. A hash function requires some data, such as a user name or password, and generates a fixed-length value representing the data passed in.

✔ **Diffie-Hellman:** Diffie-Hellman is a method used to decide upon keys that will be used to secure subsequent messages. The significance of Diffie-Hellman is that the negotiation about the key is done over an insecure connection, such as over the Internet.

✔ **message digest:** A message digest is a smaller version of a message. A message digest isn't created so that someone can read a message quicker. Rather, a message digest is a smaller, numeric representation of the original message. A message digest is a hash of the original message. It is usually to verify a message received is the same as the one sent.

✔ **MD2, MD4, MD5:** These three acronyms refer to message digest algorithms. MD4 and MD5 are the latest of this set of algorithms. MD5 is said to be harder to crack than MD4, though its performance is slower than its predecessor.

✔ **SHA, SHA-1:** SHA and SHA-1 are algorithms used to generate hashes. SHAR stands for Secure Hash Algorithm.

Cryptography has two elements:

> ✔ **Encryption:** When you encrypt information, you create the scrambled, unreadable version of the information you want to protect. It is usually the sender's job to encrypt.

> ✔ **Decryption:** When you decrypt information that has been previously encrypted, you create a readable version of the information. It's usually the job of the recipient to decrypt. You can't decrypt information unless it has been encrypted in the first place.

One of the critical elements to cryptography is that the party looking at the encrypted information must know the technique that was used to encrypt the information in order to understand it.

For example, if the following message:

```
Computer hackers eat with their elbows on the table
```

were encrypted as

```
elbat eht no swoble rieht htiw tae srekcah retupmoC
```

the person looking for the information must know the super-secret *write-it backwards* key in order to decrypt and then read the message.

Secret and public key schemes

Encryption is the best method to make sure that private information is kept private. Naturally, the No. 1 requirement for making an encryption scheme work is that the party receiving the encrypted message knows how to decrypt it. Make sense? This No. 1 requirement has a name, and its name is a key. A *key* is a piece of information that describes how information is encrypted and how that same information may be decrypted. In any encryption scheme, making sure that both parties have the correct key(s) is probably the top priority. Otherwise, there would be no way for the recipient to decode the coded message.

A key is usually nothing more than a piece of software on your computer or on a network server. A key sometimes is delivered in the header of an e-mail message. You usually do not have to hunt through your hard drive to track down your key. A key is usually stored in a location known by an application that needs to use the key. For example, if messages you exchange with your e-mail system are encrypted, your e-mail program will know how to find the key on your computer to decrypt or encrypt a message.

Key systems come in two types. Like life, a key scheme can be

✔ Secret

✔ Public

Windows 2000 supports a number of different security infrastructures, such as support for certificates (a.k.a. protocols), and keys are a critical component of most of them. Where do keys come from? Whether secret or public, keys can be generated or acquired from any of a number of third-party certificate authorities. The Windows 2000 certificate server also can generate keys.

✔ **Secret keys:** In a secret key scheme, only one key exists, and this key is kept very, very secret. Why is the key very, very secret? This key is used both to encrypt *and* decrypt. If one were to acquire this secret key, one could decrypt any message sent by any party using the same key. You'll see how this type of system contrasts with public key systems in a little bit. One of the benefits to secret key technology is speed. Messages can be decrypted much faster in secret key systems than in other schemes.

In secret key systems, both the recipient and the sender agree on the type of key to use. Next, a key is generated by one of the parties, and it is passed to the other party. This last step reflects the problem with secret key systems. The sender and deliverer must figure out a way to safely exchange the key. Considering they're concerned enough about security to encrypt a message, using that same medium to send the key is probably not a good idea. So, exchanging and maintaining this single key is usually a difficult problem with secret key infrastructures.

✔ **Public keys:** Public key schemes rely on a pair of keys as compared to the one-key approach in secret key schemes. Both keys in the pair are needed to encrypt and decrypt a message. One of the keys is a public key, the other key is a private key. These two keys are a matched pair. You cannot use a public key from one pair and a private key from another pair.

Public and private keys are used to perform encryption and decryption duties. It doesn't matter which key performs which function, only that the other key in the pair performs the other function. The same key cannot perform both functions. For example, a public key can be used to encrypt a message, and then the matching private key is used to decrypt it. Or, a private key can be used to encrypt a message, and the public key is used to decrypt. What's the benefit of a public key system? Well, in order for any information secured with a public key system to be useful, two keys are required, and one of them, the private key, is normally very difficult to acquire.

In public key schemes, any user or service that needs to exchange encrypted information, whether this information is in the form of e-mail or information exchanged over the Web, must have a pair of keys: one private and one public. The public key is made . . . public. That is, the public key is made easily available to anyone who might need to exchange secure information that could be encrypted or decrypted with the private key. A public key might be available on a network resource, or it might be distributed, usually in the form of a digital certificate. In a practical example, if Fred needs to send a secure message to Barney, Fred would locate Barney's public key and encrypt the message with the key. More likely, Fred's e-mail program would, behind-the-scenes, ensure that it encrypts the message with Barney's public key. When Barney receives the message, his e-mail program decrypts the message with his private key.

Certifying safety with certificates

Certificates are becoming one of the most widely used components of computer and network security, especially on the Web and on Intranets (and now in Windows 2000). A certificate is nothing but a computer proof-of-identity. This proof-of-identity can be used by you, a Web site you browse to, or a corporate server you connect to. Here are ways the security-obsessed world uses certificates:

- ✔ You can use a certificate to authenticate yourself on Windows 2000.

- ✔ You can view a certificate to verify the identity of the publisher of software you download from the Internet.

- ✔ A site you visit on the Web presents a certificate (really to your browser) that positively confirms the site isn't posing as another site.

- ✔ You use a certificate installed on your workstation to verify your identity to Web sites and other persons with whom you exchange information.

A certificate works in the network and Internet world the way any other proof-of-identification works in the real world. If you need to prove who you are, you usually need to produce a driver's license, a birth certificate, or a passport. In everyday life, your proof of identity has to be real and authentic. You really can't prove your identity by scribbling your name, birth date, and social security number using a crayon on the back of a used envelope.

Another way in which a certificate works like the real world is that this proof-of-identity must be provided by an entity that everyone trusts. If I presented an ID that was signed by *bigshoes the clown,* you might not think the certificate was valid. If an ID I presented, though, was embossed with a seal of the state of North Carolina, you might show me some respect. This is the same in the Internet and network world. A certificate must be certified by a well-known and trusted *certificate authority (CA).*

Certificates are very related to public key technologies. If you are unfamiliar with public key technologies, refer to the "Secret and public key schemes" section earlier in this chapter. Certificates rely on the availability of public keys. The public key associated with a certificate a user bears is stored with the organization that issued the certificate. The certificate stores the private key. So, how does a certificate vouch for the bearer's identity? By the positive relationship established by the bearer's private key on the certificate and the bearer's public key. You can find details on certificates in Chapter 10.

TIP

Certificates and IE: Partners in anticrime

Here is how Internet Explorer uses certificates. You identify for Internet Explorer the certificate authorities you trust. Actually, certificates for these certificate authorities are installed on your workstation. You specify for what tasks you trust these certificate authorities. For example, you might trust a certificate authority when it is used to certify the identity of a network server you try to attach to, but not when it is used to verify the publisher of software you download from the Internet. When you browse to some entity on the Web, and that entity produces a certificate from one of the certificate authorities you trust, Internet Explorer will automatically trust that entity. Whatever rules you apply to trusted sites are applied to this entity. For more detailed information on safe Web browsing, refer to Chapter 13.

Digital signatures

A *digital signature* is a technique used to help secure e-mail. Many of today's most popular e-mail applications support this feature. A digital signature does two extremely important jobs:

- ✔ A digital signature verifies once and for all that the sender of the message is the same as expressed on the return address.
- ✔ A digital signature verifies a message has not been tampered with.

A digital signature is a piece of information, actually a pile of undecipherable letters and numbers, which is a composite of the text of the message and a unique, protected identification of the sender. This composite is known as a hash. If a message is tampered with, the digital signature fails verification by the recipient e-mail program.

Browser-proofed technology

Internet Explorer (IE), which is bundled with Windows 2000, provides more security features than you can shake a hacker at. Why is a browser an element in corporate security? Well, the browser has become one of the critical information delivery tools at the user's desktop. A properly configured and security-feature-loaded browser can certainly diminish some of your Internet-related security risks.

In addition to providing support for Internet/Intranet security technologies (for example, certificates, SSL, TLS, PCT, and 128-bit encryption), IE includes a number of features that make your browser more of a defense against attacks rather than an invitation. As an example, you can divide the Internet and your corporate intranet into zones. These zones represent the level of trust you have in the Web sites you have assigned to those zones. You also establish the browsing ground rules for each zone. For example, you might allow the download of programs and other software, even without confirmation first, from sites you have assigned to your Trusted zone. But, you might deny download of any content from sites you have assigned to the Untrusted zone.

Using this feature, your users can browse the Web and Intranet confidently, knowing the correct security policy is applied regardless of where browsing takes them. This way, there is no need to reconfigure the security features in the browser based on the site they have browsed to.

Other browsers available today certainly have security features. IE, though, seems to have the most powerful set. You can find a mountain of information about IE in Chapter 14.

Smart cards

As if a discussion of cryptography, security, and private keys isn't enough (see preceding section), this discussion of smart cards will definitely make you a junior-007-secret agent in training. Smart card technology is somewhere today between novelty and the thing progressive companies use. Soon, smart card technology may be the de facto standard for providing security in a public-key infrastructure.

First of all, the smart card's purpose in Windows 2000 is to authenticate a user and to provide e-mail certification. This means a smart card confirms you are who you say are when you log onto the network. A smart card is a credit card on steroids. In fact, a smart card is the size of a credit card, making it portable and storable in one's wallet, purse, or back pocket, key ring, front pocket next to the pocket protector, or knapsack.

A smart card stores a set of credentials for the possessor of the card, such as a user's private key, their name, and any other positively identifying information. The user uses the smart card to log onto the network. To do so, the user inserts his smart card into the smart card reader attached to his computer and then enters a PIN. This process assuredly authenticates the user because of the confirmed association between the bearer of the card, the credentials burned into the card, and the PIN the bearer enters.

In addition, the smart card also can store all the credentials needed for the user to access various secured components of the networks. This way, users can be immediately authenticated to all the network resources they have access to automatically when they log on with their smart card.

Associated with a smart card is a smart card reader. This is the device you insert your smart card into. Smart card readers are available for desktop computers and laptop computers alike. Don't think you can upgrade your security instantly by instructing your users to run to the computer store to buy their own readers or by entering a purchase request for a few hundred readers. You must configure your network to accept smart cards.

You can find information on how to configure smart card use in Windows 2000 in Chapter 15.

Protecting the physical assets

Passwords, protocols, keys, and smart cards all help lock the door to cyber-snoops. You can deter (and really aggravate) those faceless and nameless rogues who prowl cyberspace by using the technology and techniques mentioned earlier in this chapter. You're wasting your time, though, if you don't protect the key components in this whole security thing: the actual hardware, especially the servers that compose your network. What good is a firewall if the door to the server room is never locked, or if the main administrative password is written on a yellow sticky stuck to the monitor?

You need solid internal security to protect all the hardware on which all that sensitive information is stored. Sure, you can lock the doors and hire a guard service, but does any of that sound like fun? Instead, the security world now provides some of the absolute coolest options for physical security. Do you think you're good at breaking into your office on weekends? Can you smooth-talk your way past the security guard? What if a retinal scanner (one that verifies your identity by scanning your retina and comparing it to an archived version of the scan) blocked your way? Do you find that pesky pay-by-the hour consultant is always in the server room? What if access to the room were allowed only after a fingerprint analysis verification? Perhaps then you'd really get work out of all the hours the consultant billed you! The security features built into the BIOS loaded on a computer also can help. Do you think it's easy to access the resources on a machine simply by booting the machine with DOS from a floppy disk? Not if you must supply a password before a speck of operating system code is run. High tech or otherwise, a great way to punctuate any series of security technologies is to be sure all the physical assets also are under lock, key, and at least two or three high-end security toys.

Policy, policy, policy

It's not a plan until it's written down, and nothing keeps order like a good dose of policy. One of the absolute keys to a secure system is the development and documentation of a corporate security policy. This policy defines the rules about security, how items are secured, who has access to what, and so on. Ideally, this policy is a living document that is modified and updated as an organization grows and changes and as technology makes more options available and creates more risk.

The policy is also useful because in one place an organization can determine its relative security level from a planning perspective and then, by executing an inspection, determine the security of the organization from an audit perspective. A third-party security company can help you build this document, or you can construct it yourself. If you need help, check out the advice for creating a corporate security policy in Chapter 18.

Hosing down the Internet inferno with a firewall

The *firewall* is the corporate network's border guard when the territory on the other side of the border is the Internet. The firewall is the border guard that checks all data headed out to the Internet, as well as all data knocking at your network's door. How companies use firewalls and how firewalls do their job varies, but not considerably. You can read about these vagaries and more in Chapter 17.

Chapter 2

6,000 or So Words on Windows 2000 Networking

● ●

In This Chapter

▶ Digging into the details about domains

▶ Quickly reviewing TCP/IP

▶ Finding out about Directory Service

▶ Checking out the Active Directory

● ●

*T*here's a very old expression that has been passed down through genera-tions and across civilizations. It goes like this: "Where you find someone worried about computer security, you will also find a computer network close by."

While this expression has been studied over the years and has been the subject of long debate as to its origin and true meaning, I'll provide a capsule review here. It means that a prerequisite to anyone being worried about computer network security is the condition of more than one person with access to the same thing on a computer network. Further simplified, you usually aren't concerned with security unless there's more than one user on the network mountain. This should tell you that an important component of dealing with security is to deal with the network or thing you are trying to secure. The thing in this case is a Windows 2000 network. It probably makes sense to know something about the network you're trying to secure, and addressing this issue is the goal of this chapter.

This chapter can help you get to know all the important aspects of Windows 2000 networking necessary for understanding how to secure it. If this book were about repairing cars, then this chapter would explain how a car works.

Dominating Your Networks with Domains

If you have read one paragraph of technical information about Windows NT or Windows 2000 networks over the past nine years, then you are almost sure to have heard about domains. The *domain* is the main unit of measure in a Windows 2000 network.

- ✔ All objects on the network are grouped into domains, including users, servers, printers, and so on.

- ✔ The domain provides centralized support and administration for its members. This means that users in the domain must access a server in the domain in order to log on to the domain and then access other domain resources, such as other computers, e-mail, and so on.

- ✔ A network might contain one domain large or small, or a network might contain a number of domains. When a network contains a number of domains, the group of domains can be referred to as the *enterprise*. A small- to medium-sized company might have just one domain. A medium to large company might have many domains, but could possibly have only one large domain.

- ✔ Domains represent security boundaries for the greater network. This means that an individual with the greatest security privileges can only administer security for a single domain. As an example, if I were granted full rights to the Sales domain for an enormous, monolithic software company, I could not create an account for the new programmer for the Development domain. Nothing would stop a person, though, who had sufficient security privileges to administer both domains.

- ✔ Domains don't necessarily need to reflect the organization of your organization. Also, a domain doesn't need to be specific to one physical location on your network; sites are used to deal with this issue. You can find information on sites and organization units later in this chapter in the "Seeing the Windows 2000 Sites" and "Organizing the Active Directory with Organizational Units" sections, respectively.

Not sure of what domain you might belong to? If you are logged into a machine on a Windows 2000 network, press Ctrl+Alt+Delete. The dialog box will show you the username and the domain you are logged on as.

A great source of information for creating domains is *Windows 2000 Server For Dummies* by Ed Tittel (IDG Books Worldwide, Inc.).

So many domains, so little time

Some networks have one domain, and others have more than one. The process of planning for your network (you do plan, don't you?) might reveal the need for more than one domain. Here are some reasons why:

- **Too many objects.** A Windows 2000 network domain can store up to 10 million objects. The objects include people, printers, and machines. Your company has got to be huge to run into this limit. If it does, though, you'll need to break up the domain.

- **Topology issues on the network.** You can have a pretty good network design and still not please everyone. Say that you have a remote site, and to appease the users there, you install a domain controller so that users do not have to connect across the seven seas to log on to the network. If the connection to a remote site on a network is unreasonably slow, then users will still scream and holler. You may need to create a domain at the site to quiet the natives.

- **The organization revolts.** The requirement for organization autonomy might also lead you to develop additional domains. If an organization or large division in your company insists on maintaining and securing its own domain (in contrast to a central IS department maintaining the network and all domains for the entire company), then you may need to give the people what they want. What they want is their own domain.

Namespaces, trees, trusts, forests, and other seemingly unrelated topics

While the domain is arguably the most important component in a Windows 2000 network, a domain isn't necessarily the biggest. If your organization is one of those with multiple domains, then those domains must be grouped into something bigger than a domain.

- The collection of a group of domains in a network is called a *forest*.

- A group of domains can be grouped together to form a *tree*. Like a tree (you know, the one you can climb or hug), the organization of domains looks something like a hierarchy, with the domains represented by branches stemming off of the trunk of the tree.

- The first domain in a domain tree is known as the *root domain*.

✔ When you create a new domain in an existing domain tree, the new domain is a child domain. For example, say that you have a domain named MYWORLD.COM, and it is the only domain in the tree. If you create a new domain in the MYWORLD.COM tree named CHARLOTTE, the name of the new domain would be CHARLOTTE.MYWORLD.COM.

✔ All domains that have the same root domain are said to belong to the same *namespace*.

✔ To create a new domain, you create a domain controller. During the process of creating a new domain controller, you are prompted whether the domain will be the first domain in a new forest, the first domain in a new domain tree in an existing forest, or a child domain in an existing domain tree (see Figure 2-1). The Active Directory Installation Wizard is used to convert a computer on which Windows 2000 Server is installed to a domain controller. The Active Directory is installed the first time you promote a Windows 2000 Server to a domain controller in a domain.

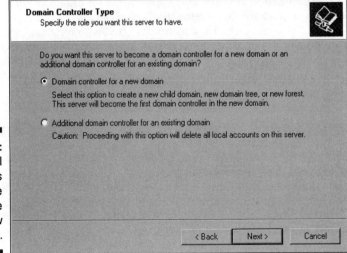

Figure 2-1:
You tell
Windows
2000 where
to create
that new
domain.

The hardware underneath a domain

The most important piece of hardware in a domain is a domain controller. Every domain needs a domain controller. The Active Directory is quite passive until you create a domain controller, so the first step in installing the Active Directory is promoting the computer where Windows 2000 is running to a domain controller. If your network only has one domain, it still might have a number of domain controllers supporting that one domain. At the same time, it is possible for a network that has more than one domain to have just one domain controller supporting each domain. A little later in this section, I explain the reasons why your organization might have more than one domain, as well as the significance of the number of servers in a domain.

Don't get the idea that the only kind of servers that can run on Windows 2000 are domain controllers. You can set up file servers, application servers, e-mail servers, web servers, and so on. Naturally, all these servers won't help manage the network. Servers like these are known as *member servers*.

Domain delegation for dummies

Considering how important domains are, you would think they're a lot of work to manage. Well, there are a bunch of chores that need to be done to keep the domain running and the users happy. All this work can be doubled, tripled, quadrupled, and whatever the word is for five-times something, and more when you add organizational units to the mix. Windows 2000 provides something called delegation to help ease the work burden. The domain administrator can allow users and groups of users to administer their own little part of their network, such as an organization unit. These users, with delegated control, can do all the typical administration tasks or just the tasks you let them handle. As if delegating control didn't save you (the administrator) enough work, there's even a wizard that's helps you set up delegation (see Figure 2-2)!

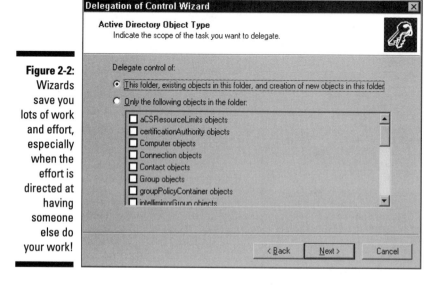

Figure 2-2:
Wizards save you lots of work and effort, especially when the effort is directed at having someone else do your work!

Organizing the Active Directory with Organizational Units

Unless your organization is unlike almost every other organization formed, then it is probably divided into departments or divisions or something like that. In fact, if your organization isn't carved up into some set of discrete parts, then it probably isn't an organization at all — it's an anarchy! In Windows 2000 networks, you can carve your domain into pieces that mirror the divisions and departments in your organization. These pieces are known as *organizational units*. In Windows 2000 networks, you can create organization units called FINANCE, SALES, MARKETING, CATERING, OBFUSCATION, or whatever.

Going on the premise that your organization is on the normal side of the ledger, the departments or divisions or whatever that comprise your organization may be divided into smaller units. For example, the SALES department might be broken down into CHANNEL, DIRECT, and TELEMARKETING groups, and they can be broken down into even smaller units, as illustrated in Figure 2-3. In Windows 2000 networking, these smaller groups are also known as organizational units, and you can model this hierarchy in Windows 2000, too. Organizational units that belong to other organization units are known as *child organizational units*. In fact, you can create as many levels of organization units as needed to duplicate your organizational hierarchy.

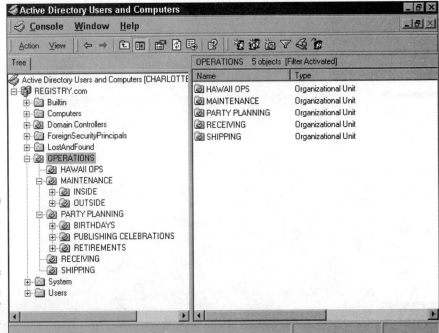

Figure 2-3: Organizational units can mirror the hierarchy of departments in your company.

Each domain in your enterprise may have its own set and hierarchy of organization units. The names of an organization unit in one domain can be the same as in another domain, but the child organization units don't need to match those in the other domain. For example, you can have a Sales organization unit in each domain, but in the North America domain, Sales could be comprised of NORTH AMERICA and CANADA, while the Sales domain in Europe could be comprised of FRANCE, ITALY, and UK.

Regarding organization units, then, you might say, "Big deal. I can draw my organization structure in half a dozen other applications!" Well, organization units are a big deal in Windows 2000 networking for a bunch of reasons. Here are reasons why OUs may be the coolest things since radio-controlled boats:

- ✔ The domain administrator can pass administrative rights to certain users on an OU basis. This allows de facto department administrators to be created that can then create users, add printers, and so on, just for their own departments. In effect, you get junior network administrators just for the OU, without jeopardizing security in the greater domain!

- ✔ The rights you create for a junior administrator who you might place in charge of the network administration of an OU can be finely controlled, such as allowing the user only to change passwords or perhaps to create users.

- ✔ The rights assigned to users in an OU don't interfere with the security in another OU, so security can be customized on an OU basis.

- ✔ Any security settings assigned to an OU can be automatically passed down to any child OUs created. This inheritance can be either turned on or off.

- ✔ By giving a user in an OU a set of rights for the OU, the local IS department doesn't need to baby-sit that small department. This gives workers in the IS more free time, which can be used to format 5¼-inch floppy disks and drink soda.

- ✔ A user who has been assigned administrator rights in an OU can also be assigned the rights to delegate security tasks to other users in the OU, or in child OUs.

Here's an example of what you can do. Say that you, the domain administrator, create an OU named FINANCE. You might give Betty Bottomdollar administrative rights to the entire OU. Betty can then add users, change passwords, and so on for all users in the Finance OU. Say that Lou Luckytobehired is hired into the AP department. Also say that Lou knows how to use spreadsheets, so he immediately assumes the role of power user in AP. Betty can delegate rights to Lou, which allows him to handle the same tasks she does, but just for the AP department.

I explain more about OU security in Chapter 3, and you can find out how to actually administer OU rights in Chapter 4.

Seeing the Windows 2000 Sites

If your company is like the vast majority of networked companies, the hierarchy of your domain and organization units probably isn't reflected in the way your network is physically organized. This means that all the departments in a division aren't necessarily located in the same place, nor are all the workgroups reporting to one really important person (RIP) located in the same place that they work.

For example, say that everyone in your company is connected via a WAN. Also say that your company houses those cranky software developers in their own building on the other side of the main parking lot. That building is also the one where the catering and travel departments are located. Now, it's likely that software development and travel and catering do not make up the same division in your organization, nor does one report to the other. (Otherwise, the only food served when you ask catering to provide meals for your lunch would be pizza, licorice, coffee, and soda high in caffeine content.) All the clients and servers in the three departments at this building, however, would belong to the same site. A site is used to group Windows 2000 network resources at the same location that might not necessarily belong to the same domain.

A *WAN* (wide area network) is a collection of connected computers in which all the computers are not in the same general geographical location. This contrasts with a *LAN* (local area network) in which all the connected machines are usually in the same location, such as a building or corporate campus setting.

Here's more of what you need to know about sites:

✔ A *site* is a set of hosts on the network that belong to the same subnet or multiple subnets. What characterizes hosts on the same subnet is fast connection transport amongst the hosts. The hosts in a subnet are usually part of a remote segment from the rest of the network.

✔ By grouping these same subnet computers into the same site, Windows 2000 networking knows where to locate the nearest domain controller. The way the logic goes is this: If your network is large enough that you need subnets, then it stands to reason that you probably will use multiple domain controllers on your network. A domain controller is typically found at each site.

✔ You may need to divide your network into smaller components. By doing so, you reap the following benefits:

- It's easier to manage something that is big that has been broken into smaller pieces than to manage the big thing as a whole.

- Things run faster when they don't have as far to go.

Replication Is Why Windows 2000 Is Like Star Trek

Replication is an important concept to understand in Windows 2000. If you understand how the replicator works in *Star Trek,* then you should have a handle on replication in Windows 2000 networking.

Replication refers to the action of making a working, usable copy of something else. In *Star Trek,* food, medicine, tools, and other items are usually replicated, though I can think of at least four things the crew never replicated but should have. (How come they never replicated a phaser when they really needed one?)

In Windows 2000, all the information about a network is replicated to different servers when a change is made in one. This makes it easy for anyone in the organization to log on to the network wherever they are, such as visiting an office other than their home office, or even from their home office. The effect of this replication is that all the important information about the network, such as the accounts, groups, passwords, what access users have to what resources, printers, computers, and more, is never centrally stored. Rather, this data is copied to a number of locations across the network.

Here are more details on replication:

✔ A Windows 2000 network replicates the entire directory to every server specified as a domain controller on the entire network.

✔ The replication scheme used in Windows 2000 is known as *multimaster replication.* In this scheme, there is no notion of one master server containing all the network information.

✔ Replication helps address a number of problems:

• What if the one server with all the critical network information went down? Without replication, the result is downtime, and while everyone likes a few minutes of rest, time is money.

• How do you deal with users on the other end of the earth connecting to the WAN potentially via a dial-up connection? When you mix the notion of sites with replication, users have a short distance to go to log on to the network, regardless of the type of connection.

• Your network had thousands of users, all usually trying to log on at the same time every work morning to the same one or two servers.

✔ Don't confuse the multimaster replication scheme with multimoron replication — this system is smart. For example, say that a user changes his password via the Charlotte domain controller. The Charlotte domain controller realizes it has a change that must be replicated to all the other domain controllers, such as the one in Portland. The Charlotte domain controller kicks off the replication, and now everyone is in synch. Now here's the question: Does the Portland domain controller realize it now has a change that must be replicated to all the other domain controllers, such as the one in Charlotte? The answer is no. Replication in Windows 2000 doesn't resemble a Three Stooges episode, with domain controllers running around in circles banging into each other and slapping each other in the forehead!

✔ Replication occurs automatically, but you can also force it to occur.

There's That Annoying TCP/IP Protocol Again!

Admit it. You're tired of hearing and reading about TCP/IP. Yeah, yeah, you say, it's the protocol of the Internet. Yeah, yeah, client-server-this and client-server-that. Well, get used to it, because TCP/IP is the primary protocol of Windows 2000 networking.

✔ TCP/IP, which stands for Transmission Control Protocol/Internet Protocol, is, yes, I'll use the word again, a *protocol*. A computer protocol in the networking world simply refers to a way in which computers speak to one another.

✔ TCP/IP is an especially effective protocol because it allows different classes, types, and flavors of computers to speak to one another. For example, using TCP/IP, a computer running Windows 2000 Professional can communicate with a Unix server. Skeptical? Provided you are running some sort of Windows operating system on your desktop right now, and provided you can access the Internet, enter this URL into your browser:

```
www.sun.com
```

which is the address of Sun Microsystems' home page on the Internet. It's a very safe bet that the Web server over at Sun headquarters isn't running Windows NT Server 3.51, 4.0, 2000, or anything else with the name Windows in it.

Does all of this TCP/IP stuff stop you dead in your tracks? Check out *TCP/IP For Dummies* by Candace Leiden and Marshall Wilensky (IDG Books Worldwide, Inc.).

What's your IP address?

When all is said and done, everything computer eventually boils down to numbers. In TCP/IP networks, like Windows 2000 networks, the most important number is the IP address. In IP networks, all machines connected to the network are known as *hosts*. Ever host is uniquely identified by an IP address. This is akin to the social security number that each citizen of the United States has. Unlike a social security number, though, the IP address assigned to a host can change.

An IP address is a 32-bit number. To make the number a bit easier to read, the IP address is broken into four pieces separated by periods. The following are examples of an IP address:

```
129.23.11.111
127.0.0.1
192.168.0.1
```

You probably will run across something named a subnet. A *subnet* is a portion of an IP network usually broken off at some geographical boundary. If your network is of a sufficient size, it might be divided into a few pieces. A *subnet mask* is used to indicate which part of an IP address specifies the subnet and which portion indicates the host. The following are examples of subnet masks you might come across:

255.255.254.0

255.255.0.0

What's my domain name with DNS?

DNS is an acronym for Domain Naming System. DNS translates IP addresses into alphanumeric names. This makes it easy for people like you and your users to refer to and specify Internet locations by name rather than number. If only a handful of hosts were on the Internet, it wouldn't be too big of a deal to refer to those hosts by their IP addresses. You probably would hear a lot of office chatter that sounded like this: "Oh yeah, send Don an e-mail and ask him to send his sales forecast. I think his address is 123.12.12.12. And when you're done, the boss wants you to download for him the new Don Knotts screen saver. I think you can find it at 123.45.67.78."

The Internet, though, is a lot bigger than a few IP addresses. A fairly large company might reserve a few thousand IP addresses just for its own uses.

While subnets can address the issue of lots of IP addresses, it is impractical to think that you can refer to every one of the many hosts you work with solely by its IP address.

DNS is a technology that maps IP addresses to alphanumeric names. This supposedly makes it easy for people like you and I to refer to network sites by their name rather than their number. This probably makes sense in most cases, but there certainly have been times where I could much more easily have remembered an IP address like 234.34.34.9 than WWW.how-2-be-a-reelly-good-writer. This isn't a really big problem, though, because any browser allows me to enter an IP address as part of a URL instead of a DNS name.

DNS isn't relevant just to the Internet, but to your network as well. Don't think that your network is special and doesn't use IP addresses. If you're running the Active Directory, it does, and DNS plays a role. If for no other reason, DNS is required for hosts on your network to be able to find domain controllers. Windows 2000 comes with its own DNS service. You can also use a DNS server on the public Internet as well.

Moving to a new address with DHCP

DHCP stands for Dynamic Host Configuration Protocol. Any computer connected to a TCP/IP network is known as a *host,* whether that box is a server or workstation. So, it would seem that DHCP is

- ✔ Something dynamic (like the author)
- ✔ Configures something, probably a host
- ✔ A protocol

All these are correct. The configuring DHCP is assigning an IP address dynamically. This means that when a host connects to a TCP/IP network, like the Active Directory, DHCP automatically assigns the host an IP address. This is good. Otherwise, some poor schlub would have the responsibility to keep track of everyone's IP address. Another advantage of DHCP is that it reduces any chance of your users misentering IP addresses. Wouldn't it be nice if the Tab key moved the cursor to the next section of the IP address, instead of the right-cursor key?

Windows 2000 Server comes with DHCP server software. This allows your network to hand out IP addresses when computers connect. You, the network administrator, need to do a little homework before firing up the server. You need to figure out what IP addresses you'll hand out, as well as be sure that they do not interfere with other IP addresses in use on the real Internet. These chores are not a big deal; you definitely won't be the first person to have done this.

Does DHCP interest you? Do you want to see this cool technology at work? Have you ever wondered what your IP address is?

1. **Open the command prompt window.**

2. **Type** IPCONFIG **and then press Enter.**

   You see your IP address on the screen, as well as the domain to which the DHCP server is attached.

   If you are a network big shot and have more than one network adapter connected to the network and configured for TCP/IP and DHCP use, you'll see the IP address assigned to each.

   If you don't like the ring of your IP address, you can always get a new one.

3. **Type** IPCONFIG /RENEW **and then press Enter.**

   The DHCP server assigns you a new IP address.

Name that computer with WINS

Another important part of Windows 2000 Network is WINS. *WINS* stands for Windows Internet Name Service. WINS is a service that runs on Windows networks. WINS is only important for networks on which computers are running with a NetBIOS computer name. A NetBIOS computer name is a required component for any computer running a Microsoft operating system that operates on a network. With Windows 2000, DNS handles the identification of computers by name. If you have any computers on your Windows 2000 network running versions of Windows other than the 2K brand, then you need to keep WINS running. If you are sure that there are no holdovers, then you can pull the power plug on WINS.

Getting Up to Speed with the Active Directory

If you have read one paragraph of publicity about Windows 2000, then it's a safe bet that you have heard about the Active Directory. *Active Directory* is the general name given to networking in Windows 2000. While you can refer to Windows 2000 networking as Windows 2000 networking, Active Directory would suffice, too. The name Active Directory refers to the fact that all the information about a Windows 2000 network has been transformed into a directory service. That thing called the Active Directory isn't just a network, but, more specifically, it is the replicated directory of all users, computers, printers, rights, certificates, and so on for the entire network. That directory exists in one place in Windows 2000, which makes the term Active Directory so handy in referring to the network in general.

So, what's the big deal about a directory service? A directory service makes information about the network available to all types of consumers. The consumers of this directory service might be

- Your end users
- Administrators like you and me
- Applications that run on the network
- Applications that need some information about your network
- The operating system on which the network servers and their clients run

All consumers want the same things: better schools, safer streets, cheaper gas. Consumers of directory service information are interested in other things. Here's the list of things a directory service can provide to the consumer:

- A list of all the network users, including their office location, e-mail address, hair color, and so on. Windows 2000 provides all of this through snap-ins like the Active Directory Users and Computers.
- A list of all the printers available on the network.
- A list of all the machines on a network, including client machines, database servers, network servers, application servers, e-mail servers, food servers, and more. The Active Directory Users and Computers snap-in provides this.
- Common access to all this stuff. Because the Windows 2000 Active Directory is replicated all over the place, a user's experience in Charlotte on the network will be the same if he travels to Chicago.

Of course, it's not impossible to get this kind of information and these features from the networks installed today that might not have what you call a directory service. You might say, "Big deal! My network works pretty well. I don't need one of these dang newfangled directory services." The difference between getting this information from today's legacy networks that might not have a directory service and a network that does read from a directory service is usually usability. For example, have you ever tried to locate and then attach to some printer you know exists on the network, like the expensive new too-many-colors-to-shake-a-stick-at presentation printer?

The following are more need-to-knows about directory services:

- A directory service is particularly important to wide, distributed networks. In large networks, users are spread across many segments of the network, and these users are administered into smaller groups. Sites in Windows 2000 address the distributed deal with networks, and the delegation of duties makes it easy for groups to manage themselves.

> ✔ A directory service can ease the pain of users trying to access resources by providing a central location or directory of all the items of interest in the network. Don't let the term central location confuse you, though. With the Active Directory, these directory services can exist in many places on the network, making it easier and faster to get the directory information. How can users expect a directory service to help them access remote objects on the network if the directory service is also at a remote location? Replication is the answer.

So, if the Active Directory is not really the entire network and is actually just the set of directory services, then why does it have such a fancy name, and what's a directory service anyway? These questions, and many others, hopefully, are answered in the next few sections.

X.500 marks the spot

The Active Directory can trace its roots back to something known as X.500. This X.500 thing is a specification defined by the International Organization for Standardization (ISO). The X.500 specification defines from a general perspective how to manage and provide a common directory for human users like you and me, servers, and applications that need directory information. This specification is broken down into the following (very) general subtopics:

> ✔ How directory information should be stored, named, and organized in the database

> ✔ How security should work in the directory

> ✔ How the directory service would work in a distributed network

> ✔ The protocols used to access an X.500 directory

> ✔ The types of information that can be stored in the directory

> ✔ How the directory can be replicated to different sites on a network

For this discussion, the subtopic that is most relevant to the Active Directory is protocols. The X.500 protocol was designed to provide a common way for networks to store information, as well as a common way for applications and users to ask questions about networks. The X.500 specification also defined the *Directory Access Protocol*. Known as DAP, this protocol defined how third-part applications would communicate with X.500 networks. The problem with DAP, as well as with this author, is that it is overweight. DAP occupies each level of the OSI network model stack. X.500 has fallen out of favor with all but organizations with large networks and with lots of money required to support those networks.

LDAP

LDAP is the directory service protocol of choice for the Active Directory. This means that whoever you are, whether using Windows 2000, a standalone application, or whatever, you need to interface with LDAP in order to work with the Active Directory. For those of you scoring at home, as well as for those of you alone, LDAP is covered in RFC 1777. LDAP was born at the University of Michigan. LDAP was developed as a TCP/IP replacement for DAP as DAP was considered to be too difficult to use. LDAP runs on TCP/IP. So if TCP/IP is not a part of your network infrastructure today (and it would be stunning if it weren't), then your network needs to graduate.

Schema

Like other directory services, the Active Directory has a schema. A *schema* defines how data is organized in a database. Yes, the Active Directory can be considered a database (at least for the purposes of this discussion). For example, in the Active Directory, a place is reserved to hold each of the pieces of information you enter in the user Properties dialog box. What if you wanted to store other information, like a user's hair color or the amount of memory installed on a computer? If Microsoft didn't account for this type of information (and it didn't), you would have to extend the schema so that the Active Directory can store it.

Understanding Kerberos Authentication in Windows 2000

One of the most important aspects of networking, Windows 2000 or other-wise, is *authentication*. Authentication is the process of users identifying themselves to the network. Windows 2000 supports two methods of authentication:

- Kerberos version 5
- NTLM

Kerberos is the default authentication method in Windows 2000. Windows 2000 ships with the client software you would install that is needed to authenticate a Windows 9x client to a Windows 2000 domain via Kerberos.

NTLM (Windows NT LAN Manager) is the Windows NT 4 authentication method. NTLM is still supported in Windows 2000 for the following reasons:

✔ A Windows NT 4 Workstation client authenticating on a Windows 2000 domain

✔ A Windows 2000 Professional client authenticating on a Windows NT 4 domain

✔ A Windows NT 4 Workstation client authenticating on a Windows NT 4 domain controller in a Windows 2000 network

Kerberos was invented at the Massachusetts Institute of Technology (MIT). The basic problem that Kerberos solves is that of authentication. Authentication is the process of checking the credentials provided by the user when he logs on against the credentials the domain has stored for the user. Kerberos goes a step further, though, in that it authenticates the user to all of the services and servers the user needs access to in the domain and in the forest, and it also authenticates the server or service the user needs access to back to the user. sense sence

This results in the following benefits to you and your users:

✔ Resources accessed by your users, such as other servers on the network, also authenticate back to the client where the user is working.

✔ Kerberos is faster than NTLM.

✔ Kerberos makes two-way transitive trusts possible. This makes it much easier to create trust relationships between multiple domains in one forest. Read Chapter 3 for more information on trusts.

✔ You can integrate Unix clients into your network by giving them accounts in the Active Directory. Kerberos can authenticate Unix machines.

✔ Users only need to log on once to access all domains in the tree. Kerberos handles the exchange of tickets (the tool it uses for authentication) between domain controllers in different domains.

Under the Kerberos hood

Kerberos uses a secret key system. In a secret key system, the same key is used to encrypt as to decrypt. You can read lots about encryption in Chapter 1.

Kerberos uses a Key Distribution Center (KDC) to generate keys when it needs them. Each domain controller runs a KDC service. Each KDC creates and maintains a secret key for each user and service in the domain. This is the key used in exchanges between the KDC and the user or service. It is known as the *long-term key*. For users, this long-term key is derived from their password. The KDC also generates session keys. A session key is generated when a client and a service need to authenticate one another.

When a user attempts to log on, the Kerberos software running on the machine where she is working converts her password into her long-term key. That long-term key is submitted to the KDC. The KDC retrieves the user's long-term key from the database where it stores all users' account information. Now, with both the long-term key generated by the password the user entered and the long-term key the KDC had stored, the KDC can figure out whether the user should be logged by comparing the keys.

The next step is to generate a ticket should the client need to authenticate itself again to the KDC.

The client requests a session ticket from the KDC. This ticket is used to authenticate the client to the KDC after the initial logon authentication. In response to the request, the KDC generates a session key that will be used by the KDC and the client. This session key is sent back to the client in the form of a *ticket-granting ticket*. The ticket-granting ticket is encrypted with the client's long-term key. The client uses its own long-term key (remember, it still has it from when it was generated when the user entered his password) to decrypt the session key. The client now has a shared secret with the KDC.

The process Kerberos uses when a client wants access to some resource in the domain is a bit different:

When a client needs to authenticate itself with a resource on the domain, the KDC generates a key at one time for both the client and the resource the client requests access to. This key is a session key. Each copy of the key is encrypted with the respective long-term key that the client/ resource server shares with the KDC. The KDC then sends both copies — that's right, both copies — to the client.

The resource's session key is delivered to the client with a bonus, though. The resource's session key also includes information about the client. This combination of session key and client data forms what's called a *session ticket*.

Now, the client is still interested in getting access to the resource. It sends the session ticket to the resource, along with something called an *authenticator*. An authenticator is nothing more than some piece of data, typically the time. When the resource receives the session ticket, the resource decrypts it using the long-term key it shares with the KDC. The server now has a session key it shares with the client. The server uses the session key to decrypt the authenticator sent by the client. If the decryption is successful, the server knows the client is legit. Why? Because the session key used to decrypt the authenticator, which was encrypted by the same session key, was provided by the KDC, which the server automatically trusts.

A point to note so far. The client does not discard the session ticket it uses with the particular resource. Every time the client wants to authenticate itself again with that server, it uses the session ticket it received from the KDC. Session tickets expire, though, at intervals determined by the system. The session ticket also expires as soon as the user logs off.

Chapter 3

Securing the Basics

● ●

In This Chapter

▶ Trusting domains

▶ Grappling with security and local groups

▶ Adding secure users to the mix

● ●

A secure network starts at the bottom. Now, your users might not appreciate being referred to as being at the bottom of anything. No offense
meant, but you need to start with a secure basis of user accounts, groups,
and domains, or else any switches you throw or permissions you set are
worthless.

As an example, what good is it to only allow administrators to perform certain
tasks if every user account is mistakenly assigned to the administrators
group? Woops! Or what use is it to enable the software setting forcing users
to supply complicated passwords if users' passwords never expire? Ouch!

This chapter helps you lay down a secure base. You see what the important
options are for creating secure user accounts. You also finally get to the
bottom of all those wacky security groups that Windows 2000 creates,
and you read about securing domains the right way.

Trusting Domains to Behave Securely

The big cheese in a Windows 2000 network is the domain. Your Windows 2000
Active Directory network will always have one domain, and there's a chance
you'll have two or more as well. The word that Microsoft uses to refer to a
network of Windows 2000 domains is *enterprise*.

Understanding trees and forests

The group of domain(s) is known as the forest. If you have more than one
domain in the forest, you need to consider how security works between them.

If you would like to read about forests, trees, and domains, see Chapter 2.

Here are a few examples of multiple domain scenarios:

✔ An example of a situation in which there are multiple domains in one organization is when two companies merge. If both organizations had Windows 2000 Active Directory domains up, it would make sense to join them in a single forest until such time that the domains are merged into one.

✔ Another example of the possible need for two domains is with organizations that are at the same time very decentralized and large enough that certain groups in the organization insist on their own autonomy and running their own network. In this case, there may be as many domains in the organization as there are divisions or business units.

Understanding trusts

As long as you have more than one domain in your network, you might as well reap the benefits. With Windows 2000 domains, users in one domain can get easy access to resources on the other domains in the forest. The relationship between domains that enable them to work together is known as *trust*. Here's all you need to know about trusts between domains:

✔ As much as domains in the same forest, and especially the same tree, act like one big happy family, the domain still represents the security boundary. An administrator can only control security within his own domain. One domain can grant an administrator in another domain appropriate administrative rights, but this is not an automatic function of trust.

✔ Trusts manage authenticating users from one domain in another. This trust doesn't necessarily mean that a user can do whatever he pleases in the domain he's visiting. All a trust does is look through the peephole of the door and recognize the person knocking at it.

✔ Domains in the same forest automatically trust one another. This trust is known as a *two-way transitive trust*.

Two-way means that domains trust one another:

If domain Doris trusts domain Paul, domain Paul trusts domain Doris.

The transitive part means that the children domains of a parent domain automatically trust the domains that the parent trusts:

If domain Alice trusts domain Bertrand and domain Bertrand trusts domain Clive, then domain Alice automatically trusts domain Clive. Get it?

As an example, Windows 2000 domains in different forests use one-way trusts. In a one-way trust, one domain trusts another, but the reverse isn't necessarily true. Here's an example: Domain Jupiter trusts domain Venus. Domain Jupiter is the *trusting* domain, domain Venus is the *trusted* domain. By virtue of the trust domain Jupiter has for domain Venus, users in the Venus domain can be authenticated on domain Jupiter. These one-way trusts are not transitive. That means if domain Venus trusts domain Mars, domain Jupiter does not automatically trust domain Mars.

✔ You can create a two-way nontransitive trust. Just have both domains create trusts for one another.

You can see the domain trusts your domain is involved in, as well as add one-way trusts (two-way trusts are set up automatically). Here's how to do it:

1. **Start the Active Directory Domains and Trusts snap-in.**

   To start the Active Directory Domains and Trusts snap-in, click the Start menu and then choose Programs➪Administrative Tools➪Active Directory Domains and Trusts.

2. **Right-click the domain you're interested in and then click Properties.**

   The Properties dialog box for the domain appears.

3. **Click the Trusts tab.**

   The Trusts sheet appears, as shown in Figure 3-1.

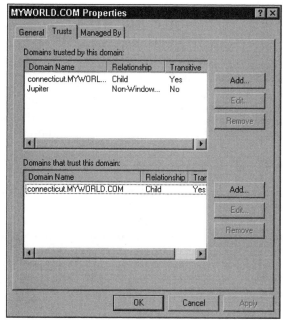

Figure 3-1:
The domain Properties dialog box.

You can select domains trusted by your domain in the top box and domains that trust your domain in the bottom box. When you see the same domain in both boxes, you know you have a two-way trust (not necessarily transitive — check the Transitive column).

4. **To create a new trust (your domain will be doing the trusting), click the Add button.**

The Add Trusted Domain dialog box appears, as shown in Figure 3-2.

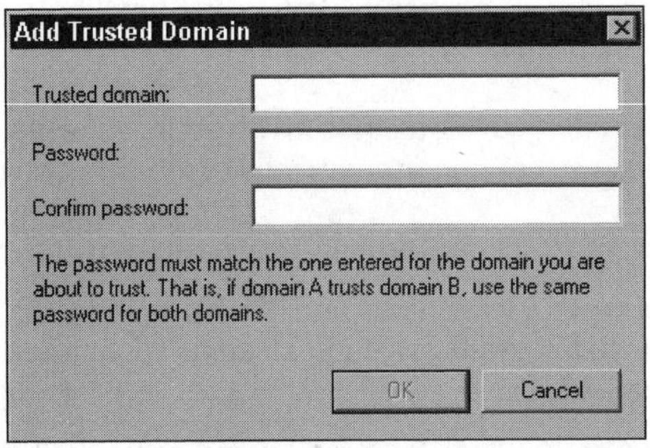

Figure 3-2:
Add a new trusted domain in this dialog box.

Add Trusted Domain	✕

Trusted domain:

Password:

Confirm password:

The password must match the one entered for the domain you are about to trust. That is, if domain A trusts domain B, use the same password for both domains.

[OK] [Cancel]

5. **Enter the full name of the domain to be trusted; also enter a password for this trust and confirm it.**

Be sure that the password you supply is the same one as supplied by the administrator for the other domain.

6. **Click OK to close the Add Trusted Domain dialog box and then click OK to close the domain's Properties dialog box.**

Now You're in Charge!

You'll probably spend a good amount of time first planning and then rolling out your Windows 2000 network. You'll be proud of your work, but now the work involved in the day-to-day administration of the network begins. Yuck! There's an option, though! As soon as you're done building your Active Directory, consider doing the next best thing: Give someone else the responsibility to look after it! Well, you might not give someone else complete control over the network you built, but you might let others in the organization take some responsibility for it. Windows 2000 lets you delegate control over certain elements of the Active Directory to other persons in your organization.

✔ You can delegate control over almost anything in the Active Directory tree, such as organizational units, folders of computers, or the entire domain.

✔ Delegate control of organizational units whenever you can. This way, an organizational unit can manage itself, adding user accounts, printers, subgroups, and more.

✔ The persons to whom delegation is passed don't necessarily need to have the same rights or belong to the same security groups as the person doing the delegating.

✔ The user who delegates control does not lose any of his permissions on the item whose control he delegates.

✔ You do not have to change the user rights or other account attributes for the person who is getting control.

✔ The rights that get passed from the *delegator* to the *delegatee* will vary based on the object whose control was delegated. For example, if you delegate control over an organizational unit, the new person in control can reset passwords, manage user accounts, and do other tasks. If you were to delegate control of the entire domain, the person being granted control can join a computer to the domain or manage group policy for the domain.

✔ You can delegate control to one user, a few users, one group, or a few groups.

Follow these steps to help answer each of the Delegation of Control Wizard's questions correctly:

1. **Start the Active Directory Users and Computers snap-in.**

   To start the Active Directory Users and Computers snap-in, click the Start menu and then choose Programs⇨Administrative Tools⇨ Active Directory Users and Computers.

2. **Right-click the object whose control you want to delegate and then choose Delegate Control from the menu.**

   The Welcome to the Delegation of Control Wizard appears.

3. **Click Next.**

   The Users or Groups dialog box appears. This is the place where you choose the user(s) and/or group(s) that you want to delegate control to.

4. **Click the Add button.**

   The Select Users, Computers, or Groups dialog box appears.

5. **Select the user or group you're interested in and then click the Add button; when you have added all the users and/or groups you want, click the OK button.**

   You can do this for as many users and/or groups as you want to delegate to. If you can't find the right user, computer, or group, they might not be a member of the domain shown in the drop-down list at the top of the dialog box. Click the list to see all the domains in the forest. Select another domain or select Entire Directory to see all the objects in the forest.

   You return to the Users or Groups dialog box.

6. **Take one last look at the persons who are getting new authority and click either Next (if the list looks good) or Remove (if you want to prune the list a bit).**

   The Tasks to Delegate dialog box appears.

   If you select a domain or an organizational unit, the options will be related to those types of objects. If you select one of the folders in the Active Directory, then you'll have the option to delegate control of one of the following:

   - All the objects in the folder you selected, including the folder itself and any new objects added to the folder

   - Specific types of objects, like computer objects, connection objects, and user objects

7. **Click the specific tasks you want to delegate and then click Next.**

   If you are delegating control of a folder, then the Permissions dialog box appears. This dialog box gives you the opportunity to specify what permissions will be delegated.

8. **Click the permissions you want to delegate. To filter the lists of permissions, click on or off the three check boxes:**

   - **General** standard permissions, like Read, Write, Read All properties, and so on.

   - **Property-specific** permissions specific to the type of folder you're delegating

   - **Child objects** permission that would allow the delegatee to manage objects created in the container being delegated

   If you need more information on permissions, be sure to read Chapter 4.

9. **Click Next.**

10. **The Congratulations dialog box appears. Click Finish to clear it.**

Grappling with Windows 2000 Groups

Windows 2000 is in love with groups. When you install Windows 2000, a handful of local groups are created. A few more show up when a computer joins the domain, and Windows 2000 even adds its own groups to groups on the local machine when the machine joins the domain party. In fact, you might even see some groups you haven't seen before when you look at the Permissions dialog box. Well, that's enough complaining.

Figuring out those built-in groups

A number of groups are created as soon as you roll out the Active Directory. You can see these groups for the first time on the domain controller you use to launch the installation of the Active Directory. As you move more computers to the Active Directory, they will be able to see and use these groups.

- **Administrators:** Members of the Administrators group can do whatever they like. Members of the Administrators group have free reign on local machines, on member servers, all over the domain, and on domain controllers. What's more, if there's some permission that has not been explicitly granted to members of the Administrators group, they can give the permissions to themselves. Being in the Administrators group is like being on the A list in more ways than one.

- **Account Operators:** This group is set up to provide a home for administrators-lite users. These users can create, delete, and manage user accounts and groups in the domain.

- **Guests:** The Guests group is used to store accounts that would have limited access to the network, including the Guest account. Members of the Guests group include the Domain Guests group, as well as the IUSR_*domain_name* account used to authenticate visitors to Web sites or FTP launched on the domain.

  Read Chapter 12 if you're interested in how the IUSR_*domain_name* account is used.

- **Server Operators:** The Server Operators group is used to house the accounts responsible for maintaining servers in the network. Members of this group can change the system time, back up and restore files, and shut down the server.

- **Users:** The users group is made up of . . . users. Members of this group have no administrative rights.

✓ **Print Operators:** Members of this group have the right to manage domain printers. They may also shut down the server and log on locally.

✓ **Backup Operators:** This group is used to house the accounts responsible for backing up and restoring files.

Windows 2000 maintains a few groups for its own use. These groups have no specific rights. Instead, Windows 2000 deploys them wherever it needs to. Microsoft suggests that you add user accounts to these groups, but if you're not sure where these accounts will be deployed, doing so may not be a great idea.

✓ **Domain Users:** Any user account created in the domain is automatically a member of the Domain Users group. You can use this group account to easily assign permissions to all the users in the domain, regardless of their level, Administrator or Users, or membership in other groups.

✓ **Domain Admins:** The Domain Admins group includes all user Administrator accounts. Ever notice how this group shows up on any computer in the domain? When a local computer, even one running Windows 2000 server, joins the domain, the Domain Admins group is added to the Administrators group on the local computer. This means that any administrator in the group gets free reign over the local PC as well. Windows 2000 uses this group whenever it needs to throw around administrator rights.

✓ **Domain Guests:** The Guest account is a member of this group. Windows 2000 deploys this group wherever in the domain it needs to represent the group of guests.

✓ **Enterprise Admins:** The administrator is a default member of this group. Microsoft recommends that this group be populated with accounts that have administrative responsibilities across the enterprise.

Windows 2000 creates another set of groups for its own use. You can't delete these groups, and you can't change the membership of these groups. Actually, the membership of these groups changes as users log on and off of the domain. You can, however, use these groups when you determine permissions for different objects.

✓ **Everyone:** Uh, take a guess who belongs to this group.

✓ **Authenticated Users:** The Authenticated Users group is the same as the Everyone group but does not include users logged on anonymously, most likely via FTP or Web server access.

✓ **Network:** This group includes any user accounts accessing a particular shared resource on the network.

✓ **Interactive:** This group includes all users logged on at a particular computer and accessing a resource on that computer.

✔ **Anonymous Logon:** This group includes connections made via the anonymous accounts, typically from FTP and web server access.

✔ **Dialup:** Members include user accounts logged on via remote access.

Lastly, Windows 2000 provides a few handy groups on the local computer:

✔ **Administrators:** Like the Administrators group on the domain, members of this group have full control over the computer.

✔ **Backup Operators:** The members of this group have the rights to back up and restore files on the local computer, even if the permissions applied to the files normally restrict access by members of the group.

✔ **Guests:** This group is reserved for the periodic visitors to a computer. Members of this group have limited rights.

✔ **Power Users:** The Power Users group is somewhere in power between users and administrators. Members of this group can create user accounts, and they can manage accounts that they create. Members of this group are not permitted to manage user accounts they did not create. Members of this group also can create local groups.

✔ **Replicator:** This group is reserved for the account that manages directory replication functions within the domain.

✔ **Users:** The Users group is the main group for nonadministrators of the local computer. These users can run programs, start and shut down the computer, and do other day-to-day chores. The only administrative right members of this group have is to create local groups.

Creating groups of domain users

The makers of Windows 2000 assume that more than one domain might be in your tree or forest. With that in mind, the groups you can create have the capability to cross a domain boundary. Here is a list of the three different types of groups you can create.

✔ **Domain Local:** Members of a domain local group can only access resources in the domain where the group was created, but the members of the group can come from all domains in the forest.

✔ **Global:** Members of a Global group are limited to user accounts in the domain where the group was created, but permissions can be created so that members of the group can access resources in any domain in the forest.

✔ **Universal Group:** The Universal Group is wide open. Membership can come from any users in any domain in the forest, and permissions can be created allowing members of the group to access resources in any domain in the forest.

Follow these steps to create a new group in the domain.

1. **Start the Active Directory Users and Computers snap-in.**

   To start the Active Directory Users and Computers snap-in, click the Start menu and then choose Programs⇨Administrative Tools⇨ Active Directory Users and Computers.

2. **Right-click the folder where you want the group created and then choose New⇨Group from the menu.**

   The New Object - Group dialog box appears, as shown in Figure 3-3.

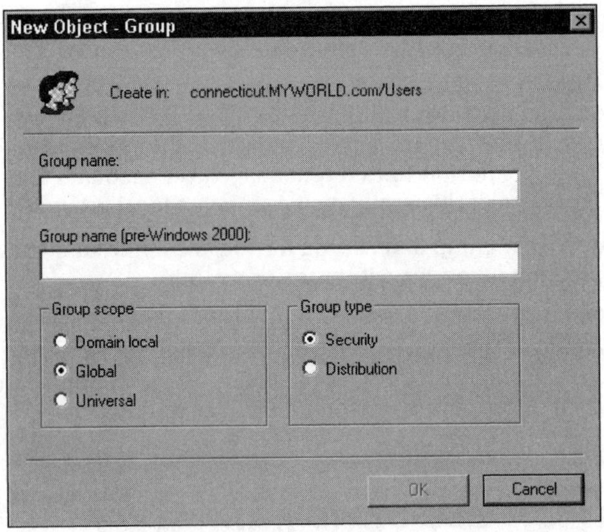

Figure 3-3:
The New
Object –
Group
dialog box.

New Object - Group	☒

Create in: connecticut.MYWORLD.com/Users

Group name:

Group name (pre-Windows 2000):

Group scope
- ○ Domain local
- ◉ Global
- ○ Universal

Group type
- ◉ Security
- ○ Distribution

OK   Cancel

3. **Enter the name of the group in the Group Name box.**

   Notice that when you enter characters in the Group name box that they also appear in the Group Name (pre-Windows 2000) box.

4. **Click the Group Scope option for the new group.**

   If the Universal option is not active, don't worry, your installation is not broken. This means your domain is running in mixed-mode, which means your domain also supports pre-Windows 2000 domain controllers. You won't be able to create a Universal group until you change the operation mode of the domain to Native mode.

5. **Click the Security Group Type option.**

6. **Click OK.**

   The group is created.

Accounting for a Secure Network

One of the most critical things you can do to be sure that your network is secure is to use your head when creating user accounts. You can set a number of important security options for each user account you create, so be sure to review each of the many tabs on the user accounts properties page. A review of the important options can be found in a paragraph or two.

In addition to being wary of new user accounts, you need to be aware of accounts that just seem to show up on your network. Windows 2000 creates a few default user accounts to get your network up and running. The accounts include the Administrator and the Guest accounts. There are a few things you should know about these accounts.

Creating user accounts the secure way

As much as group policy and security settings define much of the security configuration for your network, the options you select when you create new user accounts will make a big impact on the relative security of your network.

Follow these steps to open the Properties sheet for a particular user and then review the guidelines that follow the steps for setting secure options for user accounts.

1. **Start the Active Directory Users and Computers.**

   To start the Active Directory Users and Computers snap-in, click the Start menu and then choose Programs⇨Administrative Tools⇨Active Directory Users and Computers.

2. **Open the Users folder.**

   You can open the folder by clicking once on the + button beside the folder.

3. **Find the user account you're interested in and then right-click it.**

4. **Choose Properties from the menu.**

5. **Choose the tab that contains the security options that you want to set.**

   If you're not sure which tab contains the options you want to set, then make sure that you check out the following sections, which describe each available tab.

6. **Complete the tab.**

   If you're not sure how to complete the tab, see the following sections where I point out the strange and extraordinary.

7. **Click OK.**

   Your options are set!

The following sections give you guidelines, by tab, for setting secure user accounts.

Account tab

The following options appear on the Account tab:

- **Logon Hours:** Click the button labeled Logon Hours to specify the days of the week and the hours during those days that the user is explicitly allowed or denied logon rights. Windows 2000 uses a fancy dialog box to let you select the hours and days. Keep in mind that you can select both permitted and nonpermitted periods.

- **User Must Change Password at Next Logon:** You can find this option in the list of Account Options. This option forces the user to change his password the next time he attempts to log on.

   Here's a typical scenario in which this option is relevant: An administrator or member of the Account Operators group creates an account for a new user. The administrator either leaves the password blank, which is a big security risk, or enters a default password for the account, which is a smaller security risk. If you set this option, you can reduce exposure to the risk posed by the administrator knowing the password for the new user account.

   You can find this option in the list of Account Options.

- **User Cannot Change Password:** Use this option to restrict a user from changing his password. The only scenario in which this option should be set is if the passwords for your organization are managed by a central security group. In this case, the group provides each user with the password for his account; this option ensures that a user doesn't change the password back to his birthday, favorite color, or dog's name. You can find this option in the list of Account Options.

- **Password Never Expires:** This option is another of those dangerous choices. There's probably not a reasonable scenario in which a user should be able to keep the same password forever. The Administrator account gets this option automatically. You can find this option in the list of Account Options.

- **Store Password Using Reversible Encryption:** This option allows passwords to be stored in a method in which they can be decrypted. This option is set to support a weak authentication requirement. It's best not to set this option. You can find this option in the list of Account Options.

✔ **Account Is Disabled:** You can disable an account temporarily by checking this option.

✔ **Smart Card Is Required for Interactive Logon:** This option requires a user to use a smart card for logon authentication. While this option is checked, the user affected will not be able to log on using the tried-and-true user ID and password approach. You can find details on the creation of smart cards in Chapter 15.

✔ **Account Is Trusted for Delegation:** This option is like giving a user a pat on the back and saying that they are doing a great job. Checking this option means that you allow this user to delegate control of part of the domain.

✔ **Account Is Sensitive and Cannot Be Delegated:** This option does not allow control of this account to be delegated to another user or group.

✔ **Do Not Require Kerberos Preauthentication:** This option determines whether a user is pre-authenticated with a Kerberos ticket before ticket exchange with a service. If a user account uses a different version of the client software than Microsoft's and that does not support the ticket-granting ticket, check this option. You can find more details on this option in Chapter 2.

Dial-in properties

Options on the Dial-in tab (see Figure 3-4) let you configure the user account for dial-in access. You can configure the account with some security-smart option, such as verifying that the phone number used to dial-in is the same one on record for the user account. Dial-in security is so important that it has its own chapter. You can read all about the secure dial-in properties in Chapter 9.

What's a password?

The word password appears in this book dozens of times. In case you're wondering, here are the details on Windows 2000 passwords:

✔ Maximum length of 14 characters

✔ Case sensitive (MyPassWord is different than mypassword)

✔ Can contain special characters except for the following:

" / \ [ ] : ; | = , + * ? < >

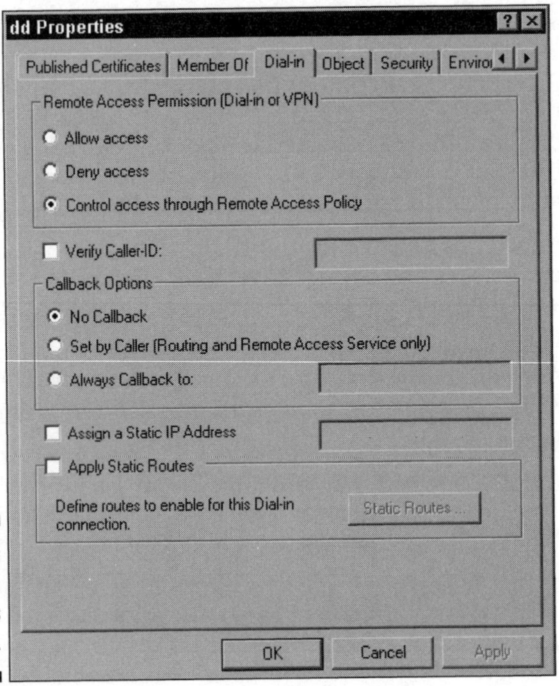

Figure 3-4:
The Logon
Hours
dialog box.

Managing that troublesome administrator account

If the Administrator account were a piece of candy, you might say about it, "How can something so sweet also taste so sour sometimes?" From a convenience and control perspective, there's nothing better than the Administrator account. From a security perspective, though, there's nothing worse than the Administrator account. Here's what you need to know:

✔ The Administrator account is the first account created on any installation of Windows 2000.

✔ The Administrator account cannot be locked out, cannot be forced to change passwords, and cannot be made to eat vegetables — now that's power!

✔ The administrator and the Administrators group have a relationship like the chicken and the egg paradox (which came first?) The Administrator account, like members of the Administrators group, is all-powerful. So, where does the power come from? Is it because the Administrator is automatically a member of the all-powerful Administrators group, or does the Administrators group get its power from its most famous member?

So what's the best way to deal with the Administrator account? I'll let you count the ways:

- Rename the Administrator account. If intruders can't find the Administrator account, then there's no way they can target it. Rename the Administrator account as soon as Windows 2000 is installed.

- Use Security Settings and group policy to rename the Administrator account on all domain computers.

- Don't use the Administrator account on a regular basis, even if you rename it. Instead, create an account with all the permissions you need. This way, you can reduce the risk of accidentally staying logged on at a domain computer with the administrator account or of someone spying on you as you enter the password.

- Create a decoy Administrator account. Obviously (hopefully), you'll have to rename the original Administrators account. Once you create the decoy account, keep a close eye on the audit log for that account. You'll be able to monitor attacks on the account. Don't forget to strip away all permissions from the decoy account!

How about that equally annoying guest account?

Windows 2000 thinks it does you a favor by creating a Guest account automatically. This account is intended for use by occasional users of the computer or as a back door for users to get on the computer if their account is disabled. No network administrator wants a guest like this one because the account is created without a password. The Guest is disabled by default (and it should stay that way).

Part II
Starting with a Good Defense

The 5th Wave   By Rich Tennant

©RICHTENNANT

"They were selling contraband online. We broke through the door just as they were trying to flush the hard drive down the toilet."

In this part . . .

A smart person once said that the best defense is a good offense. If that were true and you could apply that to Windows 2000, you might be tempted to go on the attack against suspected hackers, intruders, and so on. Maybe you would deploy a weapon that would send packet-encapsulated power surges to the target computer, zapping the target's computer and frying the modem. Keep dreaming.

This part is the alternative. The best defense is a good defense. Read on to find out how to establish password rules, permissions on files, folders, rules about user accounts, and a huge amount more.

Chapter 4

Avoiding Promiscuous Permissions

. . . .

In This Chapter

▶ Figuring out what permissions are

▶ Sorting out permissions and inheritance

▶ Applying permissions

▶ Mixing permissions

▶ Sampling permissions

. . . .

*P*ermissions show up almost wherever you try to secure anything in Windows 2000. You use permissions to secure everything from files to domains in Windows 2000. You get to specify who can do what to which. Permissions can be used with a single user, a group of users, a group of groups, a computer, and even Web-browsing users. You also see permission used to lock down computers that aren't even part of the Active Directory. (See Chapter 2 for more on the Active Directory.) Permissions are so powerful that you can assign permission to assign a permission (that wasn't a mistake).

A Primer on Permissions

Permissions are the straw that stirs the security drink. Permissions are probably the most important component of Windows 2000 security. Permissions determine who has access to what in your Active Directory and users' workstations. While authentication identifies the person who attempts to access some secured element in Windows 2000 (see Chapter 3), like a file or a printer or some service, permissions determine what the user can and can't do with that thing, such as edit a file, clear a printer queue, or start a fax service.

Permissions also are used to secure things on a local computer whether that PC is part of an Active Directory or not, but this chapter looks a bit closer at networked objects.

Permissions are easy to figure out when you think of the two things they affect:

✔ **Objects:** You apply permissions *for* the Windows 2000 objects you want to protect. These objects can be network resources, such as a printer that has been purchased for public use, an organizational unit, a shared folder, or a Web page, or they can be things that sit on a local user's computer, such as a file, folder, shortcut, whatever. You might also read how you can "create permissions for" this or that.

✔ **Users, computers, and groups:** Permissions are assigned to users, computers, or groups (UCG). When you define permissions for an object in the Windows 2000 Active Directory, you pick from the list of all users, computers, and groups in the Active Directory to determine who may or may not have access to the object (see Figure 4-1). If the object you're securing is on a computer that is not part of the Active Directory, then the list of persons who may or may not have access to the object is limited to those accounts and groups that are set up on the computer.

Figure 4-1:
If you create permissions for an object in the Active Directory, you can give or deny access to any user or computer or group in the Active Directory.

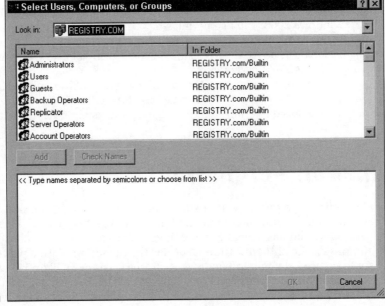

Here are some examples of permissions at work:

- Rachel can see the contents of a certain folder on the network, but she can't add or delete folders or files to that secured folder.

- Members of the Domain Administrators Support Group can create objects in the Active Directory, but cannot apply changes made to group policy to all objects in the Active Directory.

- Allison can change the properties for the laser printer in the Finance department, such as specify a separator page or change the hours at which a printer is available, but she cannot view the list of documents queued to be printed. Allison also has full control over the printer in Engineering, including control over documents waiting to be printed.

- All the members of the Accounts Payable department have full control over all the documents in the AP folder. These same folks have no access to any computer in the Quality Engineering lab.

- Victoria can see all the computers in the Shipping organizational unit, but she can't add any computers to the organizational unit or delete any, either.

So many objects, so many permission types

Permissions are not just a yes/no proposition, meaning that permissions determine more than just whether a UCG has access to an object. Like you and maybe me, permissions are smart. They know about objects and what a UCG might want to do with one. For example, when you set the permissions for a file, you can specify whether a UCG can open the file, read the file, run the file, change its attributes, and more. If you know anything about printers, you know that you can't really open, read, or run one. You can, however, manage a printer and the documents queued-up to be printed by one. This is an example of the different types of permissions you can set for two different types of objects. Windows 2000 lets you set permissions that are relevant to the type of object you're working with. Figure 4-2 shows the permissions you can set for a printer, and Figure 4-3 shows the permissions you can set for a file or folder. (To find out how to set a permission, see the section "Set a basic permission," later in this chapter.)

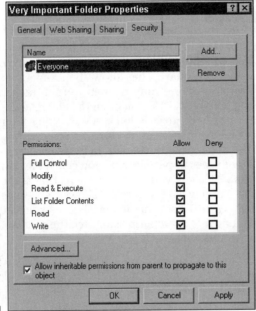

Figure 4-2:
Permissions
you can set
for a printer.

Figure 4-3:
Permissions
you can set
for a file or
folder.

So many users, so many permissions

Once a user is permitted access into your network, permissions determine what the user can do and can't do. These users aren't just the people you can see and touch, like Larry in Purchasing, who sits in the cube next to the cappuccino maker, or Fran in Development, who keeps a guppy-filled aquarium in her office. These users with permissions are also those who connect to your network over the Internet via FTP and Web sites your company raises. These users, like all others, also are subject to the permissions you create.

As an example, when someone connects to a Web site hosted by Windows 2000, a real user account is used to determine what the visitor can see and do. This user account has the name IUSR_*computername* where *computername* is the name of the server where the Windows 2000 Internet server is running. Any permissions you establish for the IUSR_*computername* account are applied to visitors to your Web site. If you mistakenly apply Full Control for the permissions server to the IUSR_*computername,* then every user who visits your Web site potentially has the rights to become your Web server's Web master! Yikes!

Naturally, there's more to consider regarding permissions for Web visitors, so read Chapter 12 for more details.

Only NTFS-permissions permitted!

Permissions are only available on drives that have been formatted with NTFS, which is the Windows 2000 preferred file system. If the object you want to secure is stored on a drive that has not been formatted with NTFS, such as FAT or FAT32, you cannot use permissions to secure the objects on the drive.

Here's more of what you need to know about NTFS and permissions:

✔ How is it possible that some resource on your network is not on an NTFS drive? Easy; here's a scenario: A computer on the Active Directory has more than one hard drive and one of them is not formatted with NTFS. This sounds like a situation where the network/security administrator is not doing an A+ job (hint, hint).

✔ How do you know whether a drive is formatted with NTFS or not? Here are a few ways:

• At the command prompt, type CHKDSK. The first message CHKDSK sends back is the type of drive. See Figures 4-4 and 4-5 for an example of each.

• Right-click a file, folder, or a drive or drive partition and then choose Properties. The next thing you should see is the Properties sheet for the drive/partition you chose. If the Security tab appears, you're in NTFS luck.

TIP

If you look at the Properties sheet of an object using the Active Directory User and Computers snap-in and do not see the Security tab, you might not be seeing the entire story. Choose View➪ Advanced Features.

```
Command Prompt                                                    _ □ X
The type of the file system is NTFS.

WARNING!  F parameter not specified.
Running CHKDSK in read-only mode.

CHKDSK is verifying files (stage 1 of 3)...
File verification completed.
CHKDSK is verifying indexes (stage 2 of 3)...
Index verification completed.
CHKDSK is verifying security descriptors (stage 3 of 3)...
Security descriptor verification completed.
CHKDSK is verifying Usn Journal...
Usn Journal verification completed.
Windows found problems with the file system.
Run CHKDSK with the /F (fix) option to correct these.

   6136798 KB total disk space.
   1731988 KB in 21703 files.
      6112 KB in 939 indexes.
         0 KB in bad sectors.
     89354 KB in use by the system.
     32736 KB occupied by the log file.
   4309344 KB available on disk.

      4096 bytes in each allocation unit.
   1534199 total allocation units on disk.
   1077336 allocation units available on disk.

F:\>
```

Figure 4-4: CHKDSK reports the file system as NTFS.

```
Command Prompt                                                    _ □ X
Microsoft Windows 2000 [Version 5.00.2128]
(C) Copyright 1985-1999 Microsoft Corp.

F:\Documents and Settings\Administrator>d:

D:\>chkdsk
The type of the file system is FAT32.
Volume COMMON created 11/10/1998 7:53 PM
Volume Serial Number is 8F66-1F5E
Windows is verifying files and folders...
Windows found errors on the disk, but will not fix them
because disk checking was run without the /F (fix) parameter.
\regwork\REGOUT Errors in . and/or .. corrected.
\regwork\regtools Errors in . and/or .. corrected.
File and folder verification is complete.
Windows found problems with the file system.
Run CHKDSK with the /F (fix) option to correct these.
   4,248,872 KB total disk space.
       5,556 KB in 182 hidden files.
       3,240 KB in 610 folders.
   2,216,412 KB in 15,958 files.
   2,023,628 KB are available.

       4,096 bytes in each allocation unit.
   1,062,218 total allocation units on disk.
     505,907 allocation units available on disk.

D:\>
```

Figure 4-5: CHKDSK reports the file system as FAT32.

✔ How do you make a non-NTFS partition into an NTFS partition? You'll have to convert the partition or drive using the CONVERT command. You use this command at, no surprise here, the command prompt. Check out *Windows 2000 Professional For Dummies* by Andy Rathbone or *Windows 2000 Server For Dummies* by Ed Tittel (both by IDG Books Worldwide, Inc.) for cool details on file system types and conversion issues.

Permissions and the Art of Parenting

Depending on the size of your Active Directory, including all the securable items on users' computers, there could be thousands of objects floating around. You've got computers, organization units, folders, files, printers, services, and a ton more. Each of these objects must be secured, and permissions are the tool to do it. So, inquiring minds want to know:

✔ How are you going to set permissions for all those objects created when you install Windows 2000, as well as when you install the Active Directory?

✔ How do you manage permissions for all those objects that you and users create every day?

Worry not! Windows 2000 applies a default set of permissions to every object it creates and you create. No fuss, no muss. What are these permissions? Like a mother gorilla caring for its young, permissions display parental care instincts. An object receives it first permissions from its parent. You're probably wondering what a parent object is, and for that matter, what a child object is. Good question. Answers are on the way in the following section.

My parent is an object!

Almost every object in Windows 2000 has a parent. The parent of an object is usually the container where an object is stored. Chapter 2 explains the whole object and container deal. Here are examples of this parent-child thing:

✔ The folder in which one or more files are stored is the parent of each of the files, as well as of any subfolders in that folder.

✔ Folders in the root folder of a drive are the children of the drive.

✔ The Registry is usually presented in a hierarchical format, as shown in Figure 4-6. Keys that belong to another key are the children of the parent key.

Registry data is stored in a handful of files on the same drive where Windows 2000 is running. This doesn't mean, then, that the parent of the Registry is the folder that the Registry files are stored in. The Registry is special. Consider the Registry to be at the top of the family tree.

✔ Active Directory objects are usually children of the thing that created them.

✔ The Computers node in the Active Directory tree is the parent of any computers you create in the Active Directory (see Figure 4-7).

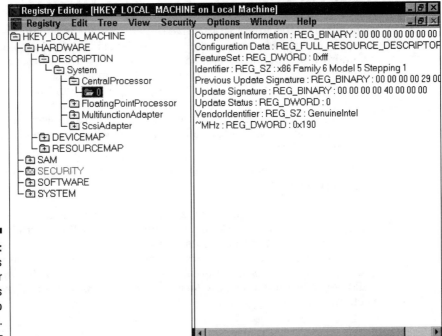

Figure 4-6:
Parent keys pass their permissions down to child keys.

The idea of parents and children is important because objects inherit permissions from their parents. When the permissions are applied to an object, they are immediately and automatically applied to any child object. When a new object is created, the object automatically receives the same permissions as its parent. The reasoning behind this seems logical: If you bother to create permissions for something, like a folder, and you create some new things in that now-secured object, like more folders, you probably would want the same permissions applied to the new things.

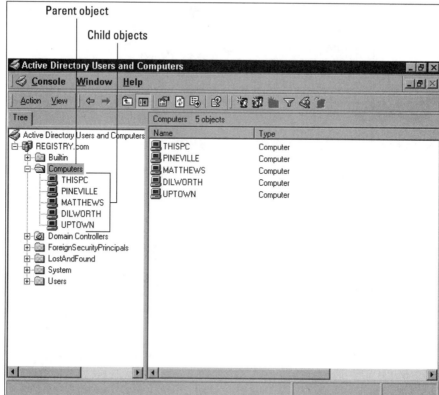

Figure 4-7:
Computers are children objects of the computer container.

If the permissions for an object appear gray (see Figure 4-8), this means that the object receives it permissions from a parent object (and that parent object might receive its permissions from its parent). If an object has permissions that are gray and some that aren't, it means that the nongray permissions were actually created at the child object. These permissions override the same permissions set at the parent.

Policy gets inherited, too

Permissions aren't the only things that get passed down from parent to child. Policy also is inherited from parent objects. Policy in Windows 2000 refers to the rules that control how computers in the Windows 2000 Active Directory are configured and used. Policy goes beyond the typical security boundary. For example, policy might determine that users cannot install software on their computers and that they cannot browse to certain sites using Internet Explorer.

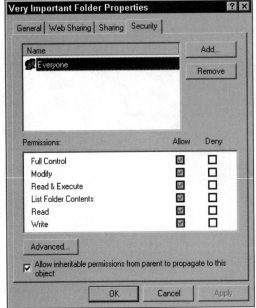

Figure 4-8:
Child
objects
aren't
required to
have their
permissions
passed
down from
their parent.

Child objects stand up for their rights!

Almost every rule has exceptions. Of course, there are some exceptions to the objects-inherit-permissions-from-their-parents rule.

Objects can be like rebellious teenagers. An object can be set up so that it *does not* receive the permissions applied to its parent. This independent-thinking object defines its own permissions. Of course, the object does exhibit this free will on its own. You must clear the Allow Inheritable Permissions From Parent To Propagate To This Object option on the object's Property sheet to keep a parent from enforcing its will.

Parent objects can loosen the reigns

Parents in the Windows 2000 world have flexibility just like in the real world. Parent objects can enforce their will to their children as much or as little as they choose (see Figure 4-9).

- ✔ Parent objects can apply their permissions only to their immediate children, not to any descendant objects of their own children.

✔ Parent objects can apply their permissions only to their children and not themselves. This is also known as the "It's different because I'm a grown-up" setting.

✔ Parent objects can apply their permissions only to themselves, not to their children.

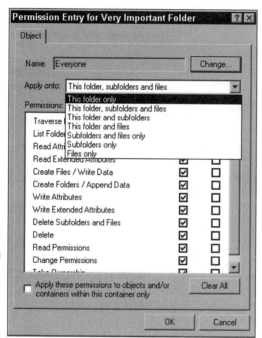

Figure 4-9:
Permissions
pass-down
options.

So, You Want to Administer Permissions?

Be proud! You're a Windows 2000 administrator (or, at least you will be soon, or you tell people that you are one). As an administrator, an important job is to set permissions. Here's how to do it:

1. **Locate the object that you want to set up permissions for.**

   The first thing to do when you want to set permissions for an object is to track down the object. This means that you must find the object, as well as have access to it. For example, if you want to tune the permissions for a group policy object, you must have sufficient rights to the domain controller where the GPO is located.

2. **Right-click the object and then choose Properties from the menu that appears.**

    The object's Properties sheet appears.

3. **Click the Security tab.**

    The Security sheet appears. An example of a Security sheet for a file object is shown in Figure 4-10.

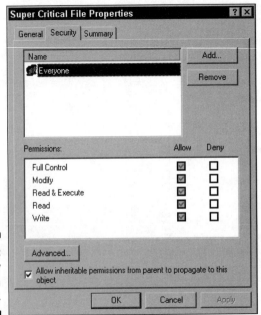

Figure 4-10: A Security sheet for a file object.

4. **Choose the permissions that you want.**

    • If permissions are set for more than one account, click the UCG to see the permissions. The list of permissions will change when you click different UCGs.

    • If the permission check boxes appear gray, then the permissions you see are inherited from the parent of the object you're working on.

Now you're ready to roll. You can find a description of how to handle your permissions chores in the sections that follow.

Add or remove a UCG

The pick and shovel work involved in setting up permissions is picking the UCG that should have access to something. There's no shortcut around this step — you've got to do it. You might also have to take a UCG off of a permission list.

1. **Open the Properties sheet for the object.**

   If you need a refresher on this, check out the beginning of this section under the "So, You Want to Administer Permissions?" heading.

2. **Remove the UCGs that don't belong.**

   If you're not interested in removing a UCG from the list, hop down to Step 4. To remove a user, computer, or group from the list, select the item you want to get rid of in the Name list.

3. **Click the Remove button.**

   The item you select disappears from the list.

   If you try to remove the Everyone group from the list, be ready for the alarms to sound. You might see a message like the one in Figure 4-11. This message is reminding you that only the owner of the object will be able to access the object.

Figure 4-11:
Everyone means EVERYONE. Are you sure you do not want anyone to have access to this object?

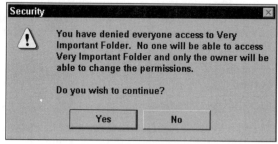

4. **If you want to create permissions for a UCG not shown in the list, click the Add button.**

   The Select Users, Computers, or Groups dialog box appears, as shown in Figure 4-12.

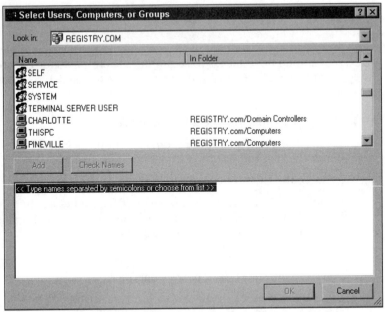

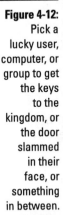

Figure 4-12:
Pick a
lucky user,
computer, or
group to get
the keys
to the
kingdom, or
the door
slammed
in their
face, or
something
in between.

5. **Select the UCG you're interested in and then click the Add button.**

You can do this for as many UCGs as you want to create permissions for.

If you can't find the right user, computer, or group, they might not be a member of the domain shown in the drop-down list at the top of the dialog box. Click the list to see all the domains in the forest. Select another domain or select Entire Directory to see all the objects in the forest.

6. **When you have added all the UCGs you want to set permissions for, click the OK button.**

7. **Click OK to close the Property sheet.**

Keep in mind that if all you did was add a user, get back to work. You need to set permissions for this user, computer, or group.

Am I on the guest list?

Sometimes you don't know whether it's better to be on a bad list than to not be on any list. In the case of Windows 2000 permissions, it doesn't matter. If the permissions for an object do not include a particular UCG, they have NO access to the object. This is the same as having all permissions for an object set to Deny.

Set a basic permission

These steps guide you through setting basic permissions on an object. This process isn't too complicated; you can usually get by with just two to four clicks.

1. **Open the Properties sheet for the object and then click the Security tab.**

2. **Select the UCG from the list.**

3. **Click the check box in the Allow or Deny for each permission.**

   That's it! You might notice odd goings-on, like check boxes clearing by their own will, when you click certain permissions.

   - If you check the Allow option for the Full Control permission, all of the other permissions in the list also switch to Allow. The same happens if you click Deny.

   - If Full Control is checked and you click another of the permissions in the list, the Full Control check box is cleared. Why? If you clear one of the permissions, then the UCG no longer has full control.

     Also, any permissions that become invalid because of the permission you check also are cleared. For example, if you check Deny for the Read permission for most any object, the Modify, Read & Execute, and Write permissions are yanked away, as well as a few others, because you can't change what you can't see!

   - Don't be afraid of the big bad gray box. Just because a permission or two is inherited from a parent does not mean that you can't enhance it. For example, if you come across a folder that grants just Read permissions for a specific user based on inheritance, there's nothing to stop you from clicking on Read & Execute to enhance the user's inherited permissions without changing any others.

4. **Click OK to call it a day!**

Change the inheritance rules

Your objects should have the right to think for themselves and, like teenagers, to choose their own friends. When an object inherits permissions from its parents, the object doesn't have this chance to be independent. You can change this. Here's how:

1. **Open the Properties sheet for the object and click the Security tab.**

   If you need help with this step, consult the steps found at the beginning of this section under the "So, You Want to Administer Permissions?" heading.

2. **Clear the check box labeled Allow Inheritable Permissions From Parent To Propagate To This Object.**

   The dialog box shown in Figure 4-13 appears. The dialog box is trying to tell you that the permissions that were created for your object by its parent aren't out of the picture yet. You need to tell Windows 2000 what to do with the permissions that have been applied to the object by the object's parent. Here are the options:

   - **Copy:** Create the same permissions directly on the object that had been applied previously via inheritance.

   - **Remove:** Delete all permissions set for the object. You need to start from scratch with this choice, adding UCGs and setting their access.

   - **Cancel:** Turn the Allow Inheritable Permissions From Parent To Propagate To This Object option back on and return to the Security sheet.

Figure 4-13:
Not so fast!
You must
clean up the
permissions
passed
down from
the object's
parental
unit.

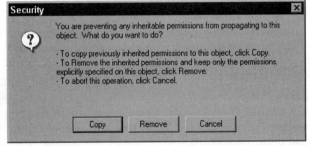

3. **Click the button to tell Windows 2000 what you want to do with those nuisance permissions.**

   You return to the Security sheet.

4. **Click OK.**

Flex your security muscles with advanced permissions

Okay, tough gals and guys — drop the gloves. Here's where you can really demonstrate how tight your security is. Use Advanced Permissions to tune the access to objects on your network and computers.

Advanced permissions also are used to override the default inheritance rules. As you see in this procedure, you can either change or just view the Advanced permissions to see any special rules regarding inheritance of permissions established for the object.

1. **Open the Properties sheet for the object and select the Security tab.**

   If you're confused with this step, good help is easy to find! Check out the beginning of this section under the "So, You Want to Administer Permissions?" heading.

2. **Click the Advanced button.**

   The Access Control Settings dialog box for your object appears, like the one shown in Figure 4-14.

   The table in the dialog box shows all permissions created for the object, as well as the type of permission (Full Control, Special, and so on) and to which child objects, if any, the permissions are applied to.

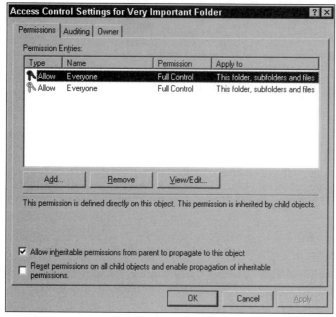

Figure 4-14:
The Access
Control
Settings
dialog box.

3. **Click the permission you want to change in the list of permissions shown in the middle of the dialog box and then click the View/Edit button.**

The Permission Entry dialog box appears, as shown in Figure 4-15.

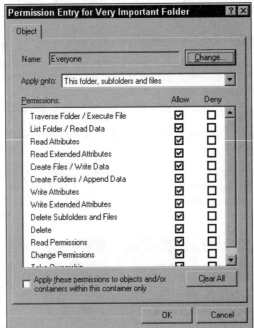

Figure 4-15:
The
Permission
Entry
dialog box.

4. **Select how you want the permission applied from the drop-down list labeled Apply Onto at the top of the dialog box.**

   This is your opportunity to fine-tune how the permissions are applied to child objects. You can choose exactly which descendants, if any, also will have the permissions you're creating applied.

   If the object you're working on cannot contain child objects, the drop-down list will be grayed out. If you look carefully and squint your eyes, you can see the words, "This object only."

5. **Click the Allow or Deny check box for each of the permissions you need to change; when you're done, click the OK button.**

   You return to the Access Control Settings dialog box for your object.

6. **Choose another permission to edit or click OK to return to the Security sheet.**

7. **Click OK to close the Property sheet.**

Signing the Deed to the Object

An administrator needs to be extremely careful as to who has permissions to what. To protect those precious objects, only the owner of an object can set its permissions. The owner also can determine what other users have the right to set permissions.

A curious user might read this and say, "Hey! This permission thing sounds great. Where do I sign up? How can I become an owner?" The owner of an object is established in a few ways.

 ✔ The user who creates an object is the owner of that object. If you create a file or a folder or add a printer, guess what — you own 'em. Naturally, the permissions and policies might not allow you to create the object you want to, but you get the idea.

 ✔ Lots of objects are created by Windows 2000 automatically when the operating system is installed, such as files, folders, and Registry settings. Your computer does not take ownership of these objects, like a futuristic thriller movie where machines like your toaster take control of the world. Rather, the Administrator account is granted ownership of objects created at installation.

 ✔ A user who is not the owner of an object can take ownership of it. This is not as easy as it sounds. Before a user can take ownership of something, the real owner of the object must first grant *take ownership* permissions of the object to the user.

Here is how someone can take ownership of an object:

1. **Right-click the object of which you want to take ownership and then choose Properties from the menu that appears.**

   The object's Properties sheet appears.

2. **Click the Security tab.**

   The Security tab appears.

3. **Click the Advanced button.**

   The Access Control Settings dialog box appears.

4. **Click the Owner Tab.**

   The Owner tab appears.

5. **Select the new owner's name from the list.**

6. **If the new owner will also take ownership of all child objects, be sure to check the Replace owner on subcontainers and objects check box.**

7. **Click OK.**

8. **Click OK again.**

Mixing a Pot of Permissions

Given the way permissions are set up in Windows 2000, it's really possible that a user might have more than one permission applied to a single object. For example, Andrea in the Maintenance department might be a member of the Engineering organizational unit, and because she is new and still on probation, she is also a member of the New Employees group. Lastly, and naturally, she is a member of the Everyone group. What happens if each of these groups has a slightly different permission level for some folder or other object?

- ✔ If two permissions affect the same object and the same UCG, the more restrictive of the permissions is applied.

- ✔ A UCG might get a double-shot of permissions. For example, suppose that a user belonged to two groups. One group had Read permissions to a folder, and the other group had Write permissions to the same folder. The user would get both the Read and the Write permissions. Permissions are cumulative.

- ✔ File permissions beat folder permissions. If a user has Read and Write permissions to a folder but has Deny permission to some file in the folder, the user will not be able to write to that file.

A Sampling of Permission Types

Permissions come in all shapes and sizes. The permissions you set for a bunch of folders at 9 a.m. won't look at all like the permissions you work with for an Active Directory object at 10 a.m. The following sections describe some of the more interesting permissions for some of the more interesting objects.

Folder and file permissions

There are probably more files and folders than anything else in your Active Directory. With this in mind, Table 4-1 lists some of the permissions you can apply to these popular items.

Table 4-1	Authentication Methods
Permission	*Description*
Full Control	Use this permission to grant or deny complete control of the file or folder. This permission allows the UCG to do any of the stuff listed in this table.
Modify	This permission lets you specify whether the file or folder can be changed.
Read & Execute	This permission lets the UCG read the contents of the object in the case of a folder or run the object in the case of a file.
Traverse Folder/ Execute File	This permission has a different purpose depending on whether it is applied to a file or a folder. For a folder, the Traverse Folder/Execute File permission determines whether the UCG can navigate through the subfolders in this folder, as well as through the subfolders of those subfolders, and so on. For files, this permission simply determines whether the UCG can run program files.
List Folder/ Read Data	This permission is another one of those that does something slightly different based on whether the object is a file or a folder. For folders, this permission determines whether the UCG can see the names of the files and subfolders contained in the folder. For files, this permission determines whether the UCG can read the file.
Advanced Read Attributes	This permission determines whether the UCG can look at the attributes for a file or folder. These attributes can be viewed by right-clicking the file or folder and choosing Properties, or by using Windows 2000 Explorer, or even by using the command prompt.
Read Extended Attributes	This permission determines whether the UCG can see the special properties for a file or folder. These special properties, known as extended attributes, are the properties of a file or folder or any other object that appear under the Summary tab of the Properties sheet.
Create Files/ Write Data	For files, this permission determines whether data in the file can be changed. For folders, use this permission to control whether new folders can be created in the target folder.
Create Folders/ Append Data	For files, this permission determines whether data can be added to the end of a file. For folders, use this permission to control whether new folders can be created in the target folder.

(continued)

Table 4-1 *(continued)*

Permission	Description
Write Attributes	This permission determines whether the UCG can change the attributes on the file or folder, such as Read-only or Hidden.
Write Extended Attributes	The extended attributes appear on the Summary tab of the file's or folder's property sheet. Use this permission to determine if the items on the Summary tab can be changed.
Delete Subfolders and Files	This permission determines whether the UCG can delete subfolders and files contained in the current folder.
Delete	This permission determines whether the UCG can delete the file or folder.
Read Permissions	Use this permission to determine whether a UCG can see the permissions applied to the file or folder. Be careful with this permission as you can effectively lock yourself out of the ability to change the permissions for a file or folder you might really need.
Change Permissions	This permission determines whether a UCG can change permissions on the file or folder.
Take Ownership	This permission allows the grantee to assume ownership of the file or folder.

Permissions for the Active Directory

Objects in the Active Directory also are secured with permissions. Examples of these objects include

- Computers
- Organizational Units
- Domains (yup, even domains)
- Policies

Table 4-2 should give you a taste of some of the permissions you can apply to Active Directory objects.

Table 4-2	Some Active Directory Permissions
Permission	**Description**
Create Child	This permission determines whether a child object can be created from the object being secured.
Delete Child	This permission determines whether any of the children objects of the current object can be deleted.
Read Property	Use this permission to set whether UCGs can look at the property sheet of the object (you know, right-click the object and then choose Properties from the menu).
Write Property	This permission determines if changing the properties of the object is allowed.
List Contents	Use this permission to specify whether the UCG can see the list of all the object's child objects.

Permissions for Sharing and Sharing Alike

You probably know that you and your users can share folders and drives with other people. This makes it easy for you and your users to give access to other people for a limited amount of time. There's no built-in time limit for sharing — when you don't want the user to have access any more, you stop sharing the item!

Permissions play a role in sharing. When a user shares something, he must figure out who gets access and the strength of that access. Hmmm; sounds like permissions, doesn't it?

By default, Everyone gets Full Control permission to any drive or folder you share. Danger! Here's how to apply permissions to shared folders:

1. **Right-click the folder to be shared.**

2. **Choose Properties from the menu and then click the Sharing tab.**

   The Sharing sheet appears.

3. **Click the Share this Folder option if it hasn't already been selected.**

4. **Click the Permissions button.**

   The Permissions sheet for the folder appears.

5. **If you want to allow access to the folder to a UCG not shown in the list, click the Add button.**

   The Select Users, Computers, or Groups dialog box appears.

6. **Select the UCG you're interested in and then click the Add button.**

   You can do this for as many UCGs as you want to create permissions for.

   You may also remove any UCGs already sharing this folder by clicking their names and then clicking Remove.

7. **For each UCG you add, click the type of access you want to give them in the Permissions list at the bottom**

8. **Click OK.**

9. **Click OK.**

Chapter 5

Using the Encrypting File System

In This Chapter

▶ Discovering the ins and outs of the Encrypting File System

▶ Mastering the art of decrypting

*W*indows 2000 does a great job of securing your network from inside and outside attack. Security isn't an afterthought at the desktop, either, as it's nearly impossible to log on to a computer, even if it's not part of a Windows 2000 network, without the correct credentials. The missing link in the overall security scheme, then, would seem to be accounting for the hardware that stores all the data that you're so interested in protecting. What happens if someone steals a hard drive? What if someone steals your laptop computer, yanks out the hard drive, and boots a computer with your hard drive installed as the second drive device? All security bets would seem to be off. Not the case with Windows 2000 and the Encrypting File System.

Seeing What the EFS Does for Your Users

The *EFS (encrypting file system)* protects data at the file level, preventing access to those assets by anyone but the person who protected them in the first place. With EFS, users can be assured that their private documents are safe. This safety is ensured regardless of the location of the drive on which the data finds itself. Here are the scenarios in which a user's files are safe (provided the user uses EFS):

✔ The user's hard drive is stolen.

✔ The user's files or folders are accessed over the network.

✔ Someone other than the user who protected the files in the first place boots the computer where the files are located.

✔ The user's files are secretly whisked away to Area 51 for inspection.

What the EFS doesn't do to your users is as significant as what it does. For one, users do not need to explicitly decrypt files and folders to use them. The decryption is done automatically.

Encrypting a Folder

To encrypt a file or folder, complete the following steps:

1. **Locate the file or folder using My Computer or Windows Explorer.**

2. **Right-click the icon for the object and then choose Properties.**

   The Properties dialog box for the file or folder you selected appears.

3. **Click the Advanced button.**

   The Advanced Attributes dialog box appears.

4. **Click the option to Encrypt Contents To Secure Data and then click OK.**

   You return to the Properties dialog box.

5. **Click OK.**

   If you encrypt a folder, the dialog box shown in Figure 5-1 appears.

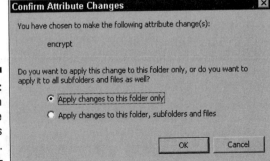

Figure 5-1:
The Confirm
Attribute
Changes
dialog box.

6. **Click the option indicating whether you want just the contents of the folder encrypted or if you want to encrypt the contents of the folder and its subfolder and files in those subfolders as well.**

   If you choose the top option, Apply Changes To This Folder Only, only the folder is encrypted, but not any of the contents. If you later add files or folders to that folder, they become encrypted. Choosing this option can later leave you with a mix of encrypted and unencrypted files, which is a scenario you want to avoid.

   A more attractive scenario would be one where you could rely on all of the contents of a folder to be encrypted or unencrypted. Period. If you choose the bottom option, Apply Changes To This Folder, Subfolders, And Files, the entire contents of the selected folder are encrypted. Further, any files or folders added to the folder become encrypted.

7. **Click OK.**

Understanding What Can, Can't, and Should Be Encrypted

Like all things new, there are some can-do's and cannot-do's associated with use of the EFS. Here they are:

✔ You may only encrypt files or folders on an NTFS partition. Files and folders on FAT, FAT16, FAT32, and other file systems may not be encrypted. This is not as unlikely as it might seem. It's not uncommon to see a mix and match of operating systems and file systems on a single machine as users play connect the dots with the operating systems.

✔ Folders are not actually encrypted. A folder is marked so that the EFS knows whether to encrypt the files in it or added to it.

✔ You cannot encrypt a system folder or a folder that has been compressed.

✔ You cannot share a folder that has been encrypted.

✔ You cannot copy a file that is marked read-only or system.

✔ You can copy or move an encrypted folder or file to any folder or drive on the machine you're running. If the drive is formatted with NTFS, the encryption comes along for the ride. If you copy or move the file or folder to a drive not formatted as NTFS, such as FAT, FAT16, FAT32, Linux, or whatever, poof, the magic dust wears off. If you copy or move the file or folder to another machine running Windows 2000, your certificate and private key must be loaded on that machine if the certificate is not available on the network (such as if the network is down or it is impossible to log on).

To copy an encrypted file or folder to a location that also supports encryption, such as and paste-and-retain encryption, you must use the Copy and Paste commands. This seems obvious, right? Well, you cannot use drag-and-drop to copy or move if you want to retain encryption, so leave that mouse where it is.

Now that you have the rules about EFS, here's the advice:

✔ Users should encrypt My Documents and any folder they may have reserved for data files.

✔ Users should encrypt the Temp directory. Also, create a folder named TMP if one doesn't exist; many applications use this folder for the storage of temporary files. Once created, encrypt it. Be sure to check for any other Temp folders created on the computer — find 'em, encrypt 'em!

✔ Microsoft Office 2000 users may want to encrypt the Auto Recovery folders. When a Microsoft Office 2000 application crashes, the Auto Recovery folders store the temporary versions of the files you had been working on. The files in these folders are real, working versions of the files you were working on when the Office app crashed, so you may want to encrypt the folders so that files created in those folders are automatically encrypted. You can find out the location of the Auto Recovery folders directly from the Office application you use.

Finding Out How EFS Encrypts and Decrypts Files and Folders

The EFS uses a public-key scheme (see Chapter 1) to encrypt and decrypt files and folders. In addition to a public key pair, the EFS uses one other type of encryption. When a file/folder is encrypted, a randomly generated encryption key is generated. This key encrypts the file. This same key is also used to decrypt the file/folder. Wait, you say, isn't that key protected? The answer is Yes. The key used to encrypt the file/folder is encrypted with the user's public key. Only the user's private key may be used to decrypt the file encryption key, and that private key is only available on the user's Windows 2000 workstation computer. Also, that private key must match up with the public key that was used to encrypt the file.

The gory details about EFS encryption

The key to the EFS is the baseline file system in Windows 2000, NTFS. If NTFS isn't used, then EFS isn't available. NTFS wasn't always so cryptography-literate. Starting with Windows 2000, Windows is now outfitted with CryptoAPI. CryptoAPI is not a wire news service written in code, nor is it a new animated-disfigured-from-nuclear-war-anti-super hero. Rather, CryptoAPI is the set of cryptography services provided to Window applications and to Windows itself. NTFS uses the services provided by the CryptoAPI to work with encrypted files.

Interested in CryptoAPI? Look for a few free weeks in your schedule to review the Windows Platform SDK (software development kit).

Every encryption scheme needs an algorithm. The EFS uses the DESX encryption algorithm. When the 128-bit encryption pack has been applied to Windows 2000, the encryption algorithm is 128-bit (duh). Otherwise, DESX is 56-bit encryption. For export beyond the borders of the United States and Canada, only 40-bit encryption is available.

The net result of this is that only the person who encrypted the file/folder can open the file/folder. This means if the file/folder is moved to a place where the user's private key cannot be accessed or authenticated, the encrypted files/folders cannot be opened. Because there always is a caveat, here's one to consider: A Windows 2000 network administrator has access to a key that can decrypt a file. See how and why later in the "Decrypting a File without the User's Private Key" section.

Decrypting a File

It's a snap to decrypt a file or folder. To do so:

1. **Locate the file or folder using Windows 2000 Explorer or My Computer.**

2. **Right-click the object to decrypt and then choose Properties.**

3. **When the Properties dialog box appears, select Advanced and then clear the Encrypt Contents To Secure Data option.**

4. **Click OK.**

   You return to the Properties dialog box.

5. **Click OK.**

   If you tried to decrypt a folder, the dialog box shown in Figure 5-2 appears.

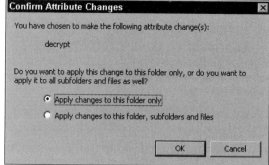

Figure 5-2:
The Confirm
Attribute
Changes
dialog box
appears.

6. **Click the option indicating whether you want just the folder selected to be decrypted or all of its contents, as well.**

   If you choose the top option, Apply Changes To This Folder Only, only the folder will be decrypted, not any of the contents. If you choose the bottom option, Apply Changes To This Folder, Subfolders And Files, the entire contents of the selected folder will be decrypted.

7. **Click OK.**

Decrypting a File without the User's Private Key

Windows 2000 provides a backdoor scheme in case a file or folder must be decrypted and either the user or the machine on which the private key of the encrypter is stored is unavailable. By default, the domain administrator has rights to decrypt a file that has been encrypted with EFS. It probably makes sense to have more than one person with this type of rights. Follow these steps to configure the system for EFS recovery.

1. **Create a user group and assign to it those persons that should have the responsibility to recover encrypted file and folder assets.**

   These folks are known as *recovery agents*. Each user in the recovery agent group also needs to request a file recovery certificate.

2. **To request a file recovery certificate, the user opens the Certificates snap-in, navigates to the Personal store, right-clicks, and chooses All Tasks⇨Request New Certificate.**

   The Certificate Request wizard starts.

3. **Each user follows the steps through the wizard to add an EFS Recovery Agent certificate.**

   You can find all the details you need about requesting a certificate in Chapter 10.

4. **Each user in the EFS recovery agent group exports their certificate along with private key.**

   This creates a certificate file with the CER extension. Users can do this by using the Certificates snap-in. You can find details on exporting a certificate in Chapter 10.

5. **Open group policy for the Active Directory item where you want to configure EFS file recovery.**

   For example, if you want to enable this feature for the domain, open the group policy for the domain. You find details on group policy in Chapter 7.

6. **Navigate down to Computer Configuration\Windows Settings\Security Settings\Public Key Policies and right-click Encrypted Data Recovery Agents and choose Add.**

   This launches the Add Recovery Agent wizard.

7. Follow the steps through the wizard to add the group created earlier.

The file or folder to be decrypted must be offloaded to a workstation machine that the recovery agent can be authenticated on. You can use any backup tool that says it's compatible with Windows 2000 as the backed-up file will retain the file's encryption. A bonus to this scheme is that the file can make non-NTFS steps along the way. When the file has arrived at the EFS recovery machine, it can be decrypted by any user logged on as an EFS recovery agent.

Restricting a Group or Computer from Encrypting

You can create policy that restricts organizational units, certain computers, or even every member of the Active Directory from using the EFS features. Why do this? There are probably two reasons:

- ✔ You want to avoid the headache of dealing with the periodic request to decrypt a file or folder for a poor schlub who has been terminated.
- ✔ You believe you do not have the need to secure a user's local file or folder assets.

To restrict some element of your organization from using EFS, follow these steps:

1. Open the group policy where you want to restrict EFS use.

As an example, to eliminate EFS use on the domain, open group policy for the domain. To restrict EFS use at a workstation, open Local Security Policy. For help with group policy, read Chapter 7.

2. Open the Public Key Policies item.

If you open group policy on an Active Directory item, such as a domain, you can find Public Key Policies under Computer Configuration\Windows Settings\Security Settings.

3. Click once on Encrypted Data Recovery Agents.

The list of certificates issued for EFS recovery appears in the details pane.

4. Delete every certificate in the list of agents.

An empty list of Data Recovery Agents will have the effect of restricting the use of EFS.

Seeing How to Do All This Stuff from the Command Line

You can use the CIPHER command at the command prompt to do lots of the things described in this chapter.

Why use the command line? Perhaps you like fixed-length fonts. Another reason is the automation ability the command line gives you. Using Windows Scripting Host or any other scripting tool, you can build automated scripts to handle any kind of encrypting or decrypting task without manual intervention. For example, you could create a script that automatically decrypts certain files in a folder to make them available to all users.

Here are some useful examples of use of the CIPHER command:

- ✔ See the encryption status for all files in the current folder: CIPHER
- ✔ Encrypt all the files in the current folder: CIPHER /E /A
- ✔ Encrypt all the folders and files in the folder named Private: CIPHER /E/ S:\PRIVATE

If the examples are not exemplary for you, here is a syntax guide to the command:

```
CIPHER [/E or /D] [/S:directory_ name] [/A] [/I] [/F] [/Q]
[/H] files
```

Where

- ✔ [ ] indicate optional switches (don't type the [or the].)
- ✔ directory name indicates a target directory for the cipher/decipher operation (must be used with /S:)
- ✔ files indicate any filename matching pattern (must be used with /A)

Table 5-1 explains the switches and their use.

Table 5-1	The Switches and Their Use
Switch	*Use*
/E	Encrypts the folders specified. This switch marks the folder so that files or folders later copied or moved to this folder also are encrypted — what automation!
/D	Decrypts the folders specified. This switch marks the folder so that files or folders later copied or moved to this folder also are decrypted — what automation!
/S	Encrypts or decrypts the directory you specify after the /S and all subdirectories of the directory specified.
/A	Encrypts or decrypts files in directories.
/I	Completes cipher/decipher operation on all files and folders specified if an error is encountered on one or more. Without this parameter, CIPHER will stop if it runs into an error, such as if a file specified is open.
/F	Forces cipher/decipher on all files and folders specified, even if they are already encrypted or decrypted.
/Q	Reports results of cipher/decipher operating summary form. Without this switch, a listing appears of all files and folders affected.
/H	Performs cipher/decipher operation of system and hidden files.

Chapter 6

Laying Down the Law with Security Settings

. . . .

In This Chapter

▶ Easing into security settings

▶ Seeing how templates can save you time

▶ Applying security around the Active Directory

▶ Applying down-home security down home to local computers

▶ Checking out (almost) all the security settings

. . . .

*Y*ou won't find a master SECURITY console in Windows 2000, nor will you find a button that says "Secure My Network." Instead, you'll find a handful of tools and modules and feature sets that you manhandle to secure your environment. Security settings are one of those areas. Less a virtual feature like permissions, which touch all kinds of things, security settings represent a big bunch of security options and features and switches. Security settings can live in a few different places, so once you figure out how to set all these options, you use the same techniques to secure anything anywhere!

Surveying Security Settings

Unless you're related to the author, you're looking at this book because you're interested in building a secure network with Windows 2000. Well, one of the most important building materials used in the construction of a secure network with Windows 2000 is *security settings*. Security settings are the set of rules that determine what users can and can't do throughout Windows 2000, both at the local workstation and across the network. These settings determine the rules when users work on the network, such as logging on and accessing network resources, as well as what activities are legal at the local workstation. The individual rules that make up security settings are known as *policies*.

Here are a few examples of Windows 2000 security policies:

- ✔ Users cannot install printer drivers on their computers.

- ✔ Only logon failure events are audited.

- ✔ Users, except for those in the Administrators group, cannot launch either of the two Registry editors that ship with Windows 2000.

- ✔ Users cannot reuse any of the last five passwords they have created.

- ✔ Kerberos authentication tickets expire every 700 minutes. You can find details on Kerberos, one of three authentication schemes used in Windows 2000, in Chapter 2.

- ✔ A certificate is available for certain users giving them the right to decrypt files encrypted by another user.

Understanding types of security settings

The group of Windows 2000 security settings is carved up into a few categories:

- ✔ **Account Policies:** This group of policies controls aspects of user's passwords (for example, how often users must change theirs), what happens when users are locked out of the network, and how the Kerberos authentication scheme works.

- ✔ **Local Policies:** Local Policies determine which users have the rights to perform certain tasks (for example, add a computer to the domain) and what kinds of events are audited. Local Policies also define a boatload of ground rules and settings (for example, clear the pagefile when the system is shut down).

- ✔ **Event Log:** Policies for the event log define the maximum size, guest access to, and other settings for the security, application, and system event logs.

- ✔ **Restricted Groups:** The Restricted Group policy helps you control the membership of user groups. The Restricted Group policy ensures that the users who do not belong in certain groups are shown the door, while making sure that users who find themselves mistakenly removed from groups to which they should belong are escorted back in.

- ✔ **System Services:** Windows 2000 does all of the things it does with the help of services. These services do just about everything but have Bill Gates deliver your laundry to your home. The System Services policy determines who can start, stop, and inspect system services running on computers.

✔ **Registry:** The Registry policy lets you slap permission on either the entire Registry database or just the keys you're interested in securing.

✔ **File System:** You define what users and groups have what kind of rights to files and folders and disks on users' workstations.

✔ **Public Key Policies:** The set of public key policies defines how certificates are applied to specialized tasks, such as how the operating system responds to requests for new certificates.

✔ **IP Security Policies on Active Directory:** The IP Security policies determine the rules and filters for using IP as a security mechanism in the network.

Inspecting security settings

You can see the security settings at work in two places:

✔ **Local Security Policy:** All the security settings at work on a Windows 2000 workstation can be inspected and/or changed with the Local Security Policy console. Workstations that are part of a domain, though, might see some policies that were set locally overridden by the policies defined for the domain. The Local Security Policy console on each workstation shows the security policies set at the workstation, as well as the effective policy, which reflects the overriding policies defined by the domain.

✔ **Group Policy:** Security settings are applied to computers in a domain by adding the settings to group policy. When group policy is refreshed on computers in the network, the security settings included in the group policy are updated on the refreshed computers. For example, say that you want to change the policy for the minimum number of days a user must keep his password before he can change it. You make this change to the group policy affecting the entire domain. Group policy is refreshed on a regular basis, by default, every 90 minutes. As soon as the new group policy is refreshed, each workstation in the domain will be updated with the new rule.

Turning security settings into law

You can use a few different approaches for configuring security settings. These same approaches are available whether you are configuring security at the local workstation via the Local Security Policy or you are defining security for all or some part of the domain via group policy. You can mix and match these techniques as you configure security every day in your organization:

- ✔ **Edit the Policy:** This is the obvious one. Just go to the group policy you want to modify and then edit the settings you want or go to the Local Security Policy and do it there.

- ✔ **Use a Security Template:** There are more than 100 individual security policies that make up security settings, and who knows how many work-stations and group policy items on the network you may have to config-ure with those security settings. Wow! Using a security template can save you lots of work.

  A Security Template is a handy device in Windows 2000 where you can define all the security policies you would want to configure for one thing or one type of thing, like the domain, or all the computers in the Sales department. You can apply a template wherever you need to. Any of the settings you've defined in the template are then configured for the thing you applied it to. You can re-use a Security Template as many times as you like, and you can change one and create new ones at any time. You can find more on security templates later in the "Working with Security Templates" section.

Whether you configure security settings directly at the policy level or in a tem-plate, they generally look the same. Windows 2000 uses the old tree/details view scheme to display security settings. This means you navigate to the place in which you're interested in the tree pane of the window, and you inspect and change the individual policy in the right pane. Figure 6-1 shows security settings loaded into a group policy object for a domain controller.

The last paragraph told you that security settings are the same regardless of where you look at them. Check that. Actually, you might not see certain set-tings if you look at the settings in certain places. For example, if you open the Local Security Policy on a computer, you won't see items such as File System or Registry. You can secure these components right at the source: in My Computer or Windows 2000 in the case of the File System and with one of the Registry editors for the Registry.

Changing security settings is not hard, but the process is different depending on what policy you're changing. Here are a few examples:

- ✔ If you are changing the minimum number of days a user must keep the same password, you'll enter a value in days, as shown in Figure 6-2.

- ✔ If you are specifying which users can and can't start, stop, or look at the Kerberos Key Distribution Center service, you'll use the handy permis-sions dialog box, shown in Figure 6-3.

✔ If you want to make sure that only the user logged on at a specific computer can access the CD-ROM drive and not users who can otherwise access the drive from across the network, you'll just click the option to enable the policy, as shown in Figure 6-4.

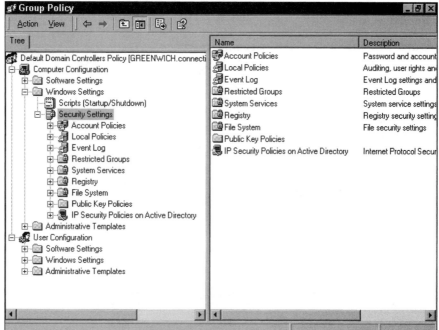

Figure 6-1:
The Security settings node in group policy.

Figure 6-2:
Sometimes you set policy by entering a value like number of days.

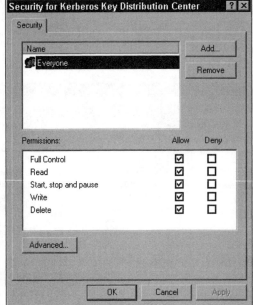

Figure 6-3:
You'll be
forced to
select users
for certain
security
settings.

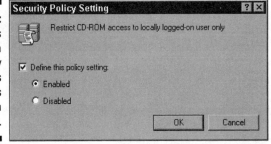

Figure 6-4:
Sometimes
enabling a
security
setting is as
simple as
enabling a
policy.

Working with Security Templates

Depending on the number of objects in your network, defining security can be a pretty tough job. You know, if you have a large network, maybe you should just ignore security for now given how tough a job this must be. Hhmm. That might not be a great idea. Instead, consider the use of security templates. New to Windows 2000, templates let you define all the Windows 2000 security settings in one place. Once defined, you can apply the template to anything in Windows 2000 that needs to be secured.

Here's more of what you need to know about security templates:

✔ You work with security templates using a management console and the security template snap-in. If you have no idea about the Microsoft management console, you can give a read to Chapter 2. Figure 6-5 shows what the Security Templates snap-in looks like.

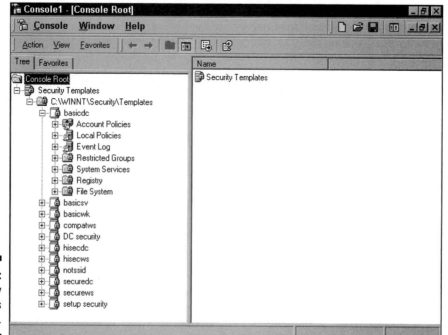

Figure 6-5:
The Security
Templates
snap-in.

✔ Security templates can save you lots of time if you have many of the same type of objects throughout your domain that should receive the same security. An example of this might be organizational units. You could easily create a security template relevant to organizational units and then apply that template to the group policy object for each organizational unit.

✔ Windows 2000 ships with a handful of prebuilt security templates. Using these templates can help you get a secure network up and running as quickly as possible. You can review the settings in each template, change the settings if you like, or create a new template based on one of these templates to suit your needs.

- **basicdc, basicsv, basicwk:** These three templates (for domain controllers, servers, and workstations, respectively) reflect the default security settings created when Windows 2000 is installed. If you want minimum security, use one of these templates. Don't read this as *zero security*, though. You wouldn't want to deploy a network with the settings in these templates, but they're better than no security.

- **compatws:** To maintain compatibility with Windows NT 4.0, local users automatically have the same permissions as the Power Users group. Your organization might feel this is too high a security price to pay just for compatibility with Windows NT 4.0. You can apply this template, which removes users from the Power Users group and also reduces the users' permissions for files and folders and registry settings that most applications use when they run or when you install them.

- **hisecdc:** This template contains settings appropriate for domain controllers. Settings in this template are designed for significant security. The settings are not compatible with non-Windows 2000 computers, so you won't be able to work with non-Windows 2000 computers after applying this template.

- **hisecws:** This template is designed for extremely secure workstations or member servers in Windows 2000 networks. The template is specific to the Windows 2000 machine, so computers that have the settings applied from the template will not be able to co-mingle with non-Windows 2000 computers on the network.

- **securedc:** The securedc template defines security settings for domain controllers. The settings are not as strong as those in the hisecdc, but they are stronger here than in the basicdc template.

- **securews:** Like the securedc template, the securews template reflects tougher security than the basicws template, but the settings are not as strong as hisecwes. This template is designed for workstations as opposed to domain controllers.

✔ A security template is really just a plain old text file. You can make changes to the template using any program that can edit text files, such as Notepad or Wordpad. Naturally, use caution when you edit the file. An extra line here or a deleted equals sign there could cause the template to become unusable. Here's what the inside of a template looks like:

```
; (c) Microsoft Corporation 1997-2000
;
; Security Configuration Template for Security Configuration
        Editor
;
; Template Name:     BasicWK.INF
; Template Version:  05.00.BW.0000
;
; Revision History
; 0000 - Original

[Profile Description]
%SCEBasicWKProfileDescription%
```

```
[version]
signature="$CHICAGO$"
revision=1
DriverVer=08/30/1999,5.00.2119.1


[System Access]
;_____
   _____

;Account Policies - Password Policy
;_____
   _____

MinimumPasswordAge = 0
MaximumPasswordAge = 42
MinimumPasswordLength = 0
PasswordComplexity = 0
PasswordHistorySize = 0
RequireLogonToChangePassword = 0
ClearTextPassword = 0


;_____
   _____

;Account Policies - Lockout Policy
;_____
   _____

LockoutBadCount = 0
;ResetLockoutCount = 30
;LockoutDuration = 30


;_____
   _____

;Local Policies - Security Options
;_____
   _____

;DC Only
;ForceLogoffWhenHourExpire = 0

;NewAdministatorName =
;NewGuestName =
;SecureSystemPartition


;_____
   _____

;Event Log - Log Settings
;_____
   _____

;Audit Log Retention Period:
;0 = Overwrite Events As Needed
;1 = Overwrite Events As Specified by Retention Days Entry
```

(continued)

(continued)

```
;2 = Never Overwrite Events (Clear Log Manually)

[System Log]
MaximumLogSize = 512
AuditLogRetentionPeriod = 1
RetentionDays = 7
RestrictGuestAccess = 0

[Security Log]
MaximumLogSize = 512
AuditLogRetentionPeriod = 1
RetentionDays = 7
RestrictGuestAccess = 0
```

Creating a console to work with Security Templates

If you're in charge of security or if you're part of the group in charge of security for your organization, then you will be spending a lot of time with security templates. It makes sense to create a console that includes the security template snap-in. This way, you don't have to create a new console and add a snap-in every time you want to work with security templates.

1. **Click the Start menu and then choose Run.**

   The Run dialog box appears.

2. **Enter MMC and then press Enter.**

   A new console window appears.

3. **Choose Console⇨Add/Remove Snap-in from the menu.**

   The Add/Remove Snap-in dialog box appears.

4. **Click the Add button.**

   The Add Standalone Snap-in dialog box appears.

5. **Scroll down the list and find Security Templates in the list; click once on it and then click Add.**

   If you drag the Add Standalone snap-in dialog box out of the way, you can see that Security Templates is added to the list of snap-ins in the Add/Remove Snap-in dialog box.

6. **Click Close in the Add Standalone Snap-in dialog box.**

7. **Click OK in the Add/Remove Snap-in dialog box.**

   Congratulations! You have created your first console. The next thing to do is to save the console so that you can use it later.

8. **Choose Console⇨Save As from the menu.**

    The Save As dialog box appears.

9. **Be sure the Administrative Tools folder is selected as the target folder, enter a name for the console, such as Security Templates, in the File Name edit box, and then click the Save button.**

    By saving the console in the Administrative Tools subfolder, you can be sure to open the console easily by just clicking it in the Administrative Tools menu.

10. **Choose Console⇨Exit from the menu to close your new console.**

11. **To test out your new console, click the Start menu, choose Programs⇨ Administrative Tools, and then click the console you just created.**

    Your new security template console should open.

Creating a new security template from a prebuilt one

If you like some but not all the settings in a prebuilt template, you can make changes to it and then save it as a different template. This allows you to re-use the prebuilt template again if you need to. This is also a much quicker method for creating a template than building one from scratch. As an example, if your security model calls for settings just a bit stronger than those reflected in the BASICWS setting but not as strong as those in SECUREWS, you might save BASICWS as CORPORATE WORKSTATION, make changes to it, and then roll it out.

1. **Open a console that gives you access to the Security Templates snap-in.**

    You can get help on creating a console for security templates in the preceding section.

2. **Open the Security Templates item.**

    You should see the various directories where security templates are stored. By default, Windows 2000 looks in just one place for the templates. You might add an additional location. Don't be alarmed, though, if you see just one location.

3. **Open the folder where the security template you want to use is stored.**

    Unless you have created a new location to store security templates, you should see just one folder.

4. **To create a new template based on the settings in an existing one, right-click the template you want to use as a template and then choose Save As.**

Be sure you click the item for the template and not one of the setting items. Otherwise, the Save As menu choice will not appear.

5. Enter the name of the new template and then click Save.

Your new template will be created. It will appear in alphabetical order in the list. If you would like to supply a description for the new template, right-click it and the choose Set Description from the menu. Enter the description in the Security Template Description box and then click OK.

You may also change any of the settings in your new template immediately.

Creating a new security template

You might find the need to create a brand-new security template with no policies already created. Doing this can take a good amount of time (there are almost 100 different policies, as well as all of the system services, file system and Registry settings), but you'll probably get a better understanding of the security applied by the template than if you used a prebuilt one and skimmed over the already-defined policies.

1. Open a console that gives you access to the Security Templates snap-in.

You can get help on creating a console for security templates earlier in this chapter in the section "Creating a console to work with Security Templates."

2. Open the Security Templates item.

You should see the various directories where security templates are stored. By default, Windows 2000 looks in just one place for the templates. You might add an additional location. Don't be alarmed, though, if you see just one location.

3. Right-click the Security Template location where you want to create the template and then choose New Template from the menu.

It's likely you'll have just one location, so don't fret if you see just one location.

A dialog box appears that looks like the one shown in Figure 6-6.

4. Enter the name of the template in the box at the top of the dialog box.

5. Enter a description for the template in the larger box at the bottom of the dialog box.

6. Click the OK button.

Your new security template will be created. It should appear in alphabetical order in the list of templates already on your system. You can work on the template now or close the console to do something else.

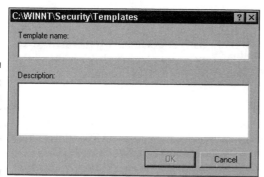

Figure 6-6:
You can
call your
template
whatever
you like.

Don't apply this brand-new template to a group policy object, say, for a domain controller, and think your security ship is watertight. When a new template is created, none of the settings are defined. If you apply this template to a group policy object or to a local computer, you won't get any of the security settings you think you might. You must edit the new template to specify all the security features you want.

Managing Security for a Local Workstation

There's a great chance that not every computer in your organization will be a happy member of the Active Directory. These lone, introspective computers do not have their security settings defined by group policy, which in turn would have its security settings applied by a template. This book focuses on security issues at the server, but you still might need to define security on the local front.

Follow these steps to configure security in a workstation with the Local Security Policy:

1. **Log on to the computer where you want to modify security.**

2. **Click the Start menu and choose Programs⇨Administrative Tools⇨ Local Security Policy.**

If you do not see Administrative Tools on the Programs menu, press the Esc key a few times to close the Programs and Start menus. Then, right-click the Taskbar and choose Properties. When the Taskbar and Start Menu properties dialog box appears, click the Advanced tab. In the list of Start Menu Settings at the bottom of the dialog box, select the Display Administrative Tools option.

Note that the console you open will not say Local Security Policy. Instead, the heading of the console will read *secpol*. This is the name given to the console that will store the security settings in force at a local computer. This is another micro-annoyance where the name of the thing you open is not the name of the thing you clicked on.

3. **Open items in the tree until the details pane displays the policy you want to change.**

4. **Double-click the policy you want to change; make the change you need and then click OK.**

5. **Close the console when you're done.**

You can use a security template to configure security for that local computer that won't play with the others on the domain. Using a template to configure a local computer is a better idea than configuring the machine by hand, trying to remember each of the security settings you applied to some other local computer, or trying your best to remember what your security policy is for local non-networked machines. Hopefully, you will not have to administer many computers that are not part of the domain, with or without templates. To load a template into a local computer policy, follow these steps:

1. **Log on to the local computer with administrator rights.**

2. **Click the Start menu and then choose Programs⇨ Administrative Tools⇨Local Security Policy.**

   The Security Settings console opens.

3. **Right-click Security Settings and choose Import Policy from the menu (Security Settings should be the node in the tree).**

   The Import Policy From dialog box appears.

4. **Choose the template file to load and then click Open.**

   The template is loaded and applied to the local computer.

Local Security Automation with the SCA

A snap-in called Security Configuration and Analysis can help you if you plan to use templates extensively to define security for lots of nondomain Windows 2000 computers. This snap-in lets you merge multiple templates and then apply the consolidated set of security settings to as many Windows 2000 computers as you like. You can also analyze security on the computer to see how local settings might differ from those established in the policy. Add the snap-in to a console and then open the console. You should use group policy as much as you can to administer security to the masses, though.

Setting Security for a Group Policy Object

The easiest way to take your security settings to the street and apply them to the users and computers in the network is to attach them to a group policy object (GPO). You attach group policy to different items in the Active Directory, such as the entire domain, an organizational unit like the domain controllers unit, or anything else. Any user or computer affected by the object would then be affected by the security defined in the GPO. You can modify the security settings from within a policy in two ways. You can

✔ Import a security template

✔ Change the policy's security settings by hand

If you need more information on using group policy to create and apply security settings, see Chapter 7.

Your One-Stop Guide for Security Settings

It will take you a good amount of time to figure out and then set each of the security settings for your domain. Some of the settings won't be relevant to your organization, and you'll ignore them; other settings you might discuss for days. This section gives you a head start on figuring out what do with each of these settings. You won't find every single security setting listed here — only the ones you should *really* know about or the ones you might have trouble with.

Account policies at the domain rule

There is a movie (can't remember the name) that takes place in a very, very large city in the northeast U.S. At some point (can't remember when) either the hero or the villain (can't remember which) yells for all to hear, "I AM THE LAW!" When it comes to account policies, the domain is the law. The account policies that are applied to the domain take precedence over any account policies applied to any other Active Directory object, like a site or computer. Actually, there is one hole in the law. An account policy applied to an organizational unit takes precedence over elements of the account policy applied to the domain. If there are multiple domains in the tree, the account policy in force at the root domain in the tree takes charge.

Setting password policy

Password policies define just about all of the rules about passwords — how big, how old, how young, how obvious, and so on. Password policies are part of the Account Policies group of security settings.

1. **Open the security template, Local Security Policy, or group policy where you want to configure Password policy.**

2. **Open Account Policies and then click Password Policy.**

   If you are changing password policy in a security template, you first have to open the folder where the security template you want to change is located and then open the specific security template. You can find details on this step earlier in this chapter in the "Working with Security Templates" section.

   The list of password policies appears in the details pane.

3. **Double-click the password policy you want to change.**

   Depending on the policy you chose, you might have to enter a value for the number of days, number of characters, or simply enable or disable the policy.

4. **Answer the prompts in the dialog box and then click OK.**

Here's a review of the individual password policies. First, though, here's some friendly advice. Carefully consider how you define password policies. While you need to think about every aspect of security in your Windows 2000 network, passwords deserve extra attention. Passwords are usually the only thing separating an authenticated, approved user from a violating, illegal user. Any hacker can figure out an account's user name. Make sure that the password part of the account isn't as easy to figure out.

✔ **Enforce password history:** Users don't like to remember too many things. They would just as soon enter their current password when the time comes to create a new password. Not too secure. This policy lets you specify how many new passwords a user must create before they can reuse an old one. The default value for this policy in the default domain policy is 1 — this means that you can't use your current password as your new password. (But you could use it again the following time the password is changed.)

✔ **Maximum password age:** This policy determines how many days a user may use a password before they are forced to change it. For the default domain policy, the value is 42 days.

Without discussion, you should force all your users to change their passwords periodically. A password is not like a fine wine that improves with age.

✔ **Minimum password age:** This policy determines the minimum number of days a user must use a password before they can change it.

You can slam the door on frequently reused passwords by synchronizing this policy with the Enforce password history policy. As an example, if you bump the minimum password age to at least one day and you set the Enforce password history to about one dozen, users must wait a minimum of days — this if they change their password every day during those 12 days — to reuse a password.

✔ **Minimum password length:** The number of characters a user must use to create a password is established by this policy. You should strongly consider using the next policy, Passwords Must Meet Complexity Requirements, to determine the complexity requirements for passwords, including their length. If you do not use that policy, specify six characters as the minimum length for a password.

✔ **Passwords must meet complexity requirements:** This policy turns on Windows 2000's special password complexity filter mechanism. If you are content with users entering short, easy-to-figure out passwords, then don't enable this policy. Otherwise, check out the "My password is red hot, your password ain't doodley-squat" sidebar.

✔ **Store password using reversible encryption for all users in the domain:** This option forces all the passwords to be encrypted in a reversible scheme.

✔ **User must log on to change the password:** This policy determines whether a user must be logged on to the computer or domain in order to change his password. A scenario in which a user who can no longer log on must change his password would be if a user's password expired while he was logged out. If you enable this policy, then users who are locked out of their accounts because of expiration of their password must place a call to the Help desk in order for their account to be unlocked.

Setting Account Lockout policy

The policies in the Account Lockout group are the bane of *Betty Big Thumbs*. You use the policies in this group to determine what happens when users fail to enter the correct password for an account. For most users, misentering their passwords is more a matter of mistyping their passwords. At the same time, the policies in this group can help ward off attempts by intruders to bombard an account with possible passwords should they figure out the user name part of the account.

To set the Account Lockout Policy option, follow these steps:

1. **Open the security template, Local Security Policy, or group policy where you want to configure Account Lockout policy.**

2. **Open Account Policies and then click once on Account Lockout Policy.**

   If you are changing account lockout policy in a security template, you first have to open the folder where the security template you want to change is located, and then open the specific security template. You can find details on this step earlier in this chapter in the "Working with Security Templates" section.

   The list of Account Lockout policies appears in the details pane.

3. **Double-click the Account Lockout policy you want to change.**

   The dialog box that appears depends on what option policy you're changing.

4. **Make whatever selections you need to in the dialog box and then click OK.**

Here is what you need to know about the individual Account Lockout policies:

- ✔ **Account lockout duration:** This policy is matched with the other account lockout polices (no kidding — they're in the same group!) This policy determines for how many minutes an account is locked out after the threshold logon attempt failures.

  The dialog box where you set this policy is tricky (see Figure 6-7). To specify some number of minutes before the account is re-enabled, enter the number in minutes in the box or use the buttons to scroll. If you want the account locked out until an administrator unlocks it, click in the box and then press the Delete key.

  If you are looking for advice on this policy, it makes sense to set this policy so that the administrator must re-enable the account. Without this check, it's harder (but not impossible) to monitor possible attacks on an account. Hackers can eventually figure out the duration and relaunch their attacks.

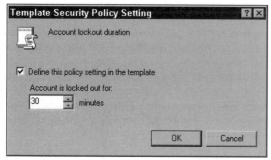

Figure 6-7:
The
Account
Lockout
Duration
policy.

✔ **Account lockout threshold:** Use this policy to specify how many attempts a user can make to enter a valid password before the account is locked. Three attempts seems to be the standard here, but there's nothing wrong with using a value of two. Keep in mind that if you use a particularly low value and you also specify that the administrator must unlock an account that has been locked because of too many failed login attempts, your Help desk will become much busier. On the other hand, the greater you set this value, the more chances you give an intruder to attempt a password before the account becomes locked.

✔ **Reset account lockout counter after:** Use this policy to determine when to reset the bad-password attempt counter to 0.

Setting Kerberos authentication policy

Kerberos is one of three different authentication methods supported by Windows 2000 (the other two are NTLM (prior versions of Windows NT) and via digital certificates). The Kerberos authentication policies determine elements of Kerberos authentication, like the lifetime of tickets. If you need background on Kerberos, read Chapter 1.

To set Kerberos policies, follow these steps:

1. **Open the security template, Local Security Policy, or group policy where you want to change Kerberos policy.**

2. **Open Account Policies and then click once on Kerberos Policy.**

   If you are changing Kerberos policy in a security template, you first have to open the folder where the security template you want to change is located, and then open the specific security template. You can find details on this step earlier in this chapter in the "Working with Security Templates" section.

   The list of Kerberos policies appears in the details pane.

3. **Double-click the Kerberos policy you want to change.**

4. **When the dialog box for the policy you selected appears, click whatever option is appropriate for the policy and then click OK.**

Here is what you need to know about the individual Kerberos policies:

- **Maximum lifetime for service ticket:** This policy determines how long, in minutes, before a newly issued Kerberos service ticket expires.

- **Maximum lifetime for user ticket:** This policy determines how long, in hours, before a Kerberos ticket issued to a user expires.

- **Maximum lifetime for user ticket renewal:** This policy determines the time, in days, for a renewed user ticket.

- **Maximum tolerance for computer clock synchronization:** Kerberos uses the time to help synchronize tickets it issues. The time is determined by the first domain controller at the root domain of the tree. This policy determines the tolerance amount between the time at the first domain controller and the time at machines on the network where Kerberos issues tickets.

Configuring Audit policy

The Audit policies component of security settings lets you specify whether Windows 2000 should audit the following events. For each of these events, you can choose to audit success events, failure events, both, or not to define the policy at all:

- Account logon events
- Account management
- Directory service access
- Logon events
- Object access
- Policy change
- Privilege use
- Process tracking
- System events

My password is red hot, your password ain't doodley-squat

If you enable the Windows password complexity filter, here are the new rules about passwords:

✔ Passwords cannot contain the user name of the account or a portion of the full name of the account.

✔ Passwords must be six characters long or longer.

✔ A password must contain at least one character from three of these four types of characters:

- English uppercase (A, B, . . . Z)

- English lowercase (a, b, . . . z)

- Numbers (0, 1, 2, . . . 9)

- Special characters, such as punctuation marks

To set the Audit policy option, follow these steps:

1. **Open the security template, Local Security Policy, or group policy where you want to change Audit policy.**

2. **Open Local Policies and then click once on Audit Policy.**

   If you are changing Audit policy in a security template, you first have to open the folder where the security template you want to change is located, and then open the specific security template. You can find details on this step earlier in this chapter in the "Working with Security Templates" section.

   The list of Audit policies appears in the details pane.

3. **Double-click the Audit policy you want to change.**

4. **Click the audit option you want and then click OK.**

Know your rights, these are your rights!

In Windows 2000, you decide which user you'll allow to perform some of the more sensitive Windows 2000 tasks. These tasks might be performed on the user's computers, or the tasks might affect something on the network. These tasks are known as *user rights*. The objective, then, for setting User Rights is to tell Windows 2000 what users in the Active Directory have permission to which user rights. It's obviously not a tough job, but you should do some planning first. There are almost 40 user rights assignments to figure out, some very sensitive, so it's worth thinking about this project before you get started on it.

Here's how to set User Rights Assignment policies.

1. **Open the security template, Local Security Policy, or group policy where you want to change User Rights policy.**

   User rights are found in the Local Policies group.

2. **Open Local Policies and then click once on User Rights Assignments.**

   If you are changing User Rights policy in a security template, you first have to open the folder where the security template you want to change is located, and then open the specific security template. You can find details on this step earlier in this chapter in the "Working with Security Templates" section.

   The list of user rights policies appears in the details pane.

3. **Double-click the user rights policy you want to establish.**

4. **To define which users are applied to the policy, click the Define these policy settings option.**

   The Add and Remove buttons light up.

5. **Click the Add button.**

   The Add user or group dialog box appears.

   You can enter the names of users or groups that get this policy in the edit box. You separate items in the box with a semicolon. A much better idea is to click the Browse button and pick the users or groups from the list. This way, you can be sure to not mistype a name. Also, you need to properly supply the name of the domain the user or group belongs to. If you let Windows 2000 put the name in the box, you can be sure that you won't make a mistake doing it.

6. **Click the Browse button.**

   The Select Users or Groups dialog box appears.

7. **Select the users or groups you're interested in and then click the Add button; when you're done, click the OK button.**

   You can do this for as many users and/or groups as you want.

   If you can't find the right user or group, they might not be a member of the domain shown in the drop-down list at the top of the dialog box. Click the list to see all the domains in the forest. Select another domain or select Entire Directory to see all the objects in the forest.

8. **Click OK again to return to the policy dialog box.**

9. **Click OK to finish defining the user rights assignment policy.**

Here is a rundown of the individual User Rights Assignments policies you can configure:

- ✔ **Access this computer from the network:** This policy lets you determine who can access the computer from across the network. This is a critical policy to apply to all domain controllers and other critical servers.

    It's a nice convenience to be able to access a domain controller from a remote point on the network, even if it's down the hall, but the convenience is not worth the risk. Strip away all permissions for this policy, including the Everyone group, the Administrators group, everybody.

- ✔ **Act as part of the operating system:** This policy is one of the few most powerful rights available. With that in mind, you won't be surprised to read that just the internal SYSTEM account is granted this right by default. This right allows access to the system as if the bearer were a part of the operating system.

- ✔ **Add workstations to domain:** This policy determines which users can add computers to the domain. This might not seem like a big deal, but imagine the fun an intruder could have by adding another domain controller to the domain!

- ✔ **Back up files and directories:** The back up files and directories right provides the bearer with the right to bypass all permission placed on the file and folder elements. Naturally, this right should be handed out with caution. Only Administrators and Backup operators, the groups that receive this right by default, should have this right.

- ✔ **Bypass traverse checking:** This interesting right allows the bearer to move through a directory path, noting its structure, but unable to see a list of the contents of a folder. This right allows a user to change the current folder to one that he does not have access rights to. He won't be able to see the contents of the folder, just move to it.

- ✔ **Change the system time:** Use this policy to determine which users can change the system time on their computer. You don't think this policy is a big deal? Guess again. All audit logs use the internal system clock to timestamp entries. An enterprising intruder can mask his activities by changing the system time.

- ✔ **Create a pagefile:** This policy determines who can create a pagefile. Administrators are the only group to get this thrilling right by default.

- ✔ **Create a token object:** Windows 2000 uses this right to create security access tokens. There's no reason why a human being should be allowed this right.

- ✔ **Create permanent shared objects:** A permanent shared object is not like a lawn mower that you and your neighbor split the cost of and share each weekend. Rather, permanent shared objects are those shares that are created automatically, like \\SYSVOL.

✔ **Debug programs:** This policy determines whether a user can use debugging tools to open and debug problem files. It really doesn't make sense to grant this right to persons other than those who really know how to debug software.

✔ **Deny access to this computer from the network:** This policy lets you shut down access to this computer from other resources on the network. As much as you'll create permissions determining who can and can't modify elements of the server, you can add a few more ounces of prevention by making sure that no one has this right.

✔ **Deny Logons:** You can explicitly deny certain users to logon using certain methods with a few handy policies:

- Deny logon as a batch job
- Deny logon as a service
- Deny logon locally

✔ **Force shutdown from a remote system:** This right allows the bearer to shut down a computer from across the network.

✔ **Generate security audits:** This right is used to add items to the list of those events being audited in the security log.

✔ **Increase quotas:** This right is used to increase a process's share of the processor's attention. While this right seems more helpful and less harmless in that it can be used to check and enhance the performance of the system, the right can be abused to create a denial-of-service attack.

✔ **Increase scheduling priority:** This right is used mainly to control who can change how a Windows 2000 process performs by assigning more processor attention to a certain process. To cut down on Help desk calls from users who mess up their system by playing with this feature, you may want to allow only Administrators to have this right.

✔ **Load and unload device drivers:** This right allows the user to load and unload Plug and Play device drivers. Absolutely no one but the operating system should have a right like this that interacts at such a low level.

✔ **Log on as a batch job:** This right allows the user the right to log on to a computer using a batch facility.

✔ **Log on as a service:** This right allows the bearer to log on to the system as a service. This is serious. Services have the run of the operating system (just about), so changing the default user rights assignment for this policy is a bad idea. Real user types like you and me — even administrators — are not granted this right by default.

✔ **Log on locally:** Not a lot of mystery here. This policy determines the users who can log on directly at a particular machine. For domain controllers, only administrators should have this right. This will prevent users other than those in the Administrators group to log on directly at a domain controller.

Match this policy with the Access This Computer From The Network policy. If you completely deny the Access This Computer policy to all users for domain controllers, and you use the Log On Locally policy, then you know that the only administration of domain controllers can occur directly at the domain controller workstation and by users in the Administrators group.

✔ **Manage auditing and security log:** Watch out for this policy. If you are too lax with the permissions around this policy, you'll have a scenario in which the inmates are running the prison in that an intruder can hide her break-in attempts by deleting the event records created in the security log. Be sure that only administrators or perhaps those in your security group are granted this policy.

The *first* event created in a security log contains details about the *last* event that affected the security log. Huh? Even if an intruder clears the security log, a new event is created that shows when the security log was last cleared. An intruder, then, will never be able to completely clear her tracks.

✔ **Modify firmware environment values:** This policy determines who can change the system variables. Naturally, this is a significant right. An industrious hacker could change the pointers to software that could enable them to hack even deeper into a system. Administrators are the only group who receives this right by default on domain controllers.

✔ **Replace a process level token:** This right is used under-the-hood by Windows 2000 to change a process's security access token. There's no reason why any human should also have this right. None do by default.

✔ **Restore files and directories:** Add this policy to the seemingly-harmless-but-really-dangerous list. Users with this right can restore files and folders previously backed up. Administrators and Backup Operators get this right by default.

✔ **Shut down the system:** You might use this policy if a particular workstation is acting like a kiosk, in which you need to be sure the machine is not shut down. You might also use this right to ensure that only administrators have the right to shut down servers.

✔ **Take ownership of files or other objects:** This right allows the bearer to take ownership of anything in Windows 2000 — anything. The owner of an object can do anything with or to the object, including giving himself Full Control rights to the object. By default, Administrators get this right out of the box.

Configuring security options

The Security Options set of security settings covers a wide range of functions, tasks, and features in Windows 2000 that probably should be secured.

Follow these steps to change one of the Security Options policies:

1. **Open the security template, Local Security Policy, or group policy where you want to change Security Options policy.**

2. **Open Local Policies and then click once on Security Options.**

   If you are changing Security Options policy in a security template, you first have to open the folder where the security template you want to change is located, and then open the specific security template. You can find details on this step earlier in this chapter in the "Working with Security Templates" section.

   The list of Security Options policies appears in the details pane.

3. **Double-click the Security Option policy you want to change.**

   The dialog boxes that appear for Security Option policies are a true mixed bag. There are definitely not enough pages in this book to show you a picture of each dialog box you might see, so you're on your own! Don't worry, there's usually no more than a button or drop-down list or edit box or two in any dialog box. Answer the prompts in the dialog box and then click OK.

Here is the list of Security Options policies:

- ✔ **Additional restrictions for anonymous connections:** This policy lets you enhance the normal permissions applied to users who access the network with the handy anonymous account. As an example, you can use this policy to restrict anonymous users from seeing a list of all the users accounts in the domain.

- ✔ **Allowed to eject removable NTFS media:** This policy determines if a user can remove a floppy disk or one of the hyper-capacity disks available today if the drive has been formatted with NTFS. Of course, if you do not set this policy, you can reduce the risk presented by users taking media by using the encrypting file system (EFS). Read Chapter 5 for details.

- ✔ **Clear virtual memory pagefile when system shuts down:** Enable or disable this policy to determine if the pagefile is deleted when the computer powers down. The pagefile is a physical file on your disk to which Windows 2000 writes data that it might need later and doesn't want to carry around in memory.

Some folks think that sensitive information could be decoded out of the pagefile. Hence, you might consider deleting it all the time. The only expense in enabling this option is an incredibly slight decrease in start-up performance. Trust me — should you enable this option, the only people who will complain about the change in performance will be the ones you told about the change.

✓ **Do not display last user name in logon screen:** This policy is another of those no-brainers. Typically, when the user presses Ctrl+Alt+Del, the user name of the last account logged on to the machine appears in the User name box. Though it takes both a user account and password to get access, why solve half of an intruder's problem by supplying them with the user ID? Enabling this policy hides the user name of the account last logged on.

✓ **LAN Manager Authentication Level:** If you are migrating from a Windows NT 4 environment, you can define what type of LAN Manager authentication to accept. See Figure 6-8.

✓ **Logon messages:** You can set policy so that a message box appears just before the prompt to logon. This message can contain any message you want to deliver to persons logging on to Windows 2000, including legal notices. You specify the text of the message, as well as the caption of the message box with the following two policies:

 • Message text for users attempting to log on

 • Message title for users attempting to log on

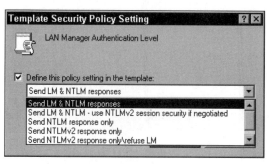

Figure 6-8:
You choose how to authenticate NTLM clients.

✓ **Prevent users from installing printer drivers:** This fairly harmless policy restricts users from installing printer drivers on their computers. Keep in mind that if you deny this right, users will not be able to update drivers for printers that are already installed.

✓ **Prompt user to change password before expiration:** Use this policy to specify how many days in advance users are warned that their password will expire.

✔ **Rename administrator account:** This policy lets you supply a new name for the administrator account. When the policy is applied, the name you enter becomes the new name for the administrator account.

✔ **Rename guest account:** This policy lets you supply a new name for the guest account. When the policy is applied, the name you enter becomes the new name for the guest account.

✔ **Restrict CD-ROM access to locally logged-on user only:** Use this policy to ensure that only the user logged on at a specific workstation has access to the CD-ROM on that machine, not users logged on at other workstations on the network. If you do not enable this policy, you run the risk of users accessing data on CD-ROM drives without the knowledge or permission of the owner or primary users of the PC.

✔ **Restrict floppy access to locally logged-on user only:** Use this policy to ensure that only the person logged on to a particular workstation can access the floppy drive. If you enable this policy, users logged on to the network but not logged on to a specific machine cannot access the floppy drive on that machine. If you do not enable this policy, you run the risk of users accessing data on floppy without the knowledge or permission of the owner or primary users of the PC.

✔ **Smart card removal behavior:** This policy lets you specify when a smart card is removed from its reader whether the system becomes locked, the logged on user is logged off, or there is no action.

✔ **Driver Installation:** You can specify whether you'll allow the installation of software, drivers or otherwise, that has not been signed. You can specify whether the installation runs without issue, whether the user is warned first, or whether the installation is halted in its tracks. The following two policies are used to control driver installations:

- Unsigned driver installation behavior

- Unsigned nondriver installation behavior

Setting event log control

You can define security settings for managing the event logs. You can set the maximum log size, how long a log should be stored, and whether the system should clear the log when it needs to or only after a certain number of days. You can define each of these policies separately for these event logs:

✔ Application log

✔ Security log

✔ System log

Follow these steps to define policy settings for the Event Logs:

1. **Open the security template, Local Security Policy, or group policy where you want to change Event Log policy.**

2. **Open Event Log and then click once on Settings for Event Logs.**

   If you are changing Event Log policy in a security template, you first have to open the folder where the security template you want to change is located, and then open the specific security template. You can find details on this step earlier in this chapter in the "Working with Security Templates" section.

   The list of Event Log policies appears in the details pane.

3. **Double-click the Event Logs policy you want to work on.**

4. **Set the details of the policy and then click OK when you're done.**

Restricted groups membership

The Restricted Groups component of security settings helps you establish and maintain the correct membership in the various security groups in the Active Directory. You're probably thinking it's not a big deal to create a group and then add some users or other groups to it. You're right. Creating groups is one of the easiest things to do in Windows 2000. It's the maintenance thing that's really tough.

Even with the tightest, most-well-documented policies and procedures, some-time users get added to groups they never should, usually just to give some-one temporary access to something. The problem comes up when someone forgets to remove that temporary user from that group. As time goes by, the membership in those private secure groups has the tendency to become public and insecure. The Restricted Groups component of security settings solves this problem.

Here are the details on Restricted Groups:

✔ When the Restricted Group security settings are integrated into group policy, every time the group policy is propagated through the network, the membership in the restricted groups is checked. Users who don't belong are kicked out; users who belong and are missing are added back in.

✔ You can protect any groups with Restricted Groups, even the powerful Administrators group.

✔ You can use Restricted Groups to create new groups that you need to protect.

Follow these steps to protect groups using Restricted Groups.

1. **Open the security template, Local Security Policy, or group policy where you want to configure a Restricted Groups policy.**

2. **Right-click the Restricted Groups item and then choose Add Group from the menu.**

   If you're changing a Restricted Groups policy in a security template, you first have to open the folder where the security template you want to change is located, and then open the specific security template. You can find details on this step earlier in this chapter in the "Working with Security Templates" section.

   The Add Group dialog box appears.

3. **Enter the name of the group you want to protect or click the Browse button to select the group from a list; click OK when you have selected the group.**

   If you want to create a group, just enter its name in the box. The group you selected (or added) appears in the list of Group Names in the details pane.

4. **To specify who should be in a group, double-click the group name in the details pane.**

   The Configure Membership dialog box appears.

5. **Click the Add button to add a user to the group.**

   The Add Member dialog box appears.

6. **Enter the name of the user you want to be sure stays in the group or click the Browse button to select the name from a list; click OK when you have selected the name.**

   If you want to create a group, just enter its name in the box. The group you selected (or added) appears in the list of Group Names in the details pane.

7. **Repeat Steps 4 through 6 for each user whose membership needs to be maintained in the group.**

8. **Repeat Steps 2 through 7 for each group you want to protect.**

Securing system services

Windows 2000 services are the small programs that launch, most times without you knowing it, and run (usually without you being able to tell), and that provide you and the operating system with whatever features and functions you need to do your thing with Windows 2000.

✔ Examples of services include networking, the Fax Service and Plug and Play (to detect and configure hardware), as well as the World Wide Web Publishing Service, and dozens more.

✔ Most services run on each and every Windows 2000 computer, like the Network Connections service, while some run just on domain controllers. Other blends of Windows 2000, like Advanced Server, have their own set of services. Most of the services in Windows 2000, though, are common to all blends.

✔ Services can be started automatically, or they can be set up to start manually. Services also can be stopped or paused.

You can use the System Services node in security settings to determine who has the right to manage services, as well as whether the services run at all. This is important. Some of these services provide basic support to the operating system. Without the support provided by certain services, the system just won't work. Modifying which services run and which don't are perfect components of a denial-of-service attack.

Some services introduce some element of risk. For example, the Computer Browser provides to one and all the list of computers on the network. Gee, it might be a good idea to deny this service so that a potential intruder cannot take inventory of the computers on the network. If you shut this service down, though, users also are denied this service. You'll have to make the decision on a service-by-service basis, perhaps by simple experimentation with each service, what services to keep, what to do away with, and what to set for manual startup.

Here is how to use the System Services node to secure services:

1. **Open the security template, Local Security Policy, or group policy where you want to configure a System Services policy.**

2. **Click once on System Services.**

   If you are changing a System Services policy in a security template, you first have to open the folder where the security template you want to change is located, and then open the specific security template. You can find details on this step earlier in this chapter in the "Working with Security Templates" section.

   The list of services you can secure appears in the details pane.

3. **In the details pane, find the service you want to secure and then double-click it.**

   The Security Policy Setting dialog box appears like the one shown in Figure 6-9.

4. **To create a policy for the service, check the Define This Policy Setting In The Template check box.**

   The options in the dialog box should light up.

Figure 6-9:
You can
secure
services
centrally by
specifying
whether a
service
should start,
as well as
which users
have
specific
permissions
to the
service.

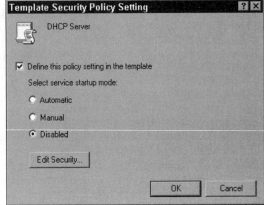

5. **Click the startup option you want for the service.**

   You can specify that the service starts automatically, manually, or not at all.

6. **To assign permissions to the service, such as to specify which users have the right to start, stop, or pause the service, click the Edit Security button.**

   This gives you access to the standard areas where you define permissions. If you need a review on permissions, you can read Chapter 4.

7. **Click OK to save the changes you made to the service's security.**

8. **Repeat Steps 3 through 7 for each service you want to secure.**

Restricting Registry key access

In case you didn't know it, the Registry is an incredibly valuable piece of Windows 2000 software. Data in the Registry controls how your computer operates from the moment Windows 2000 begins the startup process until just after you power Windows 2000 down. The Registry stores information about the user logged on to Windows 2000, the network the user might be attached to, and hardware and software installed.

The Registry policy in security settings lets you secure the Registry on each user's computer. You can secure the individual keys of the Registry or the entire Registry. Using the tools provided in security settings also means that you don't need to pack your bags to travel to each user's desktop to do the securing.

Considering how critical Registry security is, there's a full chapter just waiting for your consumption that covers everything you need to know about Registry security. Check out Chapter 8 to find out how to lock down the Registry.

Using security settings for the file system

The File System component of security settings helps you apply permissions to files, folders, and drives. You might secure files and folders on users' computers to be sure that users do not delete certain files, or you might use this setting to be sure that certain programs are not run, or you might protect a certain partition on users' computers.

If you know anything about permissions in Windows 2000, you know that it's not such a big deal to apply permissions to file system items using either My Computer or Windows 2000 Explorer. What would you do, though, if you needed to secure the files and folders on a few thousand PCs, or even just a few hundred? This is where security settings get involved.

You can use the File System component of security settings to apply permissions to the file system objects on all the computers in the network. This means that you, as the administrator, can stretch the long arm of the law to determine what users can and can't do with the files and folders and drives on their computer, all from the comfort of your domain controller. Talk about administrator control!

Here is how you establish security on files and folders:

1. **Figure out these three things:**

   - What items on the user's file system you want to secure

   - The most likely location for the files and/or folders

   - The groups of users that should and shouldn't have access to file and folders and drives, as well as any special rights they should have

   A little planning goes a long way.

2. **Open the security template or group policy where you want to configure a System Services policy.**

3. **Right-click File System and choose Add File from the menu.**

   The Add A File Or Folder dialog box appears, as shown in Figure 6-10.

   Now here's the tricky part. The dialog box shows the drives on the machine where *you're* defining this security setting. Don't let this confuse you. Your job is to pick out the files and folders you want to secure. It's Windows 2000's job to figure out where those files and/or folders are located on the local computer.

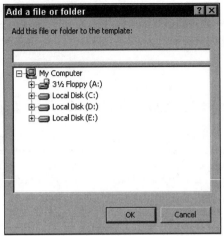

Figure 6-10:
You pick the
files or
folders or
drives you
want to
secure on
your
computer.

4. **Open the drive and then the folders until the file or folder you want to secure appears.**

5. **Click the item you want to secure and then click OK.**

The Security dialog box appears for the selection you made. Notice the caption of the dialog box, which shows the name and location of the file or folder you selected. Rather than refer to the file or folder you selected with its absolute location (for example, C:\MYFILE.DOC), Windows 2000 uses a system variable to refer to the location.

For example, if you select a file stored in some folder on the same drive where Windows 2000 is installed, such as C:\MONKEY\CHEESE.TXT, Windows 2000 will save the location with a variable for the drive, such as %SystemRoot%\MONKEY\CHEESE.TXT. When the security setting is applied to a local computer, the %SystemRoot% variable will be resolved to the drive letter where Windows 2000 is installed on the local computer.

Another note about the dialog box: This is the standard dialog box used to assign permissions to all kinds of Windows 2000 objects, like files or folders. If you need to brush up on permissions, you may want to read Chapter 4.

6. **Create the permissions you need for the file or folder and then click OK.**

The Template Security Policy Setting dialog box appears.

This dialog box lets you determine whether the permission you create is applied to children of the file or folder you selected:

- The Propagate option means that child objects of the ones you're securing will inherit the permission you're securing if those children allow inheritance.

- The Replace option means that the child objects of the ones you're securing will inherit the permission you're securing regardless of whether they allow inheritance.

You may also click Edit Security to change the permissions you created earlier in Step 6.

7. Click OK.

You return to the console.

8. Repeat Steps 3 through 7 for every file or folder or drive you want to secure.

PK and IP Settings

Public Key setting and IP Security are important settings in Windows 2000 security. In fact, they're so important, they're covered in their own chapters! If you're interested in public key policies, open Chapter 10. You can find information about IP Security in Chapter 14.

You cannot define settings for either in a template.

Chapter 7

Reinforcing Security with Group Policy

*A*dministrators who start to throw around policy in their networks invariably get a bad reputation. They are accused of being control freaks, turning users into automatons, and acting like Big Brother. Of course, some administrators would appreciate that evaluation. No one criticizes the administrator, though, when his preparation fends off a hacker attack or if a security audit of the network returns a passing grade.

Group policy helps administrators get passing security grades. Group policies act as the delivery vehicle for getting security settings out to the field. In addition, you can use a bunch of group policy settings to enhance security.

Letting the Author Pontificate on Group Policy

Group policy is the set of features that tell your user community that you're in charge (you're an administrator, aren't you?). Group policy is the rules about computer configuration and user behavior in your network. Group policy is developed by administrators in a Windows 2000 network. The users and computers in the network, including the administrators who develop the policy and the computers they operate, are subject to the rules.

You can have variations of policy throughout the domain. The same set of rules need not apply to every user and every computer.

Individual group policies are known as group policy objects. You see these referred to as GPOs in this chapter.

Group policy is refreshed periodically throughout the network. As long as a computer is connected to the network, it gets its group policy updates. When a computer is disconnected from the network, any policies the computer received previously are still in force. Group policy is stored primarily in the registry in each computer.

Here are some examples of group policy.

- ✔ Remove the Add/Remove Programs applet from the Control Panel.
- ✔ Install software on users' computers — automatically and without the need for the user to answer prompts.
- ✔ Configure every user's installation of Internet Explorer to use the proxy server.
- ✔ Restrict users from browsing to sites on the Web with adult content.
- ✔ Force the list of recently opened documents to be cleared when the user logs off.
- ✔ Restrict users from deleting printers.

Seeing how group policy works with security

You may be wondering what group policy has to do with security. Good question, and here's the answer.

- ✔ The security settings node in group policy (see Figure 7-1) contains a huge number of options you can use to control security in the domain, such as the rights specific users have to perform certain tasks, rules about passwords, such as how often they should be changed, what events are audited, and a bunch more. So, when group policy gets applied, so do the security settings in the group policy.
- ✔ Group policy includes some options you might consider related to security (all right, *the author* considers them related to security) that are not included in the security settings node.

If you need a review of what just about every one of these settings do, as well as how to change the settings, read Chapter 6.

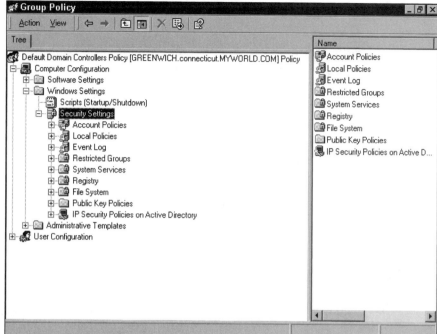

Figure 7-1:
Security
settings are
just another
node in
group
policy.

Taking inventory of group policy

There are a number of components of group policy. Figure 7-2 shows what group policy looks like. As you can see, the tree is filled with branches, and each branch is filled with folders.

Group Policy is divided into two parts: User Configuration and Computer Configuration.

- ✔ **User Configuration:** Policy created in the User Configuration area lets you legislate user's activities no matter where he is! Policy in this area is applied to every user affected by the policy, regardless of what computer he's working on.

- ✔ **Computer Configuration:** Policy created in this area affects all computers regardless of who is doing the driving at the computer.

Each of the folders contains either policies you can change or other folders. The name of the folder tells you what type of policies it contains. Also, Microsoft did you a favor by providing help about each policy. This way, you can get a better idea about the impact of a policy setting than by going down the trial-and-error road. Figure 7-3 shows an example of the hints our friends in the western United States provide us. You click the Details tab to display the text.

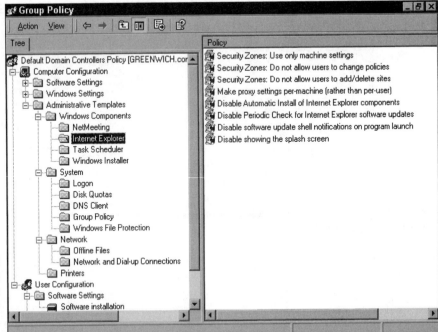

Figure 7-2:
The Group
Policy
console.

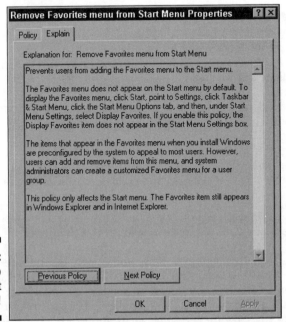

Figure 7-3:
No need to
guess about
policy!

Seeing who gets group policy

Group policy is not for everyone! Think of group policy as being applicable to the items in Windows 2000 that contain groups of other things, such as the domain, organization units, and more. It doesn't make sense to create group policy for a single workstation, though you could do so.

Here are the things to which you apply group policy:

- ✔ **Domains:** Every domain can enjoy group policy. Anything in the domain is affected by the rules established in the domain's group policy.

- ✔ **Sites:** A site can have its own group policy. This enables you to create elements of group policy that are applicable just to a site. Don't forget — a site can contain computers from more than one domain, so you need to consider the order in which group policy is applied.

- ✔ **Organizational units:** Computers and users that belong to an organizational unit (OU) are affected by any group policy applied to the OU. As an example, an OU is created automatically when you install the Active Directory. This OU is called *Domain Controllers*. A default group policy is created and applied to the Domain Controllers OU as soon as at is created. This means that server where you installed the Active Directory is subject to that default group policy, as well as any domain controllers you add to the domain.

- ✔ **Computers:** Each computer has its own group policy. This policy is created when Windows 2000 is installed on a computer. This policy is known as the Local Security Policy. Think of the Local Security Policy as the weakling who gets sand kicked in his face at the beach.

    The Local Security Policy is the first policy applied to a computer, and elements of that policy can be overridden by policy applied by the site, OU, or domain the computer also belongs to.

You can apply different policies to different instances of these objects. For example, the Sales OU can have a different policy than the Marketing OU. Also, you can apply more than one policy to a single object.

The order of policy

Some persons do not like getting direction from too many people. Some individuals in the workforce work much better when just one person is telling them what to do. Unfortunately, computers in the Active Directory must deal with having too many generals. Consider that a computer can be located at a site, naturally be part of a domain, and just might be a member of some organization unit. Also, consider that each of the objects might have one or two GPOs slapped in them. So, what's a computer to do? The following is the order in which policy is applied:

1. Local Security Policy, 2. Site, 3. Domain, and 4. OU.

Now, pay about 10 percent more attention here. Just because the number 1 appears next to Local Security Policy does not mean it really is No. 1, most important, king of the hill, whatever. In fact, being No. 1 isn't so great when it comes to the order of group policy application. Any policy you configure can be overridden if the same policy is configured with a different value by a GPO applied later.

Here are a few more rules:

- In cases where there is more than one GPO for an object, group policy is applied in the order in which the GPOs appear in the list (see Figure 7-4).

- In cases where the computer or user receiving policy belongs to a child OU, the policy from the top level parent in the OU structure is applied first. For example, if you belong to the Charlotte OU, which is a member of the Southeast OU, which is a member of the Sales OU, policy in the Sales OU is applied first, then Southeast, and then Charlotte.

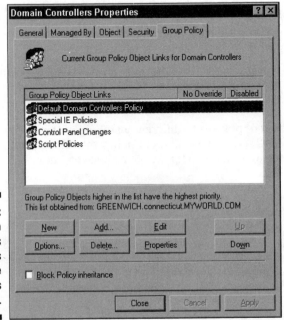

Figure 7-4:
You can
create as
many GPOs
for one
object as
you need.

Seeing how policy rolls downhill

Group policy can be inherited. Most persons like to inherit money, not rules. Unfortunately, rules are passed down with group policy. A GPO applied to some container, like an OU, also is applied to any child OUs contained in the OU where you assigned the GPO, and to that child's OUs, as well. As an example, say that in the Engineering OU there are two child's OUs: Programming and Quality Engineering. If you create a policy at the Engineering OU that installs a new Fortran compiler (so users can get the jump on Y3K bugs), the members of the Programming and QE OUs also will be the proud new users of that new compiler. Hurray for them!

Here are a few more items on policy:

✔ Policy elements that are not configured are not inherited. As an example, if the parent OU does not configure the Disable Changing Wallpaper policy, a child OU can enable that policy, and it would be applied successfully to member computers and users.

✔ Any container can block inheritance. That means a child container can stand up for its rights and say, "I will determine my own group policy." However . . .

✔ Any container can force its policy to its children, even if the children try to block inheritance.

Opening a Group Policy Object

You have a choice of how you would like to open a group policy object. Your choice is kind of dependent on your perspective. If you think that group policy is a powerful element that you cultivate and tune and apply to items in your domain, then go with the Using a Console to Open Group Policy option. If you think the domain, OU, or site is most important, and group policy is just another in the long list of properties, go with the Opening Group Policy from the Object Being Policed option.

Using a console to open group policy

You can open a GPO directly from a new management console. When you add group policy to the new console, you're asked what GPO you want to edit. This, in effect, associates one GPO with one console. This enables you to create a console for each GPO in your domain. While this could result in a large number of consoles, the benefit is that you get quick access to any GPO.

Here's how to open a GPO from the management console and, at the same time, create a permanent console to manage the GPO.

1. **Click the Start menu and choose Run.**

   The Run dialog box appears.

2. **Enter MMC in the box and then click OK.**

   A new management console window appears.

3. **Choose Console Add/Remove Snap-in from the menu.**

   The Add/Remove Snap-in dialog box appears.

4. **Click the Add button.**

   The Add Standalone Snap-in dialog box appears.

5. **Scroll down the list and find Group Policy in the list; when you find Group Policy, click it and click Add.**

   The Select Group Policy Object dialog box appears, as shown in Figure 7-5.

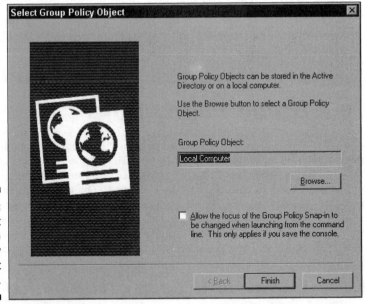

Figure 7-5:
The Select
Group
Policy
Object
dialog box.

6. **If you are working on group policy for the computer you're working on, click Finish and then skip down to Step 10.**

   Your objective here is to choose the object to which the GPO you're interested in is attached.

7. Click the Browse button.

The Browse for a Group Policy Object dialog box appears, as shown in Figure 7-6.

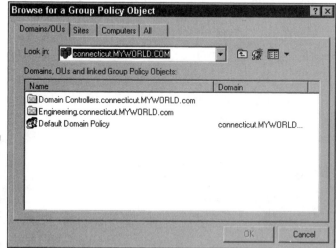

8. Click the tab for the type of GPO you want to edit.

9. Click the GPO and then click OK.

You may have to open a folder to find the GPO. To do so, double-click the folder.

You return to the Select Group Policy Object dialog box.

10. Click Finish.

The Add Standalone Snap-in dialog box appears.

11. Click the Close button.

The Add/Remove Snap-in dialog box appears.

12. Click the OK button.

You probably will want to save the console so that you can easily open the GPO in the future.

13. Click Console⇨Add/Remove Snap-in from the menu.

The Save As dialog box appears.

Be sure that the Administrative Tools folder is selected as the target folder. By saving the console in the Administrative Tools subfolder, you can be sure to open the console easily by just clicking it on the Administrative Tools menu.

14. **Enter a name for the console, such as GPO for . . . , in the File name edit box and then click the Save button.**

15. **Choose Console⇨Exit from the menu to close your new console.**

16. **To test out your new console, click the Start menu, choose Programs⇨ Administrative Tools, and then click the console you just created.**

    Your new GPO console opens.

There is nothing to stop you from adding Group Policy to a single console for each GPO you edit often. This way, you create one console with access to all of the GPOs you want. The disadvantage to this is size. Group policy contains a relatively large number of nodes, so a console with many GPOs would become very large and possibly tough to navigate.

Opening group policy from the object being policed

An easy to way to access the group policy affecting an object, or just to create a new GPO for an object, is to access that object. For example, if you are interested in the GPO affecting the Engineering OU, then track down the Engineering OU.

Here is how to open group policy via the object being policed:

1. **Find your way to the object receiving the group policy you're interested in.**

   You could end up in two different places with this step. If you are interested in the GPO affecting a site, then you'll probably open the Active Directory Sites and Services snap-in. If you are interested in the GPO affecting a domain or an OU, then you should head to the Active Directory Users and Computers snap-in. Both of these snap-ins are available on the Administrative Tools menu, which you can find on the Programs menu.

2. **Right-click the object and then choose Properties from the menu.**

   The Properties dialog box for the object appears, as shown in Figure 7-7.

3. **Click the Group Policy tab.**

   The Group Policy sheet appears.

4. **In the list of Group Policy Object Links, click the GPO you want to edit and then click the Edit button.**

   That's it!

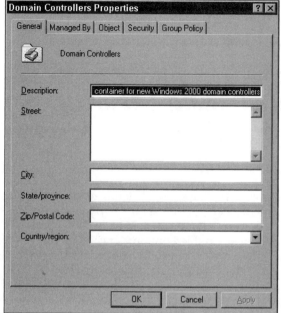

Figure 7-7:
The
Properties
dialog box
for a domain
controller
OU.

Legislating New Policy

Once you've created a new GPO for a site, domain, OU, or computer, policy is at work; there's nothing left to do. All you have to do is wait for the policy to be refreshed across the domain. Here are the quick steps involved in creating a new GPO:

1. **Right-click the lucky site, domain, or OU that will receive a new GPO and choose Properties from the menu.**

2. **Click the Group Policy tab.**

   The Group Policy tab appears.

3. **Click the New button.**

   A new group policy object is added to the list of GPOs. You'll notice a default name is given to the new GPO and the name is highlighted. This is your opportunity to name the new GPO.

4. **Just start typing; when you have entered the name for the GPO, press the Enter key.**

   As long as the text around the default name for the new GPO is highlighted, you can just enter the new name for the GPO. If you mistyped or want to change the name, right-click the GPO in the list and then choose Rename from the menu. Type the name for the GPO and press Enter.

5. **To start editing your new GPO right away, be sure that the GPO is selected and then click the Edit Button.**

   You'll find the policies are set with the default value.

Changing Policy (And Security Settings) By Hand

Enough of this setup stuff! It's time to make policy. Here's how to do it.

Depending on the policy, you'll need to click this or click that. The options you see in the dialog box depend on the type of policy you're working with. None of the polices are very complicated. Most of the policies will ask you to click either the Enabled or Disabled option. Some might ask you for more information. Some might even take you to a different dialog box. Figure 7-8 shows an example of a policy fairly simple to configure.

Enable means yes, go ahead and apply this policy. Disable means No, do not enforce this policy. When you enable or disable a policy, you are said to be configuring the policy. This is important:

   ✔ **Not configured** means you don't care. A policy that is not configured at one GPO might actually see the light of day if it is configured at a GPO applied later.

   ✔ **Disabled** means you do care. The disabled option means do not execute the rule defined in this policy.

Figure 7-9 shows an example of a more complicated policy in which you have to do more than click an option.

Follow these steps to configure group policy.

1. **Open the GPO you're interested in.**

2. **Browse through the tree until the setting you want to change appears in the details pane.**

   Just click the + button beside the name of the setting group to open the group; click the - button to close the group.

3. **Double-click the policy setting you want to modify.**

   A dialog box pops up on the screen.

4. **Make the change to policy and then click OK.**

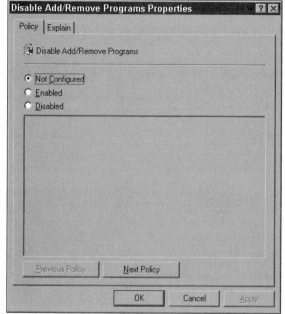

Figure 7-8:
The Disable
Add/
Remove
Programs
Properties
dialog box.

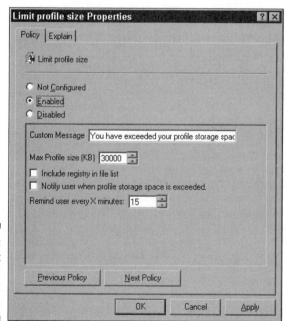

Figure 7-9:
The Limit
Profile Size
Properties
dialog box.

Waiting on your policy friend

You might be an impatient person. In fact, you might be so impatient that you become grouchy waiting for someone, like the author, to give you another thing to be impatient about. You won't be disappointed.

Group policy refreshes across the domain network every 90 minutes. If you can't wait that long, you can change the values by modifying the Group Policy refresh interval for users policy in the User Configuration\Administrative Templates\Group Policy group.

Keep in mind that if you set the interval rate too low (setting the value to 0 means 17 seconds),

your domain controller will be incapable of doing any tasks other than refreshing policy.

To force a refresh immediately, use the SECEDIT command at the command line:

```
SECEDIT /REFRESHPOLICY
MACHINE_POLICY /ENFORCE
```

or

```
SECEDIT /REFRESHPOLICY
USER_POLICY /ENFORCE
```

Applying a Security Template to a GPO

You might notice the large number of policy options you can set, as well as the large number of security settings.

The quickest way to apply security settings to a group policy object (GPO) is to apply a security template to the GPO. The settings stored in the template replace any settings set previously in the GPO. The settings loaded from the template are the same ones shown in the Computer Configuration\Windows Settings\Security Settings group.

 You really don't gain much value from using a security template just once. Rather, you gain value by using the same template with as many GPOs as you can, thus helping to ensure that the same security settings are in place in as many corners of the network as possible. If you need a review of the creation of security templates, as well as of changing the security settings in one, check out Chapter 6.

1. **Locate an object that uses the GPO to which you want to load the template.**

2. **Open the GPO where you want to apply the security template.**

3. **Open Computer Configuration\Windows Settings and then right-click Security Settings.**

4. **Choose Import Policy from the menu.**

   The Import Policy From dialog box appears. The dialog box shows all the templates stored in the default security templates folder.

5. **Click the template you want to apply to the policy and then click Open.**

   The settings in the template are applied to the policy.

Play the Family Feud of Policy

Parent and child objects in the domain feud a bit in determining what GPOs are applied. A child applies a GPO, but the parent squashes use of the child GPO, insisting its GPO is applied instead. The child object answers back with the Block Inheritance option, but the parent shows it muscle with the No Override option.

Blocking GPO inheritance

There might be some element of group policy that is so critical to your organization that you want to ensure that there is no chance of it being overridden by another GPO, like a parent.

1. **Find the object whose GPO you want to change, such as an organizational unit, domain, computer, or site.**

2. **Right-click the object and then choose Properties from the menu.**

3. **When the Properties dialog box appears, click the Group Policy tab.**

   The Group Policy tab appears.

4. **Click the GPO you want to work with and then check the Block Policy Inheritance option at the bottom of the dialog box.**

   This option ensures that the policies in the GPO will not be overridden by another GPO.

5. **Click the Apply button and then click Close.**

Blocking the block inheritance option

In group policy, parents do have some rights. As much as a child object might use the Block Inheritance option to keep GPOs defined at the parent from applying, the parent object can override that setting. This is known as the No Override option.

As an example, say that you have uncovered a significant problem in the way computers are configured across the network. Say that someone forgot to implement the policy to restrict Internet Explorer from downloading potentially dangerous content. Uh, oh! You must, without issue, update the policy at the parent to fix Internet Explorer, and you must be sure that the new GPO is applied to all children, regardless of what GPO is applied at children organizational units. You would use the No Override option to achieve this.

Here's how to do it:

1. **Find the object whose GPO you want to change.**

2. **Right-click the object and then choose Properties from the menu.**

3. **When the Properties dialog box appears, click the Group Policy tab.**

   The Group Policy tab appears.

4. **Click the GPO you want to work with and then click the Options button.**

   The Options dialog box for the GPO you selected appears, as shown in Figure 7-10.

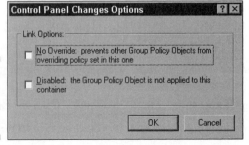

Figure 7-10:
The Options dialog box for a GPO.

5. **Check the No Override option and then click OK.**

6. **Click the Apply button and then click Close.**

Changing the Order of GPOs

You might create more than one GPO for the same object. You might create separate GPOs to maintain parts of the overall group policy separately, especially if you have lots of group policy settings. This way, it's easier to troubleshoot problems, disable just the policy you need to if need be, and provide access to a particular policy to certain individuals without giving them access to all of the group policy you've defined.

If you have more than one GPO assigned to a domain or site or OU, you may want to tune which GPO is applied in which order. The GPO at the top of the list is applied first and the GPO at the bottom of the list is applied last.

Follow these steps to change the order in which GPOs applied to the same object are applied:

1. **Find the object whose GPO(s) you want to change.**
2. **Right-click the object and then choose Properties from the menu.**
3. **When the Properties dialog box appears, click the Group Policy tab.**

   The Group Policy tab appears.
4. **Click the GPO you want to move and then click either the Up or Down button.**
5. **When the order is as you like it, click the Close button.**

Temporarily Disabling the Policy

You might need to disable a policy temporarily. You might find a serious problem with a policy and need to halt its settings from being updated on client computers. You might also need to temporarily disable the policy for testing purposes. Keep in mind that when you disable a policy, the settings in the policies are reversed the next time.

Follow these steps to disable a group policy object:

1. **Find the site, domain, or OU where the group policy object you want to disable is applied.**
2. **Right-click the object and then choose Properties from the menu.**

   The Properties dialog box appears.
3. **Click the Group Policy tab.**

   The Group Policy tab appears.
4. **Click the Options button.**

   The Policy Options dialog box for the Active Directory object appears.
5. **To disable the group policy object, check the Disabled check box.**

   Windows 2000 sounds an alarm, like the one shown in Figure 7-11.

   Worry not.
6. **Click Yes, then click OK, and then click OK one more time.**

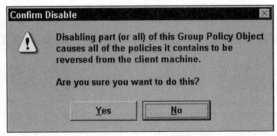

Figure 7-11:
Windows
2000 warns
you about
reversing
policy.

Picking Up the Policy Pace by Disabling Configuration

You might not use every element of every Windows 2000 policy in every GPO. For example, you might control all computer configuration and software installation policies from the GPO applied to all top-level parent OUs. The children OUs would have no reason to apply, or even check, any of the computer configuration part of their GPO. You can configure a GPO to disable either or both of the Computer Configuration or User Configuration nodes in a GPO. Doing so results in a performance boost.

Follow these steps to disable either User Configuration or Computer Configuration:

1. **Find the object whose GPO you want to change.**

2. **Right-click the object and then choose Properties from the menu.**

3. **When the Properties dialog box appears, click the Group Policy tab.**

   The Group Policy tab appears.

4. **Click the GPO you want to work with and then check the Properties button.**

   The Properties dialog box for the GPO you selected appears, as shown in Figure 7-12.

   At the bottom of the dialog box notice the two check boxes for the GPO configuration options.

5. **Click the configuration you want to disable and then click OK.**

   A dire warning appears on the screen letting you know that policy will be reversed on client computers.

6. **Click OK and then click OK once more in the Properties dialog box.**

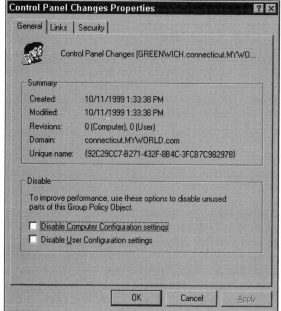

Figure 7-12:
The
Properties
dialog box
for a GPO.

Controlling Who Is Affected by Group Policy

By default, users and computers are subject to the GPO(s) applied to the Active Directory containers to which they belong, such as the domain, OUs, and sites. You can fine-tune the application of the GPO so that only the users and computers you specify are affected. For example, if you create a GPO for the domain that disables certain elements of Internet Explorer, you can specify that members of the Marketing group are not affected by the policy, even though that group is clearly a member of the domain.

By default, a new GPO is created with permissions allowing the GPO to be applied to all members of the Authenticated Users group. This means that you are not forced to explicitly specify who should or should not have a GPO applied when you create a new GPO for a domain, OU, or site.

To control who is affected by group policy, you use the standard permissions features that are used to control access to files, folders, and the like. You can find details on permissions in Chapter 5. The types of permissions you create for GPOs are different, naturally, than those you would create for a printer. Table 7-1 shows the permissions applicable to GPOs, as well as the result of creating the permissions and applying them to a user.

Table 7-1	GPO Permissions
Objective	*Method*
To force a GPO to be applied	Set both the Read and Apply Group Policy permissions to Allow.
To restrict a GPO from being applied	Set either the Read or Apply Group Policy permissions to Deny.
To neither force nor restrict a GPO from being applied	Clear both the Allow and deny check boxes for both the Read and Apply Group Policy permissions.

Note that if a user belongs to more than one group to which a GPO permission is applied, the Deny permission wins. If the permissions applied to a group to which the user belongs result in a GPO not being applied, but the user also belongs to a group in which the permissions for the same GPO specify the GPO should be applied, the GPO will not be applied.

Follow these steps to control the application of a GPO via permissions:

1. **Right-click either the domain, site, or OU to which the GPO is applied and then choose Properties from the menu that appears.**

   The Properties dialog box appears.

2. **Click the Group Policy tab.**

   The Group Policy sheet appears.

3. **Click once on the GPO you want to modify and then click the Properties button.**

   The Properties dialog box for the GPO appears.

4. **Click the Security tab.**

   The Security sheet appears.

5. **Create the permissions you need for the GPO; when you're done, click OK.**

6. **Click OK to close the Properties dialog box for the GPO.**

Part III
A Few More Ounces of Protection

The 5th Wave   By Rich Tennant

"I guess you could say this is the hub of our network."

In this part . . .

You wouldn't refer to Windows 2000 with adjectives like small, or underpowered, or feature-lite. Trying to secure this monster isn't easy, and hopefully you're not doing this job alone. You should consider getting help. No, don't bother asking; the author is booked. Here's another option.

Stop reading for a moment, look to your right. If the first person you see seems even a bit smart, ask them for help. In fact, assign them the areas covered in the chapters in this part. Also, you may want to warn your new assistant — they're about to become experts in the registry, digital certificates, and remote access.

Chapter 8

Keeping the Registry Locked Down and Secure

● ●

In This Chapter

▶ Getting reacquainted with the Registry

▶ Checking out the free Registry editors

▶ Checking out solutions for protecting the Registry

▶ Using the Registry to secure Windows 2000

● ●

The Registry is really worth protecting. The Registry is the Fort Knox of configuration details about a computer where Windows 2000 is installed. This idea of a centralized warehouse probably sounds great, but there's a big problem with it. Anyone who wants to learn about the configuration of a computer, including details about the network it attaches to, knows where to look. This chapter helps protect the Registry from prying eyes and APIs.

You read about some drastic measures for securing the Registry. While corporal punishment is not recommended in this chapter as an appropriate punishment for your users who browse through HKEY_CLASSES_ROOT, you can go through lots of effort to protect your precious keys.

What's This Registry Thing I Keep Hearing About?

The Registry is probably the most important component of a Windows 2000 system, server, advanced server, professional, data center server, or any other packaging of features Microsoft marketing comes up with. The Registry is a database that stores configuration information for Windows 2000, the hardware installed on the machine where Windows 2000 is running, and the applications you use with it. The Registry has a bit of personality in it as well.

It also stores preference information for the users. The next time you log on to a Windows 2000 machine and notice the nice Lilac Windows scheme working the way it was the last time you logged on, take a moment and thank the Registry.

Given the data the Registry stores, it's highly advisable to secure it. Here's a sampling of some of the more sensitive data found in the Registry stores:

- Architecture snippets about the network to which the computer belongs.
- The internal security identifier, known as a SID, of the user currently logged on. You can find details on SIDs in Chapter 2.
- Username of the account last logged on to the computer.
- Details about every software application installed on the computer, including any private information the application might have asked the user and then stored in the Registry.
- IP addresses.
- Location of system files.

Wow, this Registry sounds valuable!

Somebody with access to the Registry and some know-how as to its organization can modify how Windows 2000 looks and behaves from startup to shutdown.

This data isn't valuable just from a read perspective; it could be valuable from a write perspective, too. It's possible for an ill-willed intruder to reconfigure Windows 2000 via the Registry to make it easier to hack either the computer and/or the network the computer belongs to.

Those valuable hives

You might think of the Registry as a single database, but the Registry really is made up of the data stored in a bunch of files. Table 8-1 shows the files that house the data you see when you look at the Registry using one of the editors, as well as the type of data stored in the file. The file with the LOG extension is the backup version of the file. An area of the Registry where the data is populated by one of the files is known as a *hive.* This contrasts with other areas of the Registry where the data is a copy of other data. Keep in mind that certain Registry data shows up in two places to make it easier for applications to get their hands on the data. Sometimes a key will read from another key for its data.

Table 8-1	Registry Hives
Hive	*File*
HKEY_LOCAL_MACHINE\SAM	Sam, Sam.log Security information
HKEY_LOCAL_MACHINE\SECURITY	Security, Security.log Security information
HKEY_LOCAL_MACHINE\SOFTWARE	Software, Software.log Software installed
HKEY_LOCAL_MACHINE\SYSTEM	System, System.log Windows 2000 startup and configuration information
HKEY_CURRENT_USER	Ntuser.dat, Ntuser.dat.log Settings for the users
HKEY_USERS\.DEFAULT	Default, Default.log Settings for a new user

Those valuable keys

Data in the Registry is organized into *keys*. Keys are much like the folders on your hard drive. Like folders, some keys contain other keys, and those keys can contain keys, and so on. Registry data isn't thrown haphazardly into keys. Keys are typically used to collect related information. As for a few examples, Windows 2000 keeps most its configuration information about what it does when someone tries to log on in one spot in the Registry, and all of its information about SCSI devices installed on your computer somewhere else.

Those valuable values

The most important part of the Registry is the individual pieces of data. These pieces of data are known as *values*. You also see them referred to as *entries*. Every value has a name. A value might be something you can recognize, such as DoubleClickSpeed, where you specify how quickly you must click a second time for Windows 2000 to figure out you have double-clicked. A value might also be quite unfamiliar to you — keep in mind, the Registry's most important customer is Windows 2000. It's not the end of the world if you can't figure out what data is stored where in the Registry.

If you've never seen the Registry, Figure 8-1 gives you a look.

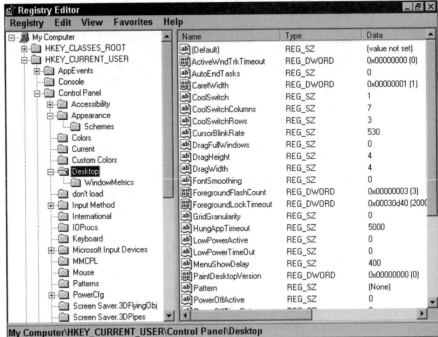

Figure 8-1:
The Registry
as viewed
from the
Regedt32
editor.

Two Registry editors for the price of none

Microsoft warns of Armageddon if you tamper with the Registry, but at the same time the company provides not one, but two editors, to help you look at and edit the Registry. This doesn't seem consistent, but because the editors come in handy, I won't argue — you shouldn't either.

Both editors let you look at the Registry and change values. You can print from the editors, export data to external files, and load from external files. The Regedit editor is a holdover from older versions of Windows. The Regedt32 editor provides a bit more features than the Regedit editor. Both editors are installed with Windows 2000. This gives any user the capability to browse through the Registry and to get into trouble. Table 8-2 gives you a quick review of editor versus editor capabilities.

Table 8-2	Registry Editor Showdown	
Feature	*Regedit*	*Regedt32*
Look at the Registry	X	X
Make changes to the Registry	X	X

Feature	Regedit	Regedt32
Create permissions		x
Make audit policy		x
Take ownership		x
Export Registry keys that can be edited and later reloaded		x
Connect to a networked computer	x	x
Copy a key name to the clipboard	x	
Print the Registry	x	x
Print just a single key and all its subkeys	x	x
Search for a key, entry name, or value	x	x
Load Registry data extracted from another computer		x

You need to be incredibly careful when you use these editors or any other tool to work with the Registry. One wrong key, and you could turn a computer into an unbootable pile of unusable hives and bytes. The Registry stores what it believes to be the configuration of the computer the last time it booted successfully. A few prior versions of working configurations are stored in the Registry as well. With this in mind, know that you can wreck your system so dramatically by misworking the Registry that it could never be booted again. Yikes! Change only what you are sure will have no ill effects and consider practicing on another machine before making Registry changes on a live computer.

If you want to find out more about the Registry from the inside out, consider *Windows 2000 Registry For Dummies* by Glenn Weadock (IDG Books Worldwide, Inc.).

Solutions for Protecting the Registry

Windows 2000 ships with a boatload of tools to help administrators administer. You can use one tool or a mix of tools to build solutions to protect the Registry.

Using group policy to secure the editors

If you use the Active Directory, you can use group policy to easily roll out permissions that restrict users from messing with the Registry editors. While this solution does not explicitly protect the Registry hives, you can be sure after applying this solution that the Registry editors aren't available for manipulating the files.

1. **Open an existing group policy object where the Registry editors will be secured or create a new group policy object and open it.**

   If you would like some hand-holding while you open or create a group policy object, check out Chapter 7.

2. **Open the Security Settings item under Computer Configuration\Windows Settings, as shown in Figure 8-2.**

   To get down to Security Settings, click the + button that appears on each step along the way.

3. **Locate the File System item.**

   This File System part of Security Settings allows you to create permissions on files and folders on Active Directory computers without having to go to each Active Directory computer!

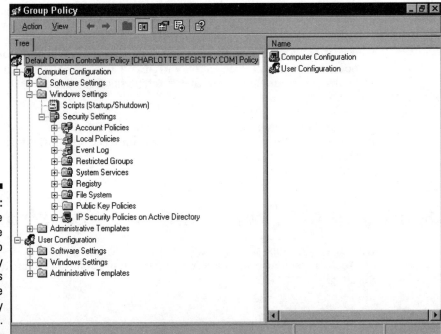

Figure 8-2:
Navigate
down to File
System to
apply
permissions
to the
Registry
editor file.

4. Right-click File System and then choose Add File from the menu.

The Add a File or Folder dialog box appears, as shown in Figure 8-3.

Figure 8-3:
Pick a file,
any file!

5. Figure out the drive on which Windows 2000 is running on the computer *you're working on*, open that drive, and then open the main Windows 2000 folder.

Don't worry if users on the Active Directory have Windows 2000 running on drives other than the one you select. For example, you might have selected the F drive, like in Figure 8-4, while your users might have Windows 2000 installed on C, D, E, or any other drives. Again, don't worry. You're working on a template, so the group policy object will figure how to work the correct way on each user's computer.

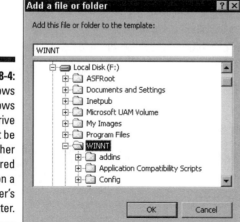

Figure 8-4:
Windows
2000 knows
the F drive
might be
some other
lettered
drive on a
user's
computer.

6. **Find the REGEDIT.EXE file, click it, and then click OK.**

The Database Security dialog box for the REGEDIT.EXE file appears (see Figure 8-5).

Do you see anything interesting about the caption on the dialog box? If you don't, Figure 8-5 points it out for you. Notice the words %SystemRoot% in the caption. The % symbols mean that SystemRoot is a variable. When the variable is used, it transforms itself into the Windows 2000 folder location.

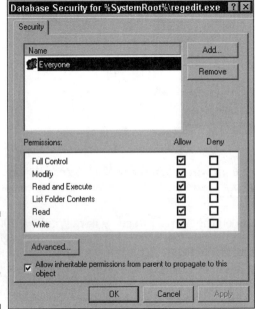

Figure 8-5:
The Database Security dialog box.

7. **Create Deny permissions on Full Control for all users except for the Administrators group.**

Chapter 4 is a great place to get pointers on creating permissions.

8. **Click OK in the Database Security dialog box, and you find yourself back at the Group Policy snap-in.**

You need to do the same thing to the Regedt32 editor.

9. **Repeat Steps 4 through 8.**

This time, navigate down to the SYSTEM32 folder under the main Windows 2000 folder and select the REGEDT32.EXE file.

Using a security template to save work and trouble

If you like the idea of using group policy to dictate Registry security but you have a lot of group policy objects (GPOs), you can save yourself some work with security templates. You can define the marching orders for either key access or Registry editor access in a template and then add that template to any GPO you want. This way, you can make the changes in one template rather than in a bunch of GPOs. This gives you more time to monitor security than administer it! Check out Chapter 6 for details on security templates.

Using group policy to secure the keys

If you want to give your users the chance to play with the Registry editors but you want to minimize their ability to break their systems, consider securing the important keys using group policy. This solution allows you to lock down keys consistently across the network without sacrificing the use of the Registry editors on users' computers.

1. **Open an existing group policy object where the Registry editors will be secured or create a new group policy object and open it.**

   If this is the first time you've heard about group policy (like when the boss says they need that report "they told you about last week" in one hour), check out Chapter 7.

2. **Open the Security Settings item under Computer Configuration\ Windows Settings.**

   To open Security Settings, click the + button that appears on each item along the way (see Figure 8-6).

3. **Locate the Registry item.**

   This Registry part of Security Settings allows you to create permissions on keys in the Registry on real computers in the Active Directory without having to go to each Active Directory computer!

4. **Right-click the Registry item and then choose Add Key from the menu.**

   The Select Registry Key dialog box appears, as shown in Figure 8-7.

5. **Navigate through the three sections of the Registry shown, select the key you want to secure, and then click OK.**

   Click the + button to open a node. If you feel like tidying up, you can click the - button to close a node.

   The Database Security dialog box appears, as shown in Figure 8-8.

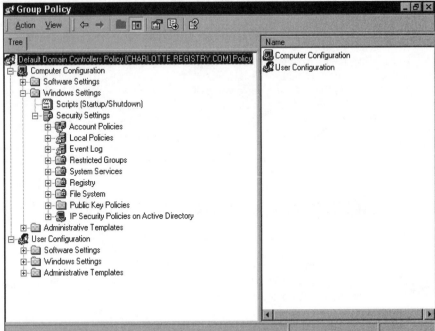

Figure 8-6:
Pop open
Security
Settings to
secure files,
the Registry,
and more.

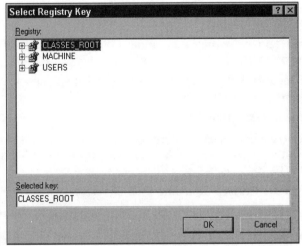

Figure 8-7:
Select a
hive to
protect.

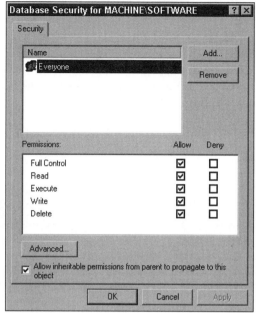

Figure 8-8:
The
Database
Security
dialog box.

6. **Create permissions for whatever users, groups, or computers that need access to the key, including some of the exotic permissions accessible by clicking the Advanced button.**

   If you need to see details on setting permissions, see Chapter 4.

7. **Click OK in the Database Security dialog box.**

8. **Repeat Steps 4 through 7 for as many keys as you need to secure.**

Using permissions to secure the editors locally

You can disable use of the Registry editors at whatever workstation you want by throwing some permissions on the two executable files that launch the editors.

Here's more of what you need to know about using permissions to secure Microsoft's registry editors on users' computers:

✔ This is a good solution (not just because the author thought of it) because it doesn't harm the editors. If you need to use the editors at some machine where you previously secured 'em, you can always log on with an account that has the rights or just use your super-administrator powers to change the permissions.

✔ If a ton of computers are on your network, you might consider using group policy to do this job for a bunch of computers at one time. If your Active Directory is not up and running, or if the workstation is not on the network, then this solution will do just fine.

✔ Don't bother with any permissions other than Full Control. If you do not want your users to play with the Registry editors, then the two files you'll secure with this solution are of zero use.

Follow these steps to use permissions to secure the editors locally:

1. **Log on to the computer with the following type of rights:**

   • Administrator

   • Ownership rights to the REGEDIT.EXE and REGEDT32.EXE files

2. **Open the main Windows 2000 folder using My Computer or Windows Explorer.**

3. **Locate the REGEDIT.EXE file.**

4. **Right-click the file and then choose Properties from the menu.**

   The Properties sheet for the file appears.

5. **Click the Security tab.**

   The Security sheet appears.

6. **Strip Full Control and Execute permissions to the file from everyone except for Administrators.**

   If you need more information on permissions, back up a bunch of pages to Chapter 4.

Using permissions to secure the keys at a computer

You can secure the Registry at any computer by applying permissions to any keys. This might not be the best solution considering you need to work with computers on an individual basis to secure them, but it's better than no security at all. For many keys, only Administrators and Windows 2000 will have Full Control access to a key; other users and groups will have just permissions to view the keys.

Use caution when you apply permissions to specific keys and be sure not to tamper with permissions already set by Windows 2000. Windows 2000 needs regular and unrestricted access to the Registry to do its job. As a general guideline, do not touch the permissions set for the SYSTEM, RESTRICTED, or Administrator user accounts or the Administrators group.

1. **Click the Start menu and then choose Run.**

   The Run dialog box appears.

2. **Enter REGEDT32.EXE in the box and then click OK.**

   The Registry Editor starts.

3. **Choose the Window menu and then choose the root key you want to secure.**

   The window for the key you selected pops up front.

4. **Click the key you want to secure.**

   You may have to navigate through the Registry to get to the key you want. Double-click any key with a + button to open it and see its sub-keys.

5. **Choose Security⇨Permissions.**

   The Permissions dialog box appears (see Figure 8-9).

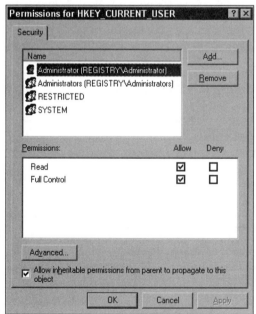

6. **Create whatever permissions you need for the key.**

7. **Click OK to close the Permissions dialog box.**

   The Permissions dialog box closes.

8. **Choose Registry⇨Close to shut down the editor.**

Removing the editors from users' machines

It can't get any easier than this. If you don't want users to play with one of those editors that come with Windows 2000, take the editors away from them.

You need to consider a few things before you remove the two Windows 2000 Registry editors from users' desktops:

- If you remove the Registry editors from users' computers, you'll be out of luck if you must diagnose a problem with one of those computers and you need to look at the Registry to do this. You can get around this problem by connecting to the troublesome computer remotely (provided you didn't remove the editors from your computer!).

- Microsoft's two Registry editors are not the only Registry editors available. Determined users can probably get their hands on some other editor if they really want to spelunk through the Registry.

- This technique is incompatible with at least one other technique described in this chapter. For example, if you yank out the Registry editors, you won't be able to give users the ability to set their permissions on certain keys. Why? Because they do this from one of the Registry editors. This might have seemed obvious, but don't write in and say I didn't tell you!

Still sound like an interesting idea? Here's how you might pull it off:

- Before you roll out new computers to users, delete the following two files:

  - REGEDIT.EXE in the main Windows folder

  - REGEDT32.EXE in the System32 subfolder off of the main Windows folder

  If you use a template to install Windows 2000 to new computers, be sure to pull the files from the template as well.

- Most system management tools, like Microsoft System Management Server, can be trained to spot certain files and delete them. Configure your tool to dust these files if they're found.

- As part of your W2K upgrade, check for and delete these files if found. You can also do a spot check for the file under the guise of a W3K check (explain that you're getting a head start).

Using read-only mode

This technique again exposes the difference between the haves and the have-nots when it comes to Registry editors. The Regedt32 editor has a read-only feature. This feature lets you switch the editor into read-only mode so that any changes you make to keys or entries are not saved. This feature does not exist with the Regedit editor.

As an administrator, you can be extremely militant in your use of this feature, or you can be a kindler and gentler administrator. You can suggest that users switch to read-only mode, with the following instructions, or you can force the issue by configuring the Registry so that the editor *always* starts in read-only mode.

Setting read-only mode in the editor

Follow these steps to switch the Regedt32 into read-only mode.

1. **Click the Start menu and then choose Run.**

2. **Enter REGEDT32.EXE in the box and then click OK.**

   The Registry Editor starts.

3. **Choose Options➪Read Only Mode.**

   If you notice that Read Only Mode is already checked when you open the Options menu, stop! Read Only Mode is one of those special toggle menus — click it once to turn it on, click it again to turn it off.

Forcing read-only mode for the Registry in the Registry

If you can't rely on your users or yourself to always set the Registry editor into read-only mode, you can rely on the Registry to do it. Here's how to change a value in the Registry so the Regedt32 editor always starts in read-only mode. First, you change the permanent read-only mode for the current user logged on, and then you change the setting for any new users.

Keep in mind that this technique only affects the Regedt32 editor. This strategy does not account for the Regedit editor, nor any third-party editors the users might acquire.

1. **Click the Start menu and then choose Run.**

2. **Enter REGEDT32.EXE in the box and then click OK.**

   The Registry Editor starts.

3. **Choose Window➪HKEY_CURRENT_USERS.**

   The HKEY_CURRENT_USER window opens.

4. **Open the HKEY_CURRENT_USER\Software\Microsoft\RegEdt32\ Settings key.**

   To open this key, double-click first on Software, then Microsoft, then Regedt32, and finally Settings.

5. **Double-click the ReadOnly entry in the Data pane, which is the right side of the editor.**

   This entry should appear on the right side of your screen in a list with about nine other entries.

6. **Change the value of the entry to 1 and then click OK.**

   The Entry dialog box closes.

   Now it's time to make sure that any new users added to this computer also get Read Only as the default mode in the Regedt32 editor.

7. **Choose Window⇨HKEY_USERS.**

   The HKEY_USERS window opens.

8. **Open the HKEY_USERS\.Default\Software\Microsoft\RegEdt32\ Settings key.**

   To open this key, double-click first on .Default, then Software, then Microsoft, then Regedt32, and finally Settings.

9. **Double-click the ReadOnly entry in the Data pane, which is the right side of the editor.**

   This entry should appear on the right side of your screen in a list with about nine other entries.

10. **Change the value of the entry to 1 and then click OK.**

    The Entry dialog box closes.

11. **Choose Registry⇨Close to shut down the editor.**

The only way to really ensure that read-only mode is used is to slap permissions on Registry keys, and that's the case here. There's nothing to stop a user from hopping into the Registry to switch the value of this key back, especially a reader who buys this book!

Cool Things You Can Do in the Registry to Enhance Security

The Registry isn't just a valuable piece of merchandise that you must secure. You can use the Registry to your benefit to add a few measures of security to your network and to users' machines. You can find a handful of Registry tweaks in this section.

Tweaking the Registry isn't for the timid. Be sure that you have backed up any Registry you plan to work on before making any changes. If you plan to trot out any of these changes using group policy, be sure to test first. You should also consider testing all the tweaks together.

Hiding the name of the last user

The logon dialog box in Windows 2000 usually displays the user name of the last account that successfully logged on to the system. This is a security no-no. The user name represents one-half of the information someone needs to logon to a system. Granted, the user name is certainly the easier piece of the puzzle to figure out, but there's no sense in giving someone with ill intentions a head start.

Here are the specifics about the Registry value to tweak to hide the name of the last user logged on at a computer:

- ✔ **Key:** HKEY_LOCAL_MACHINE\SOFTWARE\Microsoft\ Windows NT\CurrentVersion\Winlogon

- ✔ **Entry:** DontDisplayLastUserName

- ✔ **Value:** Change the value to 1 to hide the user name of the last account logged on.

Displaying a warning at logon

You might want to display an ominous warning at logon. Now, most serious hackers are going to laugh at any warning you display, but you may be able to scare off a few with weak hearts. A Registry tweak lets you set the text that appears in the caption of a dialog box that appears at logon, as well as the text of the message. Here are the Registry specifics you need to set this up:

- ✔ **Key:** HKEY_LOCAL_MACHINE\SOFTWARE\Microsoft\ Windows NT\CurrentVersion\Winlogon

- ✔ **Entry:** LegalNoticeCaption

- ✔ **Entry:** LegalNoticeText

- ✔ **Value:** Change these values to whatever text you want to appear.

Inducing amnesia in your pagefile

Unless a computer has a huge amount of memory, Windows 2000 will create a file on which it stores data it doesn't need right away. Windows 2000 will do this either when it runs out of RAM or when it simply chooses to dump some of its memory to disk. It's tough to tell what's in this thing called a pagefile, but you can bet the file might be of some interest to someone trying to break into a computer or a network.

Windows 2000 does not automatically delete the pagefile when the O/S closes up shop. It would seem that doing so would be a pretty good idea. Here's how to do it:

✔ **Key:** HKEY_LOCAL_MACHINE\SYSTEM\CurrentControlSet\Control\ Session Manager\Memory Management

✔ **Entry:** ClearPageFileAtShutdown

✔ **Value:** Change this value to delete the pagefile when Windows 2000 shuts down.

Chapter 9

Locking Down the Remote Connection

....

In This Chapter

▶ Finding out about the remote access risks

▶ Doing inventory on the remote access server security tools

▶ Assessing authentication

▶ Encrypting the connection

▶ Logging details about the authentication and the connection

▶ Setting the rules with remote access policies

▶ Consolidating control with IAS

....

*M*ost discussions about remote access wax poetic about how today's organizations aren't bounded by physical walls and how only the limits of virtual connections limit the span of our business. Uuggh! Here are the facts.

A company of almost any size will permit remote access to the network at some point, and that's the point at which network and security administrators grow another gray hair (as if they had any nongray hair left)! Remote access means no local control. Remote access means opening your network up to a different form of attack and to a new set of risks. This chapter is here to help. You read about the fancy features Windows 2000 packs into remote access to secure the service and your network. Read how to slam the door on rogue packets and establish the rules for connections. Read on and hold off on the hair color treatments (for now).

Remote Access Risks

The remote access server in Windows 2000 allows users to connect to and log on to the network without being directly connected to the network. Remote access provides remotely connected users the same type of accessibility to network resources and services (IP address through DHCP, shared folder, printers, and so on) as if they were plugged into the network down the hall from the domain controller. This remote connection can be through plain old dial-up modems, over the Internet using VPN technology, via a cable modem, DLS, ISDN, whatever.

So, what's the worst thing that can happen by allowing remote access to your network? Well, the risks presented by remote access are not much different then any of the risks present in the same building or room where a domain controller is located: illegal access, theft, data destruction, data tampering, Web site defacement, and so on. The real question is what effect does remote access have on the standard network security risks:

- ✔ Remote access creates a dangerous element known as the *anonymous user*. You can see and touch and usually recognize the users who log on to your network from computers that are directly connected to your network. You usually can't see and touch persons trying to connect to your network remotely. It's impossible to monitor the activities of remote users, the person spending countless hours trying to hack their way into your network via a dial-in modem hub.

- ✔ Not knowing the phone number at which a remote access modem is waiting is not a deterrent for a determined network hacker. A technique known as war dialing can reveal one or more of your remote access phone numbers. War dialer software, also known as scanners, can dial zillions of phone numbers, listening for the familiar tonal response from a modem. Once a hacker knows the phone number into your remote access, the next task is to pound the server with user ID and password combinations.

- ✔ If your remote access server provides virtual private network (VPN) service, in which users use the Internet to connect to your network, then your data is exposed to the open, sometimes treacherous waters of the Internet.

Remote Access Security Components

A handful of components of Windows 2000 contribute to a secure remote access environment for you and your network. Here is list of the components you use to protect your network from attack over phone lines, cable modem connections, and every other newfangled connection scheme.

- ✔ **Accounting:** No, your organization's AP department will not also have the responsibility of authenticating remote access users. Accounting in the remote access world refers to the logging of remote access server activity.

- ✔ **Authentication:** Windows 2000 supports a bagful of tools you can use to be sure that you know who is trying to log on to your network from afar.

You can use authentication methods like PAP, which simply exchanges a user ID and password in clear text, all the way to EAP-TLS, which makes it so you can use smart cards and other so-called next generation security gadgets. You can find details about authentication a little later in the "Auditing Authentication Methods" section in this chapter.

✔ **Encryption:** What? You don't want the data that your remote users exchange with your network to be read by cybersnoopers trying to peak at it? You can use one of four different levels of encryption to scramble the data passing between your network and remote users.

✔ **IAS policies:** If you have a bunch of remote access servers, you can run them all from the Internet Authentication Service (IAS). You can police all the remote access servers that IAS manages with policies. These policies let you lay down the remote access laws by defining who can connect, with what protocol, using what kind of connection type, at what time of day, on what days, and more.

✔ **Remote Access Policies:** You can configure rules that determine the who, what, when, where, and how of connections. These rules — Windows 2000 calls them policies — let you filter connections success based on time of day, protocol used, type of service requested, and more.

✔ **User Dial-in Properties:** Each user has a set of properties that apply to their dial-in access to the network. You can get to these properties via the dial-in tab on the user's property page, which you can get to by tracking down the user in the Active Directory Users and Computers snap-in. The properties include a big switch that enables you to either explicitly allow or deny the user access via dial-in.

To Connect or Not to Connect

What do you think is the most important job for a remote access server? The answer is *connect remote access users*. That was easy. What do you think is the second most important job? The answer is *decide whether to connect a user*. That was easy, too. The decision whether to connect a remote user is not arbitrary. The remote access server doesn't play favorites — there's real science in determining whether a connection is made. Here are the steps.

Step 1: Are there policies?

The first check made is of the list of remote access policies for the server the client is attempting to connect to. A *remote access policy* is a set of rules you create that determine the eligibility of a connection attempt to be successful. If there are no policies, the connection is dropped. You can see the list of policies by clicking the Remote Access Policies items for the remote access server you're interested in in the Routing and Remote Access snap-in. If there is at least one policy, the check in Step 2 starts.

Step 2: Checking those policy conditions

If at least one policy is found for the server, the first policy in the list is checked. If not all of the conditions in the first policy are met, the second policy is checked. If not all of the conditions of the second policy are met, the next policy is checked, and so on. If the last policy in the list is reached and each of the conditions in that policy cannot be met, the connection is dropped. As soon as all the conditions in any policy are met, the checks in Step 3 kick off.

Step 3: Inspecting the user's properties

When all the conditions in one policy are met, the dial-in properties of the user trying to dial-in are checked next. Figure 9-1 shows a picture of the dialog box where those properties are set. If you need a review of setting those properties, check out the "Tuning Security for a Specific Dial-in User" section a bit later in this chapter.

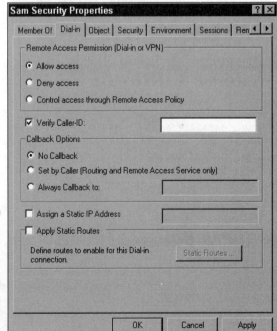

Figure 9-1:
The Dial-in
properties
for an
Active
Directory
user.

The default remote access policy

A default policy is created on every server when the Routing and Remote Access service is installed. This policy is called Allow Access If Dial-In Permission Is Enabled. Here are the details about the policy:

✔ **24x7:** Connection is permitted on any day and at any hour.

✔ **Deny:** Deny access if the user dial-in property is not set to explicitly allow access.

✔ **Default:** The default properties of the profile are in place.

Here's what happens when a user's dial-in properties are checked:

✔ If the user's dial-in remote access property is set to Deny Access, the connection is dropped.

✔ If the user's dial-in remote access property is set to Allow Access, the check in Step 4 kicks off.

✔ If the user's dial-in remote access property is set to Control Access through Remote Access Policy, then the properties of the remote access policy that the connection attempt cleared in Step 2 are checked. If the Grant remote access permission option is selected, then the connection attempt continues. If the Deny remote access permission is selected, then the connection attempt is dropped.

Step 4: Peruse the profile on the property sheet of the policy

The last check made before a remote access connection is allowed is of the profile specified for the policy. The profile can use one or both of the following tests. If either of these tests fails, the connection is dropped:

✔ Day of the week and time of the day in which connection is allowed

✔ Media used by dial-in, such as ADSL, ISDN, VPN, modem, and so on

Auditing Authentication Methods

In the remote access world, authentication is the process of checking the credentials of the user knocking on the remote access server's door. The Windows 2000 remote access server lets you choose from a bunch of authentication methods.

Not all authentication methods, though, are the same. Some are strong; some are weak. Why are weak authentication methods supported at all? Well, not every network will be Windows 2000 pure. Some of the remote users connecting to your Windows 2000 network using remote access might not use an operating system or remote access software capable of any sophisticated authentication.

Here's an audit of the authentication methods you can use with a Windows 2000 remote access server. If you need a review of some of the encryption and cryptography concepts that follow, such as hashing, refer to Chapter 1.

✔ **EAP:** EAP stands for Extensible Authentication Protocol. This protocol is used to support any exotic authentication gadgets, like smart cards. Does using this protocol mean that you can plug in any cool gadget you find at the local spy-supply store? Nope. Devices that work with EAP plug in directly to the Point-to-Point protocol (PPP) that Windows 2000 uses for remote access. The software that accompanies these devices registers itself with Windows 2000 devices. These extensions (get it — *EAP*) are known as *methods*. You can see the methods set up on your server in the EAP methods dialog box, as shown in Figure 9-2. You can see how to view the EAP later in the "Configuring authentication" section.

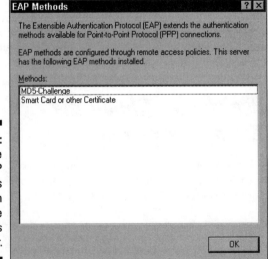

Figure 9-2:
You can see all the EAP extensions installed on the remote access server.

✔ **CHAP:** CHAP refers to the Challenge Handshake Authentication Protocol. CHAP calls for the remote access server to challenge the remote client to produce a certain coded value based on data sent to the client from the server. If the remote client responds with the correct data, the user is authenticated (you can assume that this authentication is the *handshake* part).

With CHAP, when a remote client knocks on the door of the server, the server responds with a few pieces of data: a session ID and a random string. The remote client receives the message and then creates a hash out of the session ID, the string, and the password of the user trying to access the server. The hash is made using the Message Digest 5 (MD-5) algorithm technique. The hash and the user ID (in clear text) are sent back to the server. The server, now equipped with the user ID of the client trying to get in, creates a hash with the same data it sent to the client (don't forget, the server *already* has the user's password). The server compares the hash it created with the hash sent by the remote client. If they match, the server and the client enjoy authenticated bliss.

✔ **MS-CHAP version 1:** This method is Microsoft's implementation of CHAP. With MS-CHAP, the algorithm used to create the hash is Message Digest 5 (MD-5); remember that CHAP uses MD-4. The biggest difference, though, is that the remote access server does not need to track down the password. Instead, the remote access server decrypts the password from the hash sent by the remote client.

✔ **MS-CHAP version 2:** The idea of MS-CHAP version 2 is based on MS-CHAP version 1, which is based on the RFC-standard CHAP. The biggest difference between this version of CHAP and Microsoft's first version is *mutual authentication*. In MS-CHAP version 1, the server is the big bully demanding the remote client provide credentials. The remote client responds sheepishly with a hash, hoping for authentication. In version 2, the remote client still returns the hash, but also sends its own arbitrary string so that the server can prove its identity. When the server returns a (presumed) success message to the remote client, it also sends a response that the client can use to verify the server's identity.

There is one other difference to note between versions 1 and 2 of MS-CHAP. Version 2 uses SHA (Secure Hash Algorithm) to create the hash. SHA is known to be more secure than MD-5 or MD-4, but takes longer to decrypt.

✔ **SPAP:** SPAP stands for Shiva Password Authentication Protocol. You would use SPAP if you use a Shiva remote access server. When SPAP is used, the client sends its user ID and encrypted password to the server. Once the password is decrypted, the Shiva server attempts to authenticate the user. Pass or fail, the server sends the remote client the result.

✔ **PAP:** PAP stands for Password Authentication Protocol. PAP might as well stand for Predators Attack Policy. PAP calls for passwords to be exchanged as plain old text. This means that any predator with a packet sniffer will be able to see the password as plainly as a number on your chest. The only time PAP should be used is when the client machine dialing in is capable of only PAP. If your clients are running Windows 2000, Windows 98, or Windows NT, this isn't an issue.

A *packet sniffer* is software that examines data exchanged between computers over a network. Data moves over networks in little containers called packets. That network can be a LAN, WAN, or even the Internet. A packet sniffer can tell the user certain information about each packet, such as the protocol used to send it, the target, and the destination.

This list of authentication methods is like the dessert menu at a great restaurant — everything looks so good (okay, some better than others). With all these authentication methods, you might wonder which to choose.

✔ The level of authentication you choose for remote access depends on the capabilities of the client machines accessing the network. If you set the bar too high — meaning you select an authentication method your client computers can't use — then there won't be a lot of activity on your remote access server (think of how quick it will be to review your security logs!).

✔ If your clients are Windows 2000 clients, crank up the security and use MS-CHAP version 2.

✔ Don't forget to configure EAP-TLS if your users are equipped with smart cards. You can become really smart about smart cards by referring to Chapter 15.

The order of authentication

The remote access server, like the author, does not do any more work than it must. In order to authenticate a user, the remote access server starts at the top of the list of authentication methods you have specified and will try each one in the list until there is a successful authentication. Once a user is authenticated with a particular method, like CHAP, the server doesn't bother checking any of the others.

The list of authentication methods the remote access server uses isn't arbitrary. Here is the order in which authentication methods are checked:

1. **EAP**

2. **MS-CHAP version 2**

3. **MS-CHAP version 1**

4. **CHAP**

5. **SPAP**

6. **PAP**

You might look at the list and notice that more strenuous methods are used first and the less strenuous methods are at the bottom. That's no accident. If a user is authenticated with the strongest possible method, why check a weaker one? This order also makes it possible for the remote access server to service a wide range of clients with differing capabilities for authenticating themselves. If you decide to leave a weaker authentication off the list, like PAP, you can still authenticate users with the strictest possible techniques.

Configuring authentication

Follow these handy steps to establish the authentication method for your remote access server.

1. **Start Routing and Remote Access.**

   To start Routing and Remote Access, click the Start menu and then choose Programs⇨Administrative Tools⇨Routing and Remote Access.

   The Routing and Remote Access snap-in appears.

2. **Right-click the remote access server you want to set authentication for and then choose Properties from the menu.**

   The Properties dialog box for the remote access server you chose appears.

3. **Click the Security tab.**

   The Security sheet for the remote access server appears.

4. **Click the Authentication Methods button.**

   The Authentication Methods dialog box appears. If it doesn't look like the one shown in Figure 9-3, then you probably did something wrong.

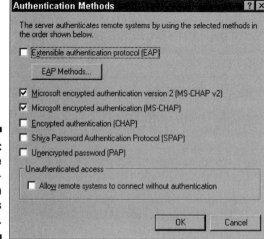

Figure 9-3:
The
Authentica-
tion
Methods
dialog box.

5. **Click all the authentication methods you want to use.**

   If you use EAP, click the EAP Methods button to see what extensions have been installed on the server. If you do not see the extension for the EAP authentication you want to use, you haven't yet properly installed the extension. Click OK to close the EAP Methods dialog box.

6. **Click OK to close the Authentication Methods dialog box.**

7. **Click OK to close the Properties dialog box.**

   An ominous message may appear asking if you want to use Windows 2000 Help to be sure that you configured everything correctly.

8. **Click Yes if you want to review Help; otherwise, click No.**

Encryption for the Remote Connection

It's a safe bet you'll want to protect the connection between your remote access server and your remote access clients. If the data exchanged between the two is even the least bit sensitive, you'll want to assign some sort of encryption scheme to protect the stream of data. Without encryption, it is possible for someone watching your network, even someone inside your network, to peek at the data exchanged between your remote users and the network.

Encryption is assigned on a per-policy basis. No user can connect to a remote access server unless at least one policy is set up, so you'll always have the chance to establish the encryption for the remote access server. If you need a review of creating a new remote access server policy, look at the "Putting Policy into Place" section later in this chapter.

There are four different levels of encryption offered by Windows 2000 remote access servers. You do not need to be a security expert to figure out which is the strongest and which is the weakest. If you need help with understanding encryption, refer to Chapter 1.

✔ **No encryption:** This encryption level means data flying around between your network and your remote users is plain as plain can be.

✔ **Basic:** Basic encryption uses a 40-bit Microsoft Point-to-Point Encryption (MPPE) key. For remote access servers working as VPN servers, a 56-bit encryption scheme is used if the protocol is L2TP. The PPTP protocol uses 40-bit encryption at the Basic level.

✔ **Strong:** The Strong encryption setting uses a 56-bit DES key. Think you might want to try breaking the key? There are 72 quadrillion possible combinations. Good luck!

✔ **Strongest:** This encryption scheme uses a 128-bit key with the triple DES encryption algorithm. Do you think this type of encryption is strong? Yup. It's so strong, the U.S. government will not allow it to be used outside of North America. This goes for the server, as well as the remote clients. Be sure to apply this encryption level to policies that would only allow access to users based in North America. You can create policies based on user groups, so it wouldn't be a big deal to apply this encryption level just to the users who you have configured with 128-bit encryption.

Follow these steps to set up encryption for a policy.

1. **Start Routing and Remote Access.**

   To start Routing and Remote Access, click the Start menu and then choose Programs⇨Administrative Tools⇨Routing and Remote Access.

   The Routing and Remote Access snap-in appears.

2. **Click the + button beside the server where the policy is located.**

3. **Locate the Remote Access Policies items and then click the + button to open the list of policies.**

4. **Over in the Details pane, right-click the policy for which you want to establish the encryption and then choose Properties from the menu.**

   The Properties dialog box appears.

5. **Click the Edit profile button.**

   The Edit Dial-in Properties dialog box appears.

6. **Click the Encryption tab.**

   The Encryption sheet appears, as shown in Figure 9-4.

7. **Click the encryption level to apply to the profile.**

   If you do not see the Strongest option, then your computer is not configured for what Microsoft calls *high encryption*. Refer to your Windows 2000 CD set or visit the Microsoft Web site at www.microsoft.com to download the encryption pack.

8. **Click OK to close the Profile Properties dialog box and then click OK again.**

   You are back at the Routing and Remote Access snap-in.

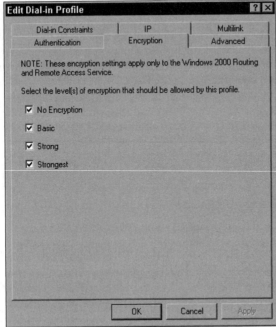

Figure 9-4:
Four easy-
to-figure-out
encryption
options.

Looking at Logging

The remote access server gives you the chance to log authentication activity on the server in a file. This gives you the opportunity to review the events on the server for possible intrusion attempts.

Here is more of what you need to know about logging remote access server activity:

✔ The file is stored in a folder named LOGFILES, which you find in the SYSTEM32 folder in the main Windows 2000 folder.

✔ The format of the file isn't easy to read. The file is comma-delimited. This means that each line of the file contains information about a single event logged by the server. Each line contains several pieces of data, such as the IP address of the remote client or the authentication method, and a comma is used to separate one piece of data from the next. Use a spreadsheet program or database to look at the file. Most spreadsheet and database applications can load comma-delimited files and load the data fields into separate columns of the table.

✔ You can also use the auditing and event logging provided by Windows 2000 server. You can find details about these features in Chapter 11.

Follow these steps to set up remote access server logging.

1. **Start Routing and Remote Access.**

   To start Routing and Remote Access, click the Start menu and then choose Programs⇨Administrative Tools⇨Routing and Remote Access.

   The Routing and Remote Access snap-in appears.

2. **Right-click the remote access server whose activity you want to log and then choose Properties from the menu.**

   The Properties dialog box for the remote access server you chose appears.

3. **Click the Security tab.**

   The Security sheet appears.

4. **Choose Windows accounting from the Accounting provider drop-down list.**

5. **Click the Event Logging tab.**

   The Event Logging sheet for the remote access server appears.

6. **Click the type of logging you want:**
   - Log errors only
   - Log errors and warnings
   - Log the maximum amount of information
   - Disable event logging

7. **Click OK.**

Putting Policy into Place

Connections to your remote access servers are either allowed or denied based on policy. This policy isn't determined by the richest man in the world (not the author) but by you, the administrator. You can use policy to control who can connect, at what time of day, and almost two dozen other conditions. You can also mix and match conditions in a policy, as well as create a bunch of policies to tune exactly what kind of connections are allowed and which are not.

Here are more details on policies:

✔ All the conditions in a policy must be met for the server to process the connection attempt. For example, if you create a policy that allows connections only between 9 a.m. and 9 p.m. on Tuesdays and only for ISDN connections, Bill's connection attempt at 9:01 a.m. with his cable modem would be rejected.

✔ Be sure to group all related conditions into one policy. Once all the conditions in any one policy are met, no other policies are checked.

✔ Place the policies with more specific conditions higher in the list. Policies higher in the list are evaluated before those later in the list. For an understanding of the role policies play in connection attempts, read the section named "To Connect or Not to Connect" earlier in this chapter.

Creating a policy

Follow these steps to create a policy for remote access server connections.

1. **Start Routing and Remote Access.**

   To start Routing and Remote Access, click the Start menu and then choose Programs➪Administrative Tools➪Routing and Remote Access.

   The Routing and Remote Access snap-in appears.

2. **Click the + button next to the remote access server for which you want to create a policy.**

3. **Find the Remote Access Policies item and then click it.**

   Notice in the Details pane any policies that have been created already for the server.

4. **Right-click anywhere in the Details pane and then choose New Remote Access Policy from the menu.**

   The Add Remote Access Policy dialog box appears, as shown in Figure 9-5.

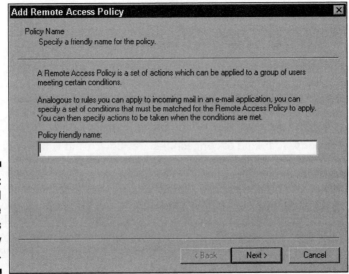

Add Remote Access Policy

Policy Name
   Specify a friendly name for the policy.

A Remote Access Policy is a set of actions which can be applied to a group of users meeting certain conditions.

Analogous to rules you can apply to incoming mail in an e-mail application, you can specify a set of conditions that must be matched for the Remote Access Policy to apply. You can then specify actions to be taken when the conditions are met.

Policy friendly name:

⟨ Back   Next ⟩   Cancel

Figure 9-5:
The Add
Remote
Access
Policy
dialog box.

5. Enter a name for the policy and then click Next.

The name you enter should be descriptive of what the policy does. For example, if you are creating a policy that restricts dial-in for all users except for those in the Dial-In Group, you probably will want to have a name more descriptive than 1-NO DIAL NOT DIG -A. Nothing wastes time like figuring out what something does. You may have to edit this policy at some point, so give the policy a name that tells what the policy does.

The Conditions dialog appears.

6. Click the Add button.

The Select Attribute dialog box appears.

7. Click the attribute you want to add to the policy and then click Add.

If you're not sure how each of the attributes works, check out Table 9-1.

Table 9-1	Remote Access Policy Attributes
Policy Attribute	*Description*
Called-Station-Id	This attribute lets you specify the phone number on which the user must call in.
Calling Station-Id	This attribute lets you specify the phone number the dial-in user can be calling from.
Client-Friendly-Name	If you use an IAS server, you can control connections based on the name of the remote access server a dial-in user is attempting to reach.
Client-IP-Address	If you use an IAS server, this attribute lets you deny or allow the connection based on the IP address of the remote access server.
Client-Vendor	If you use an IAS server in an environment with remote access servers from non-Microsoft operating systems, you can filter access based on the vendor. For example, if the IAS server you're running with Windows 2000 also minds a remote access server running 3Com software, you can explicitly deny connection attempts made to Microsoft remote access servers while allowing connection attempts to 3Com servers.
Day-And-Time Restrictions	You can specify days of the week and times during those days in which dial-in is either allowed or denied.

(continued)

Table 9-1 *(continued)*

Policy Attribute	Description
Framed-Protocols	This attribute lets you filter connection attempts based on the framing protocol used with the IAS server.
NAS Identifier	This attribute lets you specify the name of the remote access server being managed by the IAS server.
NAS-IP-Address	This attribute lets you filter remote connection attempts based on the IP address of the remote access server managed by the IAS server.
NAS-Port-Type	You can deny or allow access based on the type of connection the user is trying to make, such as ISDN, modem, or ADSL.
Service-Type	This attribute lets you allow or deny access based on the type of service being requested. Examples of service types include authenticate only, login, callback, and callback login.
Tunnel-Type	This attribute lets you allow or deny dial-in access based on the tunneling protocol being used to connect.
Windows-Group	This attribute lets you filter connection attempts based on the user, account, or user group.

A dialog box appears asking you for more information. The dialog box will differ based on the attribute you choose. For example, if you choose Date-Time Constraints, a dialog box with a cool way to choose days of the week and hours in the day appears. If you choose Called-Station-ID, a dialog box appears with just a single field where you enter a phone number.

8. **When you have supplied the information the attribute needs, click OK.**

   You return to the Select Attribute dialog box.

9. **Repeat Steps 7 and 8 for as many attributes as you need for the policy; when you're done adding attributes, click Next.**

   A dialog box appears asking you whether the policy should grant or deny connection to users not explicitly granted or denied connection privileges.

10. **Click whether to allow or deny access for those users who can't make up their own mind and then click Next.**

    The User Profile dialog box appears.

11. **To establish the encryption level for the connection, click the Edit profile button, click the Encryption tab, and then click the encryption level you want to use for the profile.**

    If you're wondering about encryption use with remote access policies, refer to the "Encryption for the Remote Connection" section found a few pages ago in this chapter.

12. **To establish the authentication methods used for this policy, click the Edit profile button and then click the Authentication tab.**

13. **Click each of the authentication methods you want to use for the profile and then click OK.**

    If you need a review of authentication use with remote access policies, refer to the "Auditing Authentication Methods" earlier in this chapter.

14. **Click Finish.**

Changing the order of the policy list

The order in which policies are listed in the Details pane of the Routing and Remote Access Server is important. Read the section "To Connect or Not to Connect" earlier in this chapter if you need a refresher why. To change the place of a policy in the list, right-click the policy and then choose Move Up or Move Down from the menu that appears.

Here is more of what you need to know about changing the order of the policy list:

✔ You can access the list of remote access policies from the Routing and Remote Access Server snap-in.

✔ If the policy you select is at the top of the list, Move Up will not appear on the menu when you right-click it. For a policy on the bottom of the list, Move Down will not appear.

Changing a remote access policy

You may need to tune a policy for dial-in. You don't need to run through each of the steps in the Add Remote Access Policy wizard described earlier in the "Creating a policy" sec- tion just to change a policy. Just right-click the policy and choose Properties from the menu. You're able to change all elements of the policy from the dialog box that appears.

Securely Consolidating Remote Access Servers with IAS

If your network uses more than one remote access server, you might use the Internet Authentication Service (IAS) to manage all the remote access servers.

Impress your remote access buddies with these IAS facts:

- ✔ To the world outside of Microsoft, this service is known as RADIUS for Remote Authentication Dial-In User Service. So, you might see the term RADIUS on the Web and other resources you might look at.

- ✔ Using IAS means you can manage all the remote access servers at one time and from one place rather than manage each of the servers individually.

- ✔ You need to tweak each remote access server ever so slightly for authentication and logging to be handled by the IAS Server. To do so, right-click the remote access server via the Routing and Remote Access Server snap-in. Choose Properties from the menu and then click the Security tab. Finally, choose the RADIUS option from both the Authentication Provider and the Accounting Provider drop-down lists.

- ✔ Use the techniques to assign authentication and encryption to remote access policies here to assign the same to IAS policies.

When you use an IAS server, the remote access policies you might have concocted on the remote access servers don't work anymore. If you want to use remote access policies for your remote access servers, you must create them on the IAS server. Follow the steps in the "Creating a policy" section, just follow them on the IAS server instead. Stop! I can hear the complaints already: You don't have the time or interest to recreate those policies. Not to worry. Microsoft has provided a method to copy policies from a remote access server to an IAS server. What will they think of next!

1. **Open a command prompt window on the computer where the remote access server is running.**

2. **Type** `NETSH AAAA SHOW CONFIG` *filename* **and press Enter where filename is the location and name of the file that will store the information that will be copied.**

   It doesn't matter what you call the file, and you can use UNC to refer to the file.

UNC refers to *Universal Naming Convention.* UNC is a standard way of referring to things on a LAN. A UNC address starts with the \\ symbol. The first part of a UNC address is the name of the server. Following the server name, parts of the address are separated by the \ symbol. Locations on the LAN are referred to by the name of the share created. A share is some folder on some machine on the network made available to many users on the LAN. A share is typically given a common name so that users can figure out what the folder contains. So, an example of a UNC address might be \\Myserver\Docs\Sales\00Plan.xls.

Remember what you entered for *filename.* You're going to have to copy that file somewhere.

3. **Copy the file created in Step 1 (hope you're not surprised) to the computer where IAS is running.**

Remember where you copied it. You're going to need that location in a second.

4. **Open a command prompt window on the computer where the IAS server is running and switch to the directory where you copied the file.**

5. **Type** NETSH EXEC *FILENAME* **where filename is the name of the file you copied from the remote access server machine in Step 3.**

Microsoft says that you don't have to shut down the server first to do this. Well, I never believe billionaires wearing glasses, so I suggest shutting down the server first.

Having fun at the remote server command line

There are a bunch of other nifty programs you can run at the command line to help you diagnose problems, as well as to just impress the person in the cube next to you.

Command	*Does This*
NETSH RAS SHOW AUTHTYPE	Shows the authentication methods in use on the remote access server running on the machine where the command is entered.
NETSH AAAA SHOW RADIUS-CLIENT-ACCTSECRET	Shows the shared secret word for your IAS server. A shared secret word is a string, and it can be anything that is entered at both the Radius client and the Radius server so that both can confirm that they are really working with the other.
NETSH AAAA SET/SHOW AUTHMODE	Displays the current authentication provider.

Tuning Security for a Specific Dial-in User

You can configure some aspects of dial-in access and security on a user-by-user basis. This can be helpful if you need to make an immediate change to some user's access rights without having to touch group policy or the remote access policy. For example, suppose that HR just told you that Sam from Sales just resigned, and he was going to work for your company's public enemy No. 1. These options also let you fine-tune the settings for a specific dial-in user.

1. **Start the Active Directory Users and Computers snap-in.**

2. **Click the Users item under the domain where the user is a member.**

3. **Find the user in the details pane, right-click the user, and then choose Properties from the menu.**

    The user's Properties dialog box appears.

4. **Click the Dial-in tab.**

    The dial-in sheet appears.

5. **To immediately shut down this user's remote access, click the Deny Access option in the Remote Access Permissions box; if the user's access has been denied and you want to allow him access again, click the Allow Access option.**

6. **To let the remote access policy determine whether the user should have access or not, click the Control access through remote access policy option.**

    You can have the server check the phone number from which a user dials-in against the number you have recorded for the user.

7. **Check the Verify Caller-ID box and then enter the phone number the system should check in the box.**

    Be sure that the modem you use for the remote access server supports caller-ID. Also, the user's phone system must be able to support caller-ID, and be sure that the user does not use a block feature to prevent his number from being identified.

    This option might not be useful at all for your organization, especially if your remote users call in from different locations. Not all remote users travel, but many do, definitely most in my organization. If you know the user is a road warrior, hopping from one city or hotel to another, then this option might not be a good idea.

You can have the remote access server call the user trying to make a connection.

8. **Click the Always Callback option and then enter the phone number the server should dial after the user has been authenticated.**

This option adds an element of security in that the server can verify the caller is who he or she says he is by calling the predetermined phone number for the user.

9. **Click OK in the user's Properties dialog box.**

Securing Your Remote Access VPN Tunnel

Your users may want to connect to your remote access server, and thereby to your network, by using their own Internet Service Providers. Whether users use ISPs or not, you might also have a situation in which different offices connect to one another using the Internet. In effect, you link the routers at each office using the Internet. With the use of the Internet, your network goes from small to REALLY BIG. This type of network is known as *virtual private network*, or VPN. You can set up a Windows 2000 remote access server to handle VPN connections. Regardless of how or why you use a VPN, data on the VPN highway is usually encrypted. Otherwise, your virtual private network will become a virtual public network.

VPN in a minute

Data that is exchanged on a VPN is said to be encapsulated. For a VPN packet, this encapsulation is a header that tells routers where the data should really go (your remote access server or your VPN client). Think of this encapsulation as placing regular mail in a special envelope that provides the postal service more detailed instructions about where your original envelope should go. While the Internet is routinely thought of as the network that connects your VPN clients and your VPN server, the middle network can be anything.

Here are some pointers about configuring a secure VPN remote access connection:

✔ You need to configure a remote access server specifically as a VPN server. If you haven't done so, do it now (it's tough to configure security on a server that doesn't exist). Otherwise, you won't have access to the VPN ports.

✔ You do not need to create new accounts for existing users who now connect with VPN. Your challenge as an administrator is to manage the secure exchange of information over the VPN (encryption), as well as to authenticate anyone who comes knocking at the VPN door.

✔ You can use one of two different protocols to establish a VPN connection: Layer 2 Tunnel Protocol (L2TP) or Point-to-Point Tunneling Protocol (PPTP). The authorization scheme used by the VPN is dependent on the VPN protocol used on the port where the VPN client is knocking.

  • For L2TP, a computer certificate is required both on the machine where the VPN server is running, as well as on each VPN client that will use L2TP. You can find details about certificates in Chapter 10.

  • If your VPN protocol of choice is PPTP, you have your choice of any of the authentication methods offered by the Routing and Remote Access Service. If your clients are capable, use either MS-CHAP version 1 or MS-CHAP version 2. Do you need to do anything special to your remote access server to specify the authentication? Nope. When you configure the authentication of either the server or the remote access policy, you're all set.

✔ The encryption used is dependent on the VPN protocol:

  • If you want to encrypt your PPTP connection, and it's hard to believe that you wouldn't, you can use MS-CHAP or EAP-TLS encryption. Naturally, if your clients will be authenticated with smart cards, then you'll have to enable EAP-TLS.

  • If you use L2TP, then IPSecurity (IPSec) is your only option for encryption. Data exchanged with IP Sec includes a special Authentication header (AH). The AH contains data that verifies the sender of the data and ensures the data hasn't been monkeyed with. You can find details about IP Sec in Chapter 14.

You need to be sure that any Internet traffic passing through your VPN server is actually VPN traffic going to and from a real VPN client. The best way to do this is to filter the interface so that only VPN traffic can pass through.

1. **Start Routing and Remote Access.**

   To start Routing and Remote Access, click the Start menu and then choose Programs⇨Administrative Tools⇨Routing and Remote Access.

The Routing and Remote Access snap-in appears.

2. **Open the server you want to work on by clicking the + button beside its name; next, open IP Routing for the server.**

3. **Click once on the General item.**

4. **In the details pane, click once on the interface where VPN traffic will run.**

   Take a look at the IP Address column and memorize the IP address. If you have too much on your mind, feel free to write the number on something.

5. **Right-click the interface you chose and then choose Properties from the menu that appears.**

   The General tab should appear. If for some odd reason it doesn't, click it.

6. **Notice the two filter buttons near the bottom of the dialog box, one labeled Input Filters, the other labeled Output Filters; click the Input filters button.**

   The Input Filters dialog box appears.

7. **Click the Add button.**

   The Add IP Filter dialog box appears

8. **Check the Destination Network check box.**

   The IP address, subnet mask, and Protocol drop-down list fields should light up.

9. **Enter the IP address you memorized or wrote down in Step 4 in the IP address field.**

   You can use the right-arrow key to move to the next section of the IP address. When you enter 3 digits, like 213 or 128, the cursor automatically moves to the next field.

   Notice how an IP address is divided into four pieces. Each of these pieces is known as an octet, although you may also see each section referred to as a field.

10. **Enter** 255.255.255.255 **as the subnet mask.**

11. **Select UDP from the Protocol drop-down list.**

    UDP refers to User Datagram Protocol, which is one of the protocols in the TCP/IP suite. UDP is useful for moving packets quickly (at the expense of error checking and resending) from computer to computer.

12. **After you select UDP, the Source port and Destination port fields should light up.**

13. **Enter 500 in both the Source port and Destination port fields.**

14. **Click OK.**

    You return to the IP Filters dialog box.

15. **Click the Be Sure To Drop All Packets Except Those That Meet The Criteria Below option.**

16. **Click the Add button again and repeat Steps 8 through 15.**

    This time, enter 1701 in the Source port and Destination port fields.

17. **Click OK.**

    You should be at the Properties dialog box for the connection you chose in Step 5.

18. **This time, click the Output Filters button.**

19. **Repeat Steps 7 through 17.**

    Note that on this pass the dialog box you see in Step 14 is the Output Filters dialog box.

20. **Click OK.**

    You return to the Routing and Remote Access Snap-in.

Using VPN to connect routers

You might use a VPN server as a router to connect a few private segments of your network. If this is the case, you need to add packet filtering to each of the router stops along the way to be sure just traffic generated by the routers is passed through.

Chapter 10

Certifying Authentication with Digital Certificates

• •

In This Chapter

▶ Finding out all the basics about certificates

▶ Becoming the authority on certificate authorities

▶ Managing certificates as a user

▶ Administering certificates as an administrator

• •

*C*ertificates have a significant impact on organizations that choose to use them. Certificates add a flexible and pretty-easy-to-administer option for organizations to both authenticate and encrypt. As more and more companies do business on the Internet, certificates will play a larger and larger role. Not convinced? How many times have you seen that message when you're browsing the Web informing you that you're about to make a secure connection? That connection isn't secure because no one is looking over the shoulder of the Webmaster who built the site. Rather, that's an indication of a certificate at work.

This chapter has two personalities. One personality is that of a user guide for users, the other as a guide for you, the administrator. You discover how to administer this certificate thing, as well as how to request your own certificates. Also, if you have no idea about certificates, you're treated to a free introduction.

Taking Certificates for 100, Alex

Certificates have an important but rather simple purpose. Certificates in Windows 2000 prove that Active Directory users are who they say they are. Certificates are subtle about their responsibility, though. They don't simply broadcast to the world that "everyone in this Active Directory is legit!" Rather, certificates provide positive user identification just to the parties that bother to ask them. If an application or service doesn't bother to query a certificate as to whether Jim@Mailroom.com is really that Jim guy who works in your mailroom, it's their loss.

Certificates provide the same services for computers in the Active Directory and for services. Certificates also verify their identity to anyone or anything that bothers to ask.

You might think all of this sounds interesting, but you can't remember anyone at the copy machine saying how much they enjoyed using their digital certificate. Here are just three ways digital certificates are used in Windows 2000:

- ✔ Windows 2000 introduced the encrypting file system (EFS). This feature lets users encrypt files and folders. A certificate is used to encrypt the folders/files, ensuring that if they're stolen from the drive where they are stored, or even if the entire drive is stolen, the files and folders cannot be decrypted.

- ✔ Windows 2000 supports smart cards for authentication. The smart card has burned on it data (a private key) that associates the bearer of the card with an account in the Active Directory via a digital certificate.

- ✔ The most sensitive Web sites, like those providing financial services, need to verify that the data they exchange with browsing users actually gets to the intended browsing users. A certificate can be used both to identify someone on the Web, as well as to encrypt the entire exchange of data between the server and user.

Certificates might sound interesting, but they're not very interesting in person. Figure 10-1 shows a certificate. Actually, the figure shows Windows 2000's presentation of the data contained in a certificate. Remember, a digital certificate is just 1s and 0s — it's software. While you might be able to get someone in the marketing department at Microsoft or VeriSign, the large public key and digital certificate provider, to draw you a picture of a certificate, no one will accept it as proof of you or your company's identity.

Certificates usually contain the following details:

- ✔ The public key of the subject presenting the certificate

- ✔ The length of time the certificate is valid

- ✔ Information about the subject, like name, address, favorite breakfast cereal, and so on.

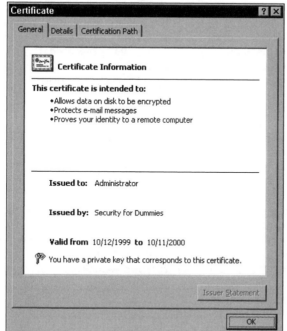

Figure 10-1:
Now that's
an important
looking
certificate!

Understanding certificate authorities

Certificates are issued by a *certificate authority* (CA). A CA can be a real organization with offices, employees, buildings, and an HR department, or simply the certificate services running on Windows 2000 server. The purpose of a CA, though, does not change regardless of the form the CA takes.

A certificate authority (CA) is an organization trusted by two groups of consumers:

✔ One group trusts the CA to issue certificates for organizations and persons that it knows and that it can verify to be the true presenter of a certificate. A CA isn't worth much if, after it issues a certificate, it cannot verify that the party who displays the certificate is the party the CA issued the certificate to.

✔ The other groups who trust CAs are those who ask the CA to create certificates for them. These groups trust the CA not to divulge any of the personal information they provide to the CA. This personal information is used by the CA to verify the identity of the party that displays a certificate issued by the CA.

A CA is also a respected organization. A certificate presented by an unknown or untrusted CA is worth as much as ID I might present at the bank that was signed by either my mother or by *Bigshoes the Clown*. Clearly, the folks at the bank are not going to fulfill my request. If an ID I presented, though, was embossed with a seal of the state of North Carolina, I might be shown some respect. This is the same idea in the digital certificate world.

Understanding how certificates work

Certificates are part of the Windows 2000 public key support. If you would like to read about public key cryptography, be sure to turn to Chapter 1.

Certificates contain private keys. When a private key is used with a public key, the two keys interact to unlock some piece of information. That piece of information is usually proof that the certificate is valid. These two keys also can be used to encrypt and decrypt data. You usually can't get the public key and the private key from the same certificate — makes sense, right?

The public key is usually held by the CA who issued the certificate. The public key is available on the CA's root certificate. This means that as long as an organization has a trusted certificate issued by a CA, it can use that CA's public key to work with the private key presented by a digital certificate issued by the same CA.

Lastly, your users will not receive a new digital certificate in office mail, nor will they receive an e-mail asking them to "bring along their certificate" the next time they're in the office. Certificate exchange and presentation is usually a function of the applications they run. Users will usually have no idea that a certificate is being used to authenticate them somewhere.

Understanding how all this affects Windows 2000

So how does this stuff about certificates and CAs apply to Windows 2000?

Organizations that trust CAs install the trusted CA's root certificate in their certificate store. If a business partner of yours trusted you, they would install a certificate from your Windows 2000 CA in their certificate store. A *certificate store* is the place where a computer keeps all the certificates it has acquired. This way, when one of your users requests access to some secured asset at your partner's site, for example, your business partner can confirm their identity by checking their certificate against the certificate you provided to your partner from your CA. Does your partner run a file compare of the two certificates? Nope. Windows 2000 does all the work, working with the public key provided in your CA's certificate and the private key in your user's certificate.

The Windows 2000 CA on your network provides the same services to users on your network when the applications they need require a public key so that users in your network can interact securely with one another, too.

Creating a Console for Certificate Care

The first order of business involved in working with certificates is to create a console. You can create a console that provides you access to the tools you'll need to administer certificates, as well as to manage them as a user. It makes sense to create a console that includes these two snap-ins. This way, you don't have to create a new console and add a snap-in every time you want to administer certificates, as well as tend to your own.

1. **Click the Start menu, choose Run, enter MMC, and press Enter.**

   A new console window appears.

2. **Choose Console⇨Add/Remove Snap-in from the menu and click Add when the Add/Remove Snap-in dialog box appears.**

   Scroll down the list and find Certificates in the list.

3. **Click once on it and then click Add.**

   The Certificates Snap-in dialog box appears.

4. **Click My User Account and then click OK.**

5. **Click Close in the Add Standalone Snap-in dialog box.**

6. **Click OK in the Add/Remove Snap-in dialog box.**

7. **Choose Console⇨Save As from the menu.**

   The Save As dialog box appears.

8. **Enter a name for the console, such as My User Certificates, in the File name edit box and then click the Save button.**

   Be sure that the Administrative Tools folder is selected as the target folder. By saving the console in the Administrative Tools subfolder, you can be sure to open the Certificate console to manage your own certificates easily by just clicking it in the Administrative Tools menu.

Mastering Certificates as a Consumer

Certificates aren't just a piece of software for administrators to roll out to users, nor are they a management tool that users will never see. Administrators like you are people, too. With this in mind, it's worth it to review the things that users will do with certificates.

Requesting certificates

If you don't have a certificate, you should see to getting one. Because there are different types of certificates for different uses, you most likely will request a certificate more than once.

To request a certificate, follow these steps:

1. **Open a console that gives you access to the Certificates snap-in.**

2. **Open the Personal folder and then right-click Certificates. Choose All Tasks⇨Request New Certificate; when the Certificate Request Wizard starts, click Next.**

   The Certificate Template dialog box appears, as shown in Figure 10-2.

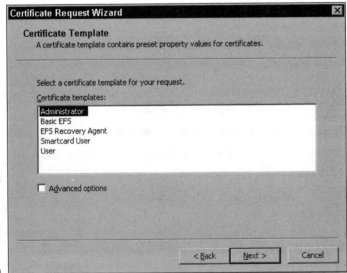

Figure 10-2: The Certificate Template dialog box.

3. **Click the type of template you need, click the Advanced Options check box, and click Next.**

   The only option available for requesting a certificate that is not considered Advanced is for a regular user certificate.

   The Cryptographic Service Provider dialog box appears.

4. **Click the type of certificate you need and then click Next.**

   If you're not sure what kind of certificate you need, click the default option of Microsoft Base Cryptographic Provider v1.0. Certain security services your organization might use will require you to make a specific selection from this list. For example, if you are requesting a certificate for a smart card, you need to know what kind of smart card you're using.

The Certificate Authority dialog box appears. Check the CA displayed in the dialog box.

5. **If this is the CA from which you want to have your new certificate issued, click Next; if there is more than one CA installed on the domain where you are working and you need to select a CA not shown, click Browse to select it.**

6. **Enter a name for the certificate and then click Next.**

   It's not likely that you'll have so many certificates that you'll get confused as to which one does what, but there are some spots in Windows 2000 where the only info you'll see about the certificate is the name.

7. **Verify the information about your new certificate and click Finish.**

   Windows 2000 charges off to create your certificate. When it's done, you'll be asked to install it.

8. **To install the certificate right away, click the Install Certificate button. If you want to look at the certificate first, click the View Certificate button. If all of this was a big mistake, click Cancel.**

   Your certificate should appear immediately in your list of certificates.

Importing and exporting certificates

Certificates aren't necessarily bolted to the computer where they were issued. You can move a certificate from one computer to another, as well as create a back-up copy of a certificate. You import and export certificates from the Certificates snap-in.

Here's how to export a certificate:

1. **Open a console that gives you access to the Certificates snap-in.**

   You can find help on creating a console for Certificate use earlier in this chapter in the "Creating a Console for Certificate Care" section.

2. **Open the folder where the certificate you want to export is located.**

   The list of certificates appears in the details pane.

3. **Right-click the certificate you want to export and select All Tasks⇨ Export.**

4. **When the Certificates Export Wizard starts, click Next.**

If you chose a personal certificate to export, or any certificate type for which you have a private key, the Export Private Key dialog box appears. If the Export File Format dialog box shows up, skip to Step 6.

5. **Select whether you want to also export your private key with the certificate by clicking on the appropriate option. Then, click Next.**

   If the option to export your private key is grayed-out, you can't export your private key for this certificate type. You can only export the private key if:

   - The certificate was made from the EFS Recovery Agent template.
   - The mark keys as exportable option was selected when the certificate was created.

6. **Pick the format of the exported certificate and then click Next.**

   You'll probably have a few choices of formats to pick from. Here's what you need to know about picking a format for your exported certificate:

   - Use the DER or Base-64 formats if you will later import the certificate into a non-Windows 2000 machine or if you're just not sure where the exported certificate will end up.
   - Only PKCS #10 format is available if you export the private key.

PKCS #10 is an odd name for a file format. PKCS stands for Public Key Cryptography Standards. The #10 refers to the standard regarding how to move around a user's certificate, including the secret keys.

If you selected the option to export the private key, you're asked to supply a password for the exported file.

7. **Enter the password and confirm and click Next.**

   The File to Export dialog box appears.

8. **Enter a location for the exported certificate and then click Next.**

   Review the information in the confirmation dialog box.

9. **If everything looks right, click Finish.**

If exporting a certificate seemed fun, try out importing a certificate. If you do not have a sample certificate to try to import, try exporting a certificate using the preceding steps.

1. **Open a console that gives you access to the Certificates snap-in.**

   You can find help on creating a console for Certificate use earlier in this chapter in the "Creating a Console for Certificate Care" section.

2. **Choose Action⇨All Task⇨Import from the menu.**

3. **When the Certificates Export Wizard starts, click Next.**

4. **Enter the name and location of the certificate you'd like to import or click the Browse button if you don't feel like typing; click Next.**

If the certificate you're importing was exported with its private key, you may have to enter a password to give you access to the certificate.

5. **Enter the password if prompted.**

You also have the option of forcing the password to be used all the time, as well as deciding whether the certificate created by the import can be exported with its secret key.

6. **Click Next.**

You're next presented with the option of placing the imported certificate in a specific folder in your certificate store or having the location chosen automatically.

7. **Select the Automatically Select option for the location of the certificate and then click Next.**

8. **Review the information in the dialog box and then click OK.**

Mastering Certificates with the Certificate Master

If you're done being a consumer, it's time be an administrator! Windows 2000 provides a CA-in-a-box via its certificate services. This means Windows 2000 can act as its own CA. This contrasts nicely and neatly with third-party companies like VeriSign, who must collect enough data in order to confidently produce a certificate for its customers. Windows 2000 needs to turn just to the Active Directory to collect the information it needs to produce certificates.

Actually, the Windows 2000 CA you implement can and should interface with third-party CAs like VeriSign. Why? The certificates that fly around your network are backed by your CA, but who is your CA backed by? If Windows 2000 trots out a digital certificate to identify a user hitting one of your partner's sites, why should the site let your user in? Your Enterprise CA probably should use a certificate distributed by a third-party CA. This way, the certificates in use in your network are backed by your CA, while your CA is backed by a known, trusted source like VeriSign.

Creating an Enterprise CA

The first step in implementing a public key infrastructure in your network is to add a trusted root certificate authority. Huh? This means that if you plan to use certificates, then you need to be able to issue certificates to the users and computers and services that want them.

If you have any experience with Windows (including 3.1, 95, 98, whatever), you might be offended by the following steps. The reason you might be offended is that you're led through the use of the relatively basic steps of using the Add/Remove Programs wizard. The installation of an Enterprise CA is integrated into the wizard, though, so it's worth the hit to your pride to follow the steps.

Follow these steps to install a trusted root CA:

1. **Click the Start menu and then choose Settings⇨Control Panel.**

   The Control Panel folder opens.

2. **Double-click Add/Remove Programs.**

   The Add/Remove Programs dialog box appears.

3. **Click the Add/Remove Components button and then click the Components button.**

   The Windows Components Wizard appears.

4. **Find Certificate Services in the list; when you find it, check the option.**

   Windows 2000 warns you that the computer on which you're installing a CA cannot be renamed or join or be removed from a domain. This is to ensure the veracity of the certificates that this CA will eventually produce.

5. **Click Yes and then click Next.**

   The Certificate Authority Type dialog box appears. This dialog box gives you the opportunity to select the type of CA you want to create.

6. **Be sure that Enterprise Root CA is selected and also check the Advanced Options box; click Next.**

   The Public and Private Key Pair dialog box appears.

If your CA will provide certificates from a cryptographic service provider other than those provided by default in Windows 2000, you need to be sure that support for the CSP is installed before you create the Enterprise CA.

7. **Click the Cryptographic Service Provider from the CSP list.**

   You'll most likely use the default choice of Microsoft Base Cryptographic Provider v1.0. If this CA will provide certificates for smart cards, be sure to pick the appropriate CSP from the list.

8. **If you already have a key pair for the CA you'd like to use, click the Use existing keys option and then select the type of certificate with which the keys are associated. Next, click the Import button. Enter the name of the file to which you exported your keys and enter the password. Click OK when you're done.**

   The CA Identifying Information dialog box appears.

9. **Enter the information about your organization and then click Next.**

   The Data Storage Location dialog box appears.

10. **Click Next to accept the default values.**

11. **Click Finish in the last dialog box.**

    That's it! Your Enterprise CA has been created and can start issuing and verifying certificates.

Understanding why to create other CAs

You're probably proud of your work in rolling out your first Enterprise CA. Well, come back to Earth because you have lots more work to do. Rarely are Enterprise CAs rolled out and set up to directly service certificate requests. Rather, a hierarchy of CAs are built under the root Enterprise CAs to provide certificate services.

There are a few different types of certificate authorities you should know about:

- ✔ **Enterprise CA:** An enterprise CA is integrated into Windows 2000 through the Active Directory. An enterprise CA validaztes the users it issues certificates for against their accounts in the Active Directory. An enterprise CA can be a root CA or a subordinate CA.

- ✔ **Root CA:** A Root CA refers to the first CA in an organization. The root CA is the most trusted CA in an organization in which there are multiple CAs. Typically, organizations will launch a root CA and then create subordinate CAs from the root CA to do all the work. This way, the risk of someone getting their hands on the private key of the root CA is reduced. Just think, if someone were to access the private key of a root CA, they could masquerade as the organization to whom the root CA represents.

- ✔ **Subordinate CA:** A subordinate CA does the real work in an organization. A subordinate CA is either a subordinate to the root CA or to another subordinate CA. A subordinate CA issues its own certificate, but the subordinate CA is certified by the parent CA. If that parent CA is also a subordinate CA, then that CA is certified by its parent, as well. A subordinate CA is typically issued to handle a specific type of request, like for smart cards.

- ✔ **Stand-alone CA:** A stand-alone CA is not automatically integrated with the Windows 2000 Active Directory. A stand-alone CA is typically deployed to deal with Internet requests for CA services.

To install a new CA, follow the instructions found earlier in the section "Creating an Enterprise CA." When you follow the steps provided, this time choose the type of CA you want to install.

Stopping and starting the CA

You may need to stop the CA running on your network for some reason. Also, certain administrative tasks will require the CA be stopped and then restarted. Windows 2000 may graciously volunteer to restart the CA service after it starts or it might not, and sometimes when it volunteers to restart the service, Windows 2000 doesn't keep its promise.

To start or stop the CA service, log on to the network with a user account with administrator level rights. Next, open a console that gives you access to the CA. Right-click the name of the CA and then choose either Start or Stop.

Determining what kind of certificates your CA can issue

The first CA you installed can generate a number of certificate types right away. There's nothing special to do. Here's the list of certificates your CA can generate immediately.

- ✔ EFS Recovery Agent
- ✔ Basic EFS
- ✔ Domain Controller
- ✔ Web Server
- ✔ Computer
- ✔ User
- ✔ Subordinate Certification Authority
- ✔ Administrator

To configure your CA to issue other types of certificates, follow these steps:

1. **Start the Certificate Authority snap-in.**

   You can find the Certificate Authority snap-in by clicking the Start menu and then choosing Programs⇨Administrative Tools⇨Certificate Authority.

2. **Open the CA.**

3. **Right-click Policy Settings and then choose New⇨Certificate to Issue.**

   The Select Certificate Template dialog box appears, as shown in Figure 10-3.

4. **Select the certificate you want your CA to issue and then click OK.**

   The new certificate template should now appear in the list of certificates.

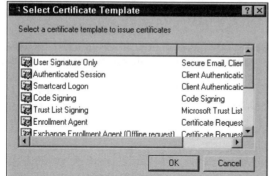

Figure 10-3:
The Select
Certificate
Template
dialog box.

Backing up and restoring the CA certificate

You need to add the root CA certificate to your existing back-up and recovery plan. You *do* have a back-up and recovery plan, don't you? Just checking!

You launch certificate back-up and restore operations from the CA snap-in. To launch either of these operations, open a console that gives you access to the snap-in, click the CA and then choose Actions⇨All Tasks⇨Restore CA or Actions⇨All Tasks⇨Backup CA.

Windows 2000 uses a wizard to walk you through the steps involved in backing up and restoring. Here's some help answering the wizard's questions:

✔ You'll choose a directory to store the backup. The backed-up certificate is a bit of a sociopath and doesn't get along well with others. That folder must be empty. You can create it ahead of time, or you can just enter the name of the folder when the backup wizard asks and then let the wizard create the folder.

✔ You'll be asked to supply a password for the backup. You'll have to supply that password if you restore from that backup.

✔ The first backup you perform should be a full backup. Perform just incremental backups after the first full backup. If you need to restore the certificate from backup, you'll need to restore the full backup first and then each of the incremental backups, in order.

✔ To restore from a backup, the CA service must be shut down. The helpful backup wizard is happy to stop the service for you, as well as to restart the service when the restore is completed.

✔ You can restore the entire certificate, including the private key, or just the log of issued certificates, including the list of certificates waiting to be issued.

Revoking certificates

You may need to revoke a certificate that your CA has issued. You might find that somehow the private key for the certificate has gotten to the open water, or that something is wrong with the certificate. Don't worry, there's no harm or embarrassment involved in revoking a certificate. Authorities from your organization will not show up at the office or cube of the person from whom the certificate is being revoked.

Follow these steps to revoke a certificate:

1. **Log on to the domain where the CA is located with an account with administrative rights.**

2. **Open a console that gives you access to the CA.**

3. **Open the Issued Certificates folder for the CA you're working on.**

4. **Click the certificate you want to revoke in the details pane.**

5. **Choose Action⇨All Tasks⇨Revoke Certificate.**

   The Certificate Revocation dialog box appears.

6. **Select the reason to revoke the certificate from the drop-down list (see Figure 10-4) and click OK.**

Figure 10-4: The Certificate Revocation dialog box.

Certificate Revocation	? X

Are you sure you want to revoke the selected certificate(s)?

You may specify a reason for this revocation.

Reason code:

Unspecified ▼

| Unspecified |
| Key Compromise |
| CA Compromise |
| Change of Affiliation |
| Superseded |
| Cease of Operation |
| Certificate Hold |

No

If you're not completely sure that you want to revoke the certificate for good, select the Certificate Hold option. This allows you to halt use of the certificate without completely revoking it. You can unrevoke the certificate if you clear up the problem with the certificate.

7. **Now, click the Revoked Certificates folder to see the certificate you just revoked.**

If you have created a hierarchy of CAs in your organization, you might wonder how all CAs find out when one CA revokes a certificate. No problem. CAs produce CRLs (certificate revocation lists). These lists are produced on a regular basis, automatically, though you can generate this list whenever you like (such as when your organization sells off that troublesome business unit). In addition, Windows 2000 can publish public CRLs so that locations to which your enterprise CA has been installed also can be made aware of revoked credentials.

Making certificates available to your users via the browser

You can make it very easy for users to request the certificates they need via Internet Explorer or whatever browser they like. While the browser runs slower than the Certificates snap-in, which is the only other option users have for requesting certificates, you can integrate certificate requests onto your Intranet.

Support for browser requests happens automatically when you install a CA. Actually, you might have noticed the option to provide the support. When you installed the CA in your domain, you selected Certificate Services from the list of Windows Components to install. Remember? If you clicked the Details button for Certificate Services, you would have noticed the option.

The default URL for web-based certificate requests is

your_web_server_name\CertSrv

Unless you change the layout of the default page, Figure 10-5 shows what your users see.

So, what's the advantage to users requesting via their browser rather than the snap-in? None, really. Sorry. Here's the list of things a user can do from the certificate request Web site:

- ✔ Request a new certificate from any of the CSPs installed on the domain, such as a basic Microsoft Base Cryptographic Provider certificate or a certificate to burn onto a smart card
- ✔ Download your CA's certificate
- ✔ Download your CA's certification path
- ✔ Download the your CA's most recent certificate revocation list

Figure 10-5:
The
Browser
interface for
certificate
requests.

Part IV

Just When You Think You're Safe

The 5th Wave   By Rich Tennant

COMPUTER SCIENCES LAB

"I'm sure there will be a good job market when I graduate. I created a virus that will go off that year."

In this part . . .

*J*ust when you think you're network is the most secure place with an IP address, Rick from Marketing taps you on the shoulder and says, "Have you seen the Web site we put up?" You scream, turn to one of the chapters in this part, and a few hours later, you calm down.

All seems well until Kevin from Sales approaches you during the company bowling outing and says, "We need our reps to be able to get pricing and inventory when they're in the field. Can we do this by Thursday?" Hmmm, you remember your last trip to Part IV of this book, recall that chapter on remote access, tell him no problem, and promptly throw a turkey.

After you return from a short vacation, Bob from Systems (your boss) says to you, "All I know is what I have learned from reading magazines. This IP Security thing seems neat. Make it happen." Off to Part IV again!

Chapter 11

Performing Your Security Due Diligence

*I*t's not enough to secure your network and then head home, content to spend your evening attending a dBase user group meeting. You need a strategy to monitor your network and watch for possible violations or, at least, attempted violations. The attention you pay to your network is your due diligence. You are obliged to monitor your network. You can use Windows 2000's auditing tools to watch for events occurring on files, folders, printers, domain controllers, and whatever other items on the network. Use auditing to watch also for specific actions taken by specific users on specific items. Windows 2000 also provides the Security Configuration and Analysis snap-in, used to audit the security configuration on every computer on the network.

Setting Up Security Auditing

Windows 2000 provides support for monitoring and recording events that occur throughout the network, including on domain controllers, member servers, and user computers. This monitoring and recording is known as auditing. If this seems like a *big brother is watching* scenario from George Orwell's *1984,* you're right, and big deal!

There are two parts to using Windows 2000 auditing:

  ✔ Pick the objects to audit.

  ✔ Monitor the audit logs on the Event View snap-in.

Figuring out what type of events to audit

The decision to audit activities on the network is an easy one. It kind of makes sense that you'd like to monitor the events on your networks, such as the comings and goings of your users. A much harder decision is *what* to audit. Basically, there are two parts to this decision:

- ✔ What type of events to monitor
- ✔ On what objects in the network to watch for those events

Now, the decision you make should not be "I want to watch for all kinds of things!" For every type of event you choose to audit, and for every object you audit those types of events on, the S L O W E R your network will run. So, consider carefully exactly what and how much you want to audit.

Here is a list of the type of events you can audit. Get to know the list. You select which of these events you want to audit when you turn on the auditing policies.

- ✔ **Account logon events:** This event is triggered when a domain controller is asked to check a user account. You do not have to do anything special to audit these types of events.

- ✔ **Account management:** This event is triggered when a user account's properties are accessed, as well as when an account is created or deleted.

- ✔ **Directory service access:** This event is triggered when some Active Directory object is accessed, such as a domain controller, domain, group policy object, site, and so on.

    In addition to selecting this event for auditing, you must also work on each Active Directory object you want to audit, as well.

- ✔ **Logon events:** A logon event is triggered when a user account logs on or logs off the domain. This event is also triggered when a connection to the network is established or broken.

- ✔ **Object access:** When a file, folder, or printer is accessed, this type of access event is triggered. This type of audit event is not automatic. You must edit the specific object, such as the file or folder, that you want to audit in order to specify the events you want to trap, as well as the users for whom you want access tracked.

- ✔ **Policy change:** This event is triggered when some aspect of the Local Polices node of security settings is changed, which includes audit policy, user rights assignments, and security options.

✔ **Privilege use:** This event does not refer to the privileged slice of processor time an application gets. Rather, it refers to the "use of a privilege." This event is fired when a user attempts to perform one of the user rights tasks. Here is a list of those rights:

- Access a computer from the network
- Act as part of the operating system
- Add workstations to domain
- Back up files and directories
- Bypass traverse checking
- Change the system time
- Create a pagefile
- Create a token object
- Create permanent shared objects
- Debug programs
- Generate security audits
- Increase quotas
- Increase scheduling priority
- Load and unload device drivers
- Lock pages in memory
- Log on as a batch job
- Log on as a service
- Log on locally
- Manage auditing and security log
- Modify firmware environment values
- Profile single process
- Profile system performance
- Remove computer from docking station
- Replace a process level token
- Restore files and directories
- Shut down the system
- Synchronize directory service data
- Take ownership of files or other objects

✔ **Process tracking:** This event is fired when a running application launches a process.

✔ **System events:** These are the events that affect the entire Windows 2000 system, like a shutdown. Windows 2000 also tracks changes made to the security log. Changes to the log generate a system event.

Flipping the master auditing switch

The first step to take in auditing events is to enable auditing for the particular event(s) you want to track. The auditing option is an element of group policy and security settings, so you'll have to think about where in the domain you want to audit. For example, do you want to enable logging for the entire domain, or perhaps just one organizational unit, or maybe just one computer? Follow these steps to turn on auditing:

1. **Open a group policy object for the object on which you want auditing to occur.**

2. **Open Computer Configuration\Windows Settings\Security Settings\Local Policies and then click Audit Policy.**

   The list of audit policies appears in the list in the details pane.

3. **Double-click the audit policy for the event you want to audit.**

   A dialog box like the one shown in Figure 11-1 appears.

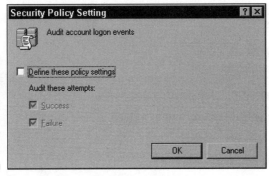

Figure 11-1:
The
Account
Logon
Policy
dialog box.

4. **Click the Define These Policy Settings option.**

   The Success option and the Failure option become active.

5. **Click one or both of the Failure and Success audit options.**

6. **Click OK.**

7. **Repeat Steps 3 through 5 for each type of event you want to audit.**

Tuning the security log

You may want to modify the behavior of the logs that store details about the events you're auditing. These modifications are done via group policy, so, as with the case of turning on auditing, you also have to consider which object in the domain you'd like to audit.

You can set these options for the security log:

- **Maximum security log size:** This policy determines the maximum size of the security log. The default is 512K.

- **Restrict guest access to security log:** This policy controls whether user accounts in the Guests group can access the security log. There's no reason why any users other than administrators, and certainly not guests, should get access to the security log. Why? If you hacked your way into a system, wouldn't the first thing you'd do be to cover your tracks by deleting the audit trail of your actions?

- **Retain security log:** This policy determines how long the security log is retained.

- **Retention method for security log:** This policy enables you to specify what occurs when the maximum log file size is reached. You can specify that events are deleted to create room for new events, that events older than the number of days you specify are deleted, or whether you are forced to delete the log on your own.

- **Shut down the computer when the security audit log is full:** This policy helps you ensure that there is no gap in any auditing you've configured should the security log fill up.

Follow these steps to configure the security log as you like it.

1. **Open a group policy object for the object where you want auditing to occur.**

2. **Open Computer Configuration\Windows Settings\Security Settings\Event Log and then click Settings for Event Logs.**

   The list of event log policies appears in the list in the details pane.

3. **Double-click the policy you want to edit.**

4. **First, click the Define this policy setting check box to enable the policy.**

   If the policy needs more information from you, such as the number of days, enter the value.

5. **Click OK when you have supplied all the information the policy needs.**

Picking out events and users to watch

Windows 2000 sometimes makes you work a little harder than you'd expect to or want to. Sometimes just picking the type of event to audit is not enough. Depending on the type of event you have decided to audit (this decided by the policies you configured), you may also have to specify the objects, the events affecting those objects, and the people causing the events.

If, as part of your audit policy, you chose either *directory service access* or *objects access*, you must directly configure auditing on each object you want to audit. So how do you know what kinds of objects to configure auditing for and which objects not to?

- ✔ If your audit policy enabled *directory service access*, then you need to configure auditing on Active Directory objects like domain controllers, Active Directory folders, organizational units, policies, and so on.

- ✔ If your audit policy enabled *object access*, then you need to configure auditing on files, folders, and printers.

Now that you know who and what to audit, here's the how part:

1. **Right-click the object to audit and choose Properties from the menu.**

   The Properties dialog box appears.

2. **Click the Security tab.**

   The Security tab appears.

3. **Click the Advanced button at the bottom of the dialog box.**

   The Access Control Settings dialog box appears.

4. **Click the Auditing tab.**

   The Auditing tab appears, as shown in Figure 11-2.

5. **Click the Add button.**

   The Select User, Computer, or Group dialog box appears.

   From this dialog box, you select which users will have their activities audited as they work with the object you selected.

6. **Select the user or group from the list and then click OK.**

   The Auditing Entry dialog box appears, as shown in Figure 11-3.

7. **Click the events you want to audit and select whether to capture failure events and/or success events.**

   If you do not select either Success or Failure, the event is not audited.

   Keep in mind that the list of events to audit will differ based on the object you're auditing.

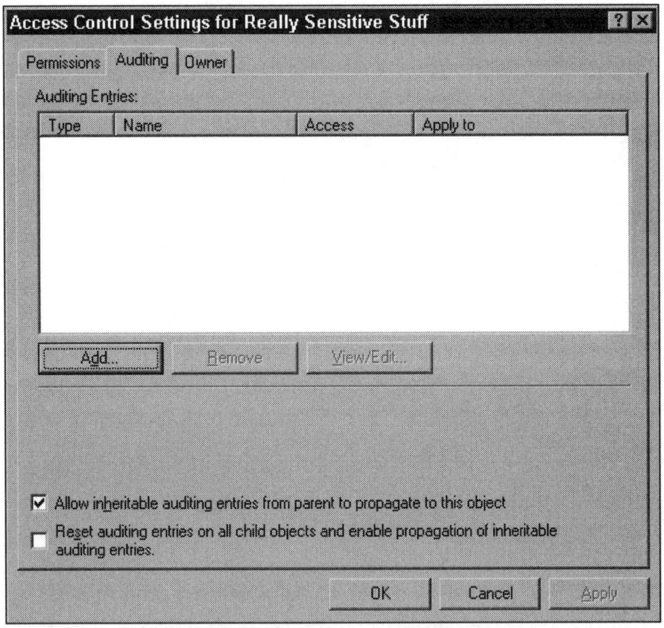

Figure 11-2:
The Auditing
Tab.

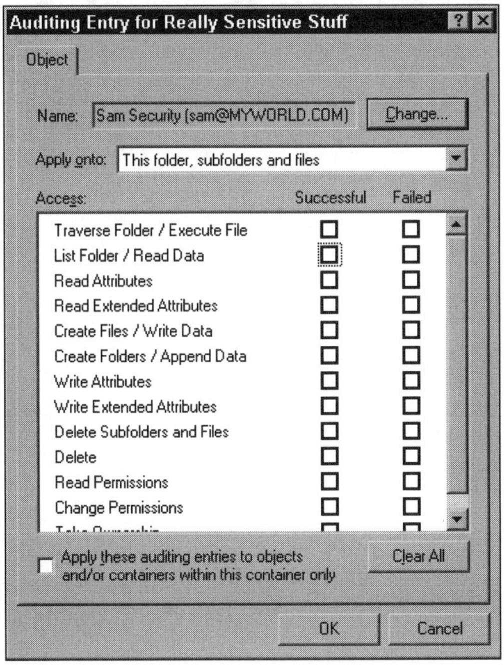

Figure 11-3:
The Auditing
Entry dialog
box for a
folder.

8. **Click OK**

   You return to the Access Control Settings dialog box.

9. **Repeat Steps 5 through 8 for each user or group of users you want to keep your eye on; when you have added all the users whose activities you want to audit, click OK.**

   You return to the Properties dialog box for the file or folder you're auditing.

10. **Click OK.**

Using the Event Viewer

The Event Viewer is probably the most important tool you'll use to audit events. To start the Event Viewer, click the Start menu and then choose Programs➪Administrative Tools➪Event Viewer. Figure 11-4 shows a picture of the Event Viewer.

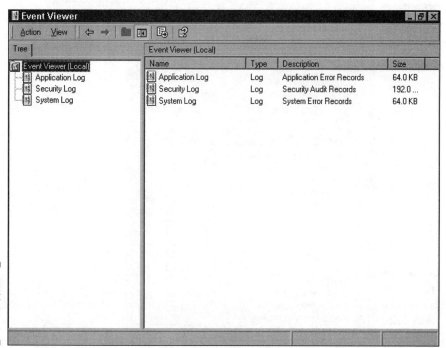

Figure 11-4:
The Event
Viewer
console.

Working with the security log

The Event Viewer gives you access to all the logs that Windows 2000 maintains. The log you should be interested in from a security perspective, of course, is the security log. The security log stores all the audited events, as well as events captured by the audit policy you define.

Figure 11-5 shows a picture of the security log from the Event Viewer.

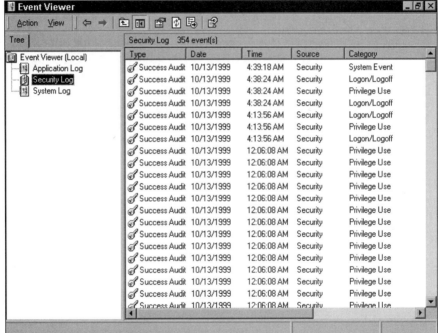

Figure 11-5:
The Event
Viewer
console
opened
to the
security log.

Here are some things you can to do to customize the presentation of events in the system log:

✔ To sort by any of the columns in the list of events, click the column header.

✔ To see all the details of an audited event, double-click the event. The Properties dialog box for the event appears.

✔ To view or increase the drive space allotted to the security log, right-click Security Log in the Event View tree.

✔ To see just certain types of events in the list, display the Security Log properties sheet. Click the Filter tab and then select any option other than the All in the Event source box. Next, pick the type of event to show from the Category drop-down list.

✔ To see only events occurring either on or before a specific date and time or on or after a specific date and time, start by displaying the Security Log properties sheet. Click the Filter tab. Next, choose Events On from the From drop-down list at the bottom of the dialog box and then select the date and time. After you click Apply or OK, only events captured on or after the time/date you specified will appear in the list. To specify the end date in the range, select Events On from the To drop-down list and then select the date and time.

✔ To see just Failure events or just Success events, or both, display the Security Log properties sheet and then click the options you want.

Interpreting system log results

You can probably figure out what the data means in the system log. Just in case you can't, though, take a look at Table 11-1.

Table 11-1	System Log Results
Audit Data	*Description*
Type	Shows the type of event captured. Typically, this field will show either Failure or Success.
Date	This field shows the date of the audited event. This date is taken from the system date. If you change group policy so that users cannot change the system date, even on their computer, you can reduce the risk of intruders covering their tracks by adjusting the date.
Time	This field shows the time of the audited event. Like the date field, this field is sensitive to the system time on the computer where the auditing occurs. Consider changing the group policy for client computers so that users cannot change the system time.
Source	This field reports which Windows 2000 subsystem generated the audited event. If you're like me, you're a lot more interested in the audit event itself and less about which of the eight bazillion lines of programming code generated the audit event.
Category	Indicates the category of the event, which is the same as the type of audit event you have set in the audit policy.

Audit Data	Description
Event	The unique numeric ID of the event.
User	Shows the name of the user associated with the event. In the event of a system event, like a shutdown, or of a failed logon attempt, the user will be SYSTEM.
Computer	Shows the name of the computer on which the event was captured.

You can see even more detail about the event by double-clicking it to display the Event Properties dialog box. The dialog box shows detail specific to the trapped event. As an example, in the case of a Logon/Logoff event, you can see the user name and the type of authentication used. Figure 11-6 shows an example of a failed logon event.

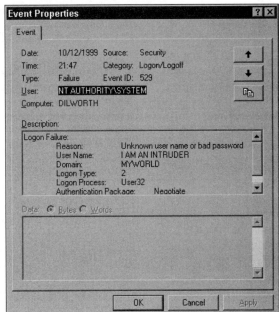

Figure 11-6:
The Event
Properties
dialog box.

Discovering the best practices for auditing

So now are you confused? Are you not quite sure what to do now that you know so much about auditing? Do you know where to start? Table 11-2 can help you grow from a novice auditor to an event-logging impresario.

Table 11-2	Best Auditing Practices
If you want to watch for . . .	*Then audit this . . .*
Someone trying to glean information about your network or your users by accessing the Registry	Use of either of the two Registry editors by an account other than the internal Windows account.
Virus attack	Successful or failed write events to just about any of your .EXE or .DLL files. There is no reason why any application should be writing to these files. Any write activity could be a virus trying to attach itself to the file. Be careful not to audit a read event for your program files. These files are typically opened for read access when they are used, so your log could fill up very quickly if you audit read events, too.
Access to your decoy accounts	Create a fake Administrator account after renaming the original.
Compromised user account information	Logon events; be on the lookout for successful logon events at night, on weekends, during holidays.
Attempts to secure objects	Object access; be sure to enable auditing on the files, folders, and printers you want to keep an eye on.
Access to the group policy (group policy controls security)	Any Failure or Success events for any group policy objects in the domain. Note that you must enable the Directory Service Access policy to trap accesses attempted or made to group policy. (See Chapter 7 for details on group policy.)

Windows 2000 ships with a great tool to check the configuration of security on each desktop in your network against a baseline that describes how the workstation *should* be set. This tool, the Security Configuration and Analysis tool (SCA for short), analyzes the configuration of security settings on the machine where you run the tool, and compares settings against a security template you load. If you need information about security settings and security templates, take a peek at Chapter 6.

Creating an SCA console

Start work with the SCA by creating a console.

1. **Click the Start menu, choose Run, enter MMC, and then press Enter.**

2. **Choose Console⇨Add/Remove Snap-in from the menu.**

   The Add/Remove Snap-in dialog box appears.

3. **Click the Add button.**

   The Add Standalone Snap-in dialog box appears.

4. **Scroll down the list and find Security Templates in the list; click it and then click Add.**

   If you drag the Add Standalone snap-in dialog box out of the way, you can see that Security Templates is added to the list of snap-ins in the Add/Remove Snap-in dialog box.

5. **Click Security Configuration and Analysis and then click Add.**

6. **Click Close in the Add Standalone Snap-in dialog box.**

7. **Click OK in the Add/Remove Snap-in dialog box.**

8. **Choose Console⇨Save As from the menu.**

   The Save As dialog box appears.

9. **Enter a name for the console in the File name edit box and then click the Save button.**

10. **Choose Console⇨Exit from the menu to close your new console.**

Analyzing security at a computer

The SCA tool does one thing, and it does it well. The SCA tool compares security settings at a local PC against the settings in a security template. This means that if you do not use a security template to apply consistent security settings around the network, then you'll only be able to compare a computer's security configuration against one of the stock security templates that Microsoft sent.

As much as you'll use group policy (hopefully) to dictate security settings, sometimes a person's settings change, perhaps exposing a security risk. If you do not legislate security settings by group policy, you'll be forced to work at each workstation on your network to configure security.

Here's how to analyze security:

1. **Open a console that gives you access to the SCA tool.**

   Be sure to open the snap-in on the computer you want to analyze.

2. **Right-click the Security and Configuration Analysis tool and then choose Open Database from the menu.**

3. **If you have analyzed security on this computer previously, select the security database you created; then skip to Step 7.**

   If you can't find the database or want to compare to a different template, continue with Step 4.

4. **Enter a name for the security database that will be created on the computer you're working on and then click Open.**

   Consider using the name of the computer with the words "Security Database."

   The Import Template dialog box appears.

5. **Select the template to which you want to compare the security configuration of the computer you're working on.**

   This is the critical step. The SCA will compare every element of security in the template against the configuration of the computer. Even if you have not spent any time with the template, such as customizing one for your corporate use, it's still worth choosing one. At the minimum, you have the opportunity to compare the computer configuration to a configuration dreamed up by Microsoft.

6. **Click Open.**

   Your security database is created.

7. **Right-click Security Configuration and Analysis and choose Analyze Computer now.**

   The Perform Analysis dialog box appears.

8. **Specify a name and location for the log file and then click OK.**

   Feel free to accept the default.

   The SCA tool now analyzes the target computer. This could take a minute or two.

9. **When the analysis is complete, the details pane is updated with results.**

10. **Click the security setting you want to check.**

    For example, to see how close the account policies on the computer are to the corporate standards (or at least what's included in the template), click either Password Policy or Account Lockout under Account Policies. See Figure 11-7.

Notice the icon beside the name of the policy. Here's what they mean:

✔ **Red X:** Computer configuration is different than template.

✔ **Green check:** Settings match.

✔ **No icon:** Security setting used on the computer is not included in the template.

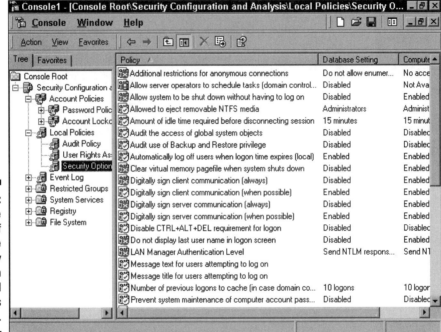

Figure 11-7:
Seeing the
results of
applying the
Security
Configuration
and
Analysis
tool.

Chapter 12

Serving the Internet Securely

● ○

In This Chapter

▶ Getting the skinny on Windows 2000 Internet Information Services

▶ Knowing who's knocking on your web or FTP server's front door

▶ Checking visitors' IP address IDs at the door

▶ Making sure that the NTFS is up to the permissions task

▶ Proving your web server's worth with certificates

▶ Caulking the leaky connection pipe with SSL

● ○

*W*indows 2000 Server isn't just about local and wide area networks. The glamour in Windows 2000 is in the great Internet services you can provide. Windows 2000 comes with a great Internet server that allows you to run FTP, Web, newsgroup, and mail servers from Windows 2000 and hardly break a sweat. That's the good news. The bad news is that the only thing between the Internet and your Windows 2000 server (and your network) is your Internet server. Yikes! It's safe to say that a locked-down, tightly secured, super-protected, caged-up, caged-in Internet server is a good idea.

Still not convinced? Keep in mind that when someone browses to some page on a Web site, they are reading a real HTML page stored in a real folder on a real hard drive on a real computer. If that Web site is running on your server, then that browser is accessing a file on *your computer*. Considering this, what's to stop someone from noodling around in some other folder on your server or even the network where the Web server is running? This situation would be called a security breach. The more common term for this situation is *disaster*.

This chapter is the source you need to be sure that your content and your network are safe from the Internet.

Internet Information Services in Windows 2000

Windows 2000 would like to be your one-stop shop for everything network and Internet related. Given that, Windows 2000 Server includes an Internet server. This Internet server is called Internet Information Services (IIS), based on the name of the standalone product from previous versions of Windows NT. This component provides you with the software tools to run the following services from Windows 2000:

- ✔ FTP server
- ✔ Web server
- ✔ Newsgroup server
- ✔ SMTP mail server

The version of IIS that ships with Windows 2000 is 5, and that's the version in this chapter.

You probably will run IIS on a machine other than the one where the server servicing your LAN or WAN is running. If this isn't your plan, you had better make it so. It makes sense to completely isolate your network from your Internet server. Only connect your Internet server to your network when you need to move content to the server from your network. This way, you can reduce almost any chance of someone on the Internet snooping into your network.

The Sequence of Security

The security features in IIS are on the sophisticated side. This means that visitors from the Internet won't be allowed access to your FTP or Web site just by using a decoder ring from a box of breakfast cereal.

There are about five steps IIS takes before it allows a visitor to get to the content it wants. Depending on how you configure the server, IIS might skip a few steps, kind of the way you run up stairs two-at-a-time to answer a ringing phone or Internet call.

1. **Ask for User ID and Password:** The first thing the web or FTP server is interested in is a user ID and password. Even if your site doesn't require an ID and password (in which case the user won't be asked for one), the server uses a special user ID reserved for this anonymous access.

2. **IP Address Check:** You might restrict access to your site based on the IP address of the host doing the visiting. If the host doesn't pass the IP address test, an "Access Forbidden" message appears and the host is denied access.

3. **Check User Account:** The next step is to verify that the user ID supplied by the browser is valid. The Internet server will check the user ID supplied by the user against the list of valid users on the Windows 2000 server where the IIS is running.

4. **Internet Server Permissions:** Each server, FTP or web, uses a default set of rules that determine what all users can and can't do, such as read content. Those rules are applied at this step.

5. **NTFS Permissions:** When the server has allowed a visitor to reach the content they want, the server will check the permission placed on the content. For example, if the visitor is trying to view a Web page, and the permissions on the file allow read access just by the Administrators group, the visitor will see an "Access Forbidden" message if he does not belong to the Administrators group.

Knock Knock Knocking on Your Internet Server's Door

If your Web or FTP site is useful and filled with great content, then visitors will be knocking on your site's door all the time. There's a chance, though, that you'll want to know exactly who's knocking at your FTP or Web door before you let them in. You might wonder why you would be concerned about the identity of visitors to your site. Here are some scenarios:

- ✔ Your Web site is an intranet, and certain content is appropriate only for certain persons from certain departments.

- ✔ Your FTP site provides downloadable files for your customers only, not the general public.

- ✔ Some of the content your Web site offers is fee-based, so only real, paying customers get access to the goods.

This process of identifying visitors is known as *authentication*. Authentication identifies the parties accessing your site, which gives you the opportunity to figure out what to let the visitors see and what to do once they're in.

You can also use authentication on a folder-by-folder or file-by-file basis. You might let everyone into your site without care for identity, but insist that a visitor provide a user ID and password if they try to access a private area.

Don't secure the safety net!

As you read through this section, you might experiment with the authentication settings and the default Web site that gets created when IIS is installed. Like all experimentation, good luck and good learning, but be careful. Any changes you make to the authentication settings will be applied to the site, and that site stores all the IIS 5.0 documentation that Microsoft ships with the product. Be careful that you do not secure yourself out of the opportunity to read the help file!

Checking authentication methods

The Internet server in Windows 2000 provides four methods for authentication. Each method handles the authentication chores a little differently than the others and has a different level of security (in fact, one of them isn't secure at all). So, you have to decide which method to use based on your requirements and network design. Table 12-1 lists the methods and the relative level of security each provides.

Table 12-1	IIS Authentication Methods
Method	*Security Level*
Anonymous	Low, actually, None
Basic	Low
Digest	Medium
Integrated	Really High

Certain authentication methods work only on a web server. Table 12-2 shows you which authentication methods are available for which type of server.

Table 12-2	Authentication Methods	
Method	*FTP*	*Web*
Anonymous	Yes	Yes
Basic	Yes	Yes

Method	FTP	Web
Digest	No	Yes
Integrated	No	Yes

You can find a description of each of the four authentication methods in the following four sections.

The no-authentication authentication method

If you don't click a button or make any choices, IIS still configures your Web or FTP site with an authentication method. Unfortunately, you get what you pay for.

The default method for authentication is called *Anonymous access*. If it sounds strange to see the word *anonymous* describe a type of authentication, then your sight is good. Anonymous access means that the visitor to your FTP or Web site does not need to identify himself. A majority of the Web and FTP sites you visit use Anonymous access (whether they use IIS or some other web server). How do you know if a Web site you visit uses anonymous access? Well, if you do not get prompted for a user ID and password when you access the site's home page, then anonymous access is used. As an example, stop by Microsoft's spot on the Web at `www.microsoft.com`. Did you get prompted for a password?

Here's what you need to know about anonymous access:

✔ Anonymous access really isn't anonymous. Windows 2000 reserves a single account for the user visiting your site with anonymous access. Whenever a person browsing your Web site wants to do something, Windows 2000 uses the reserved account to figure out whether the person has the rights to do it. This account is IUSR_*computername*. So, if the name of your computer is WACKY, then the account IUSR_Wacky is used to impersonate visitors to your site.

✔ Windows 2000 automatically places the anonymous account in the built-in Guest group. So, whatever rights are granted to the Guest group also are granted to Windows 2000 when it tries to do things at the request of an anonymous visitor.

✔ You are free to create an account for the anonymous user, as well as create a user group that controls the access for the anonymous user. Be sure to assign the appropriate permissions to the new user, or be sure that the group you assign the user to also is properly locked down. Also, you must give the account Log on Locally rights.

✔ If you manage multiple Web sites in Windows 2000, you can create a different anonymous user account for each. Oh, the flexibility!

✔ You do not have to worry about whether the browser on the other end of the connection supports anonymous access — they all do!

✔ When you create a new FTP site, it is configured automatically for Anonymous authentication.

(Really) basic authentication

If you need a minimal amount of authentication for a user browsing your Web or FTP site, you can use Basic Authentication. Basic authentication is the no-frills, cheapo method for authenticating visitors. Basic authentication also falls into the you-get-what-you-pay-for category.

In case you're wondering, yes, Basic Authentication forces the person browsing to your site to supply a user ID and a password. However — and here's the catch — the user ID and password are sent sailing across the connection unencrypted to the server. That's right, when you use Basic Authentication, the user ID and password are fair game for anyone with the capability and willingness to peek at your network traffic.

So, given the insecure nature of this security feature, why would you use it? Well, if the server uses SSL to secure the connection between the browser and the Internet server, then you do not have much to worry about. You reap the benefits of basic authentication in that you can give certain access to certain visitors based on their ID, and you can also track their activities via logging, neither of which are possible with Anonymous access. Not a bad deal!

The following are the basics on basic authentication:

✔ Because Windows 2000 will impersonate each of the user accounts that log on using Basic Authentication, each account must have the Log on Locally right.

✔ Most browsers available support Basic Authentication.

✔ IIS will authenticate the user ID and password against an account on the Windows 2000 domain where the IIS server is running. If the server is running on a different domain, you must supply that domain's name. This means that you must create a Windows 2000 account for each user ID and password combo you expect a user to enter when they access your site.

✔ When you create a new FTP site, it is configured automatically to accept Basic authentication if a visitor tries to access a protected folder. You can turn this option off so that FTP *only* accepts anonymous authentication. It makes sense to turn this option on to reduce the chance of someone sneaking onto your site with rights other than anonymous, which potentially could give them powerful rights to your server or network.

Digest authentication

Microsoft added the Digest Authentication to IIS in Windows 2000. This authentication is reminiscent of the *Goldilocks and the Three Bears* children's story.

Basic authentication is too soft, and Integrated Windows Authentication is too hard, but Digest Authentication is just right!

Digest Authentication is much like Basic Authentication in that it prompts the browsing user for a user ID and a password (see Figure 12-1). The difference with Digest Authentication, though, is that the user ID and password are protected as they cross the wire to the server for authentication by a hash. Does this mean that all the characters in the password are replaced with the # symbol? Nope. The server sends data to the browser that will be used to create the hash. The browser uses the data sent from the server plus the user ID and password to create a hash, which is sent back to the server.

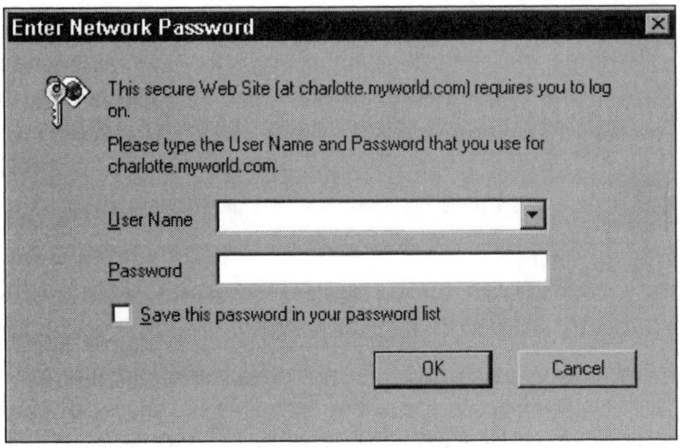

Figure 12-1:
Using Digest
Authentica-
tion means
your
Internet
visitors are
greeted with
a warm wel-
come when
they knock
on the door.

> **Enter Network Password**
>
> This secure Web Site (at charlotte.myworld.com) requires you to log on.
>
> Please type the User Name and Password that you use for charlotte.myworld.com.
>
> User Name [   ]
>
> Password [   ]
>
> ☐ Save this password in your password list
>
> [OK]   [Cancel]

✔ The Digest Authentication scheme is supported by HTTP 1.1. A user browsing with a browser that does not support HTTP 1.1 cannot be authenticated against a server using Digest Authentication, which leads to the next point . . .

✔ Digest Authentication is supported only by domains with a Windows 2000 domain controller.

Integrated windows authentication

Integrated Windows Authentication (IWA) is actually our old friend from the previous version of IIS, Windows NT Challenge/Response Authentication. This scheme relies on the browser to provide the Internet server with the credential data the server needs to allow the visitor access. The advantage of this method is that it does not commit the cardinal sin of passing a user's ID or password over the network, even encrypted.

This authentication is a bit like the admission process to a private club: You get a ride to the club in a taxi. You knock on the door and say, "Let me in!" The bouncer at the door says, "I don't know you!" He turns to the taxi driver and says, "You know this guy?" The cab driver says, "Yeah, he's okay. Let him in." The taxi driver winks at the bouncer, and then you're admitted to the club.

Like the taxi driver, the browser never tells the server a password. Instead, encrypted data is sent to the server, like the cab driver's wink signal to the bouncer.

There are some restrictions on the use of IWA:

- ✔ IWA does not work if a firewall or proxy server sits between the server and the browser.
- ✔ The only browser that supports IWA is Microsoft Internet Explorer, Version 2.0 and later.

Assigning authentication

Now that you know the ground rules, here's how to configure authentication on your web server or FTP server:

1. **Open the Internet Services Manager tool and then click + next to the Windows 2000 server to see all the web and FTP servers.**

    Internet Services Manager appears on the Administrative tools menu, which you can find on the Programs menu.

2. **If you want to assign authentication to the entire site, right-click the site node for the server you want to secure; if you want to work on a file or folder on the site, open the site and then right-click the file or folder.**

3. **Choose Properties from the menu.**

    The Properties dialog box for the server you selected appears.

4. **If you're working on an FTP server, click the Security Accounts tab. If you're working on a web server, click the Directory/File Security tab.**

5. **If you're working on an FTP server, skip to Step 6 — I'll be with you in a minute; if you're working on a web server, click the Edit button.**

    You're now at the point where you can define any authentication options you like.

6. **Click the options you need.**

   Here are your options:

   - To deny Anonymous connections for an FTP server, clear the Allow Anonymous Connections check box.

   - To use *only* Anonymous connections for an FTP server, check the Allow Only Anonymous Connections check box.

   - To change the account used for anonymous connections, click the Browse button for FTP servers. Click the Edit button in the Anonymous Access box for a web server.

   - If you click Basic Authentication, you will see an annoying message confirming that you really want to send user IDs and passwords unencrypted, as shown in Figure 12-2. If you're sure, click Yes.

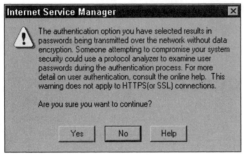

Figure 12-2:
Windows
2000 asks
you to
confirm that
you want to
allow users
to pass their
user ID and
password
in an
unencrypted
form to the
server.

   - If you choose Basic Authentication and visitors will be authenticated on a domain different from the one the web server is running on, click the Domain button. Enter the domain where the user can be authenticated and then click OK.

7. **Click OK (twice for Web) to return to the Internet Services Manager.**

Mixing and matching authentication

You might wonder about the effect of mixing authentication methods, as well as some of the particulars about authentication.

✔ If there is a conflict between the access allowed for the anonymous account and the access setup for a user account, the more restrictive access is applied.

✔ If you do specify Anonymous Access, then the Login dialog box will appear for any user who tries to access your site.

✔ If the only access you will allow to your site will be by anonymous authentication, then you do not need to create new user accounts. It's unlikely, though, that your site won't have at least one area that needs secured protection. In that case, you'll need to apply authentication other than anonymous to the folder or file that should be secured.

✔ If you force visitors to identify themselves when they access certain areas of your site, then you'll have to create the user accounts that match the information you expect them to enter when the logon dialog box appears at their browser.

✔ The authentication method you apply to a site is applied to all the folders in the site. You can override that site setting by assigning a different authentication method to a particular folder. You can override that folder setting by assigning a different authentication method to a subfolder, and so on to a file.

IP-Bias Based Access

You can control access to your FTP or Web site based on the IP address of the host hitting your site. If the terms IP address, host, or DHCP seem foreign to you, you may want to get your hands on *TCP/IP For Dummies,* 3rd Edition, by Candace Leiden and Marshall Wilensky (IDG Books Worldwide, Inc.). In order to use this feature, you need to know the IP addresses of the hosts you want to deny or allow access. Getting the addresses isn't impossible, but the process could chew up lots of time.

Windows 2000 lets you use one of two methods for filtering access to your site based on an IP address:

✔ **Method 1:** Allow everyone in, but restrict access to those hosts you identify.

✔ **Method 2:** Deny everyone access except for those hosts you identify.

What method you choose depends on the use of the site. If the site will be used to support a small population of folks that you know, such as persons for whom you make available some downloadable files via FTP, you might just lock down the entire site using Method 2. If you want to make it difficult for your competitors to see your Web site, you might just use Method 1.

Keep in mind that unless you use an authentication method other than anonymous, it is almost impossible to confidently block access to your site on the open Internet based on an IP address. Why? It's a snap for anyone to get on the Internet with a different IP address than the one they used previously.

You can also filter access to your site based on the domain name of the host. This means if you know the DNS name associated with the firewall at your closest competitor, you can block admission to your site for any host originating from your competitor's network. Be careful; this option can slow performance of your site down to a crawl as it requires your server to search the Internet every time a host hits your site to see whether the IP address resolves to one of the DNS sites you specified.

Here's more of what you need to know about IP-based access:

- ✔ If you plan to allow access to just some of the persons from one organization, you may be out of luck. If the organization uses a firewall, the only IP address the Internet server will be able to identify from that organization might be the IP address of the firewall. This means you won't be able to filter in just the visitors you want.

- ✔ You can specify grant or deny access for a group of computers as long as they belong to the same subnet. To do so, you must know the IP address of the router for the segment where the computers live, as well as the subnet mask (which indicates what portion of the IP address tells TCP/IP the actual real host's address).

- ✔ You'll have trouble filtering hosts whose IP address is dynamically generated by DHCP and who do not live behind a router or firewall. In these cases, the IP address of the host probably changes often, possibly every time the host logs on to the Internet. These types of hosts are probably individuals (as opposed to company employees) on the Internet who subscribe to services from an Internet Service Provider (ISP). The ISP dynamically configures the host with an IP address generated by DHCP (dynamic host configuration protocol).

- ✔ Some ISPs use a static domain name for the hosts on their network. This domain name is a combination of the customer's account number and the ISP's domain name. This makes it easy to reliably refer to a host whose IP address changes because of DHCP. For example, if the name of your ISP is SECURITYFORDUMMIES, and your name is Rachel, and your account number is 0525, then your DNS name might be RACHEL0525 .SECURITYFORDUMMIES.COM.

Follow these steps to establish IP filtering for access to your FTP or Web site.

1. **Open the Internet Services Manager and then click + next to the Windows 2000 server to see all the web and FTP servers.**

   The Internet Services Manager appears on the Administrative Tools menu, which you can find on the Programs menu.

2. **Right-click the site node for the server you want to secure and then choose Properties from the menu.**

   The Properties dialog box for the server you selected appears.

3. **Select the Directory Security tab.**

4. **If you are securing a Web server, click the Edit button in the frame labeled IP Address And Domain Name Restrictions. If you're working on an FTP server, take a two-second break as your web server administrators catch up.**

   Depending on the type of server you are working on, either a dialog box labeled IP Address and Domain Name Restrictions (Web — Figure 12-3) or one labeled *your site name* Properties" (FTP — Figure 12-4) should be on the screen.

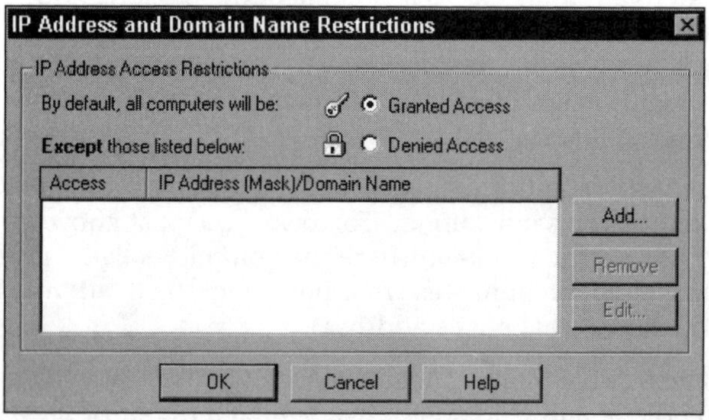

Figure 12-3:
IP address
filtering gets
its own real
estate if
you're
running a
web server.

5. **Click either the Granted Access or Denied Access option, which specifies the default access for all hosts except for those you specify in the next few steps.**

   Now you need to define the exceptions.

6. **Click the Add button.**

   Depending on the default behavior you specified in Step 5, a dialog box labeled either Deny Access On or Grant Access On appears (Figure 12-5 and Figure 12-6).

7. **To specify the IP address of one computer, enter the IP address in the IP Address field; click OK.**

8. **To specify the IP address for a group of computers, click the Group Of Computers option and then enter the IP address of the router for the segment and also the subnet mask; click OK.**

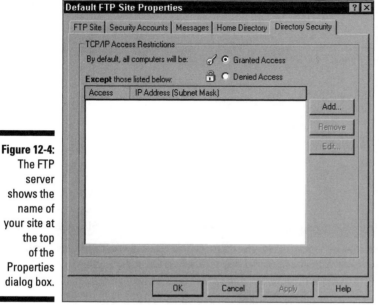

Figure 12-4:
The FTP server shows the name of your site at the top of the Properties dialog box.

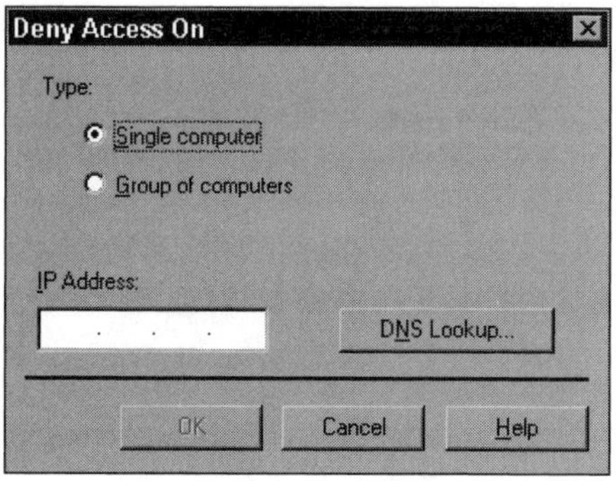

Figure 12-5:
You can grant access to everyone on the Internet except for those IP addresses from the bad side of town.

9. **To deny or grant access based on the DNS name of the host, click the Domain Name option and then enter the full domain name of the host; click OK.**

10. **To change the address or name of an entry already in the list, click the entry and then click Edit.**

Figure 12-6:
You can
create an
exclusive
club of
Internet
visitors by
allowing in
just the IP
addresses
you name.

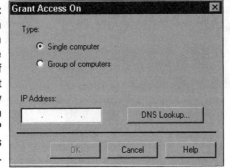

11. **Edit the entry that appears in a dialog box and then click OK.**

12. **To remove an entry from the list of IP addresses or domains explicitly denied or granted access to the site, click the entry and then click Remove.**

    The entry you selected disappears from the list.

13. **When you have completed entering, editing or removing IP addresses or names from the list, click OK.**

    The Directory Security tab of the Properties dialog box for the site you're securing appears.

14. **To have the changes take effect now, click Apply.**

FTP and Web Server Permissions

You can save yourself lots of work by defining server permissions that apply to the entire site, regardless of user or content. For example, you can specify what visitors can and can't do with each folder and file on your Web or FTP site. For example, if you are truly embarrassed by your HTML coding skills, you can specify that browsers visiting your Web site not have the right to view the source HTML code for a particular page. You would probably give visitors the right to view the pages on your site using a browser; in this example, you're just restricting the inspection of the code. The rights that are specific to a web server are known as *Web server permissions*.

FTP and web server permissions are not the same permissions you apply to files and folders on your Windows 2000 server. FTP and web server permissions only apply when someone tries to access the content on your site using FTP or HTTP. Also, FTP and web server permissions apply to all visitors, regardless of their Windows 2000 account.

Don't think that server permissions give you a vacation. You should still secure all content using NTFS permissions, and you can read how to do that in Chapter 4. FTP and web server permissions help you secure the typical things people do on your site, like look at a file.

Table 12-3 explains the permissions you can set on FTP and web servers.

Table 12-3	Web Server Permissions	
Permission	*Secures*	*Type of Server*
Read	Use this option to define whether visitors can read content on your site. If this option is not checked, visitors cannot view pages on the Web site, including the home page, or see the contents of the FTP site	FTP and Web
Write	This option specifies whether visitors can change a file, change the contents of a directory, or change an attribute of an item on the site	FTP and Web
Script Source	This option specifies whether a user can look at the HTML code that displays a page in a web browser.	Web only
Directory browsing	Use this option to specify whether browsers can see and navigate through the directory structure that makes up your Web site if they access a directory that does not have a default page	Web only
Execute Permissions	Use this option to determine what kind of programs can be run from your site.	Web only

Follow these steps to set FTP or web server permissions.

1. **Open the Internet Services Manager tool and then click + next to the Windows 2000 server to see all the web and FTP servers.**

   The Internet Services Manager appears on the Administrative tools menu, which you can find on the Programs menu.

2. **Right-click the FTP or web server you want to secure and then choose Properties from the menu.**

   The site tab appears for the server you selected.

3. **Click the Home Directory tab.**

   The Home Directory tab appears for the site you selected. If your site is an FTP site, you'll see only a few options in the FTP Site directory group in the middle of the dialog box. The only options you see should match the list of FTP permissions shown in Table 12-3.

4. **Specify the appropriate options by checking or clearing the Script source access, Read, Write, and Directory browsing options.**

   You might notice the Log Visits and Index This Resource check boxes. The Index option really isn't security specific, and logging is covered later in this chapter, so ignore both for now.

5. **If you are securing a Web site, select the appropriate option from the Execute Permissions drop-down list.**

   The following list will help you figure out which option to pick:

   • **None:** Visitors cannot run any script or program on your site.

   • **Scripts Only:** Visitors can run scripted programs, such as Active Server Pages.

   • **Scripts and Executables:** Visitors can run scripted programs, such as Active Server Pages, as well as programs.

6. **To have the changes take effect now, click Apply.**

Using NTFS Permissions to Protect Your Server and Network

Though you probably chose and configured an authentication method to identify visitors to your site, you still must secure every last piece of data on the server. Why? Keep in mind that when a visitor hits your Web or FTP site, most times they are viewing files in folders that physically reside on the computer where the web server is running. Yikes! Unless you do a great job of securing the server, you can easily have ill-intentioned visitors snooping all over your server. In addition, if your Web server is part of your Windows 2000 domain, access gained from the Web could possibly give a user access to your entire network.

This is where NTFS permissions get involved. You use NTFS permissions to secure the folders, files, and other resources on your IIS server and your network. This advice is no different than the advice given to the Windows 2000 network administrator to secure his LAN or WAN or from the advice given to the Windows 2000 Professional user to secure his computer from other persons who use it.

If you are not using the NTFS file system, then you should convert to it immediately. If you are new to NTFS, then be sure to see Chapter 4.

Here are more details on NTFS Permissions:

✔ You must use Windows 2000 Explorer or My Computer to assign NTFS permissions. Typically, you assign permissions by right-clicking the folder you want to secure, choosing Properties from the menu, and then clicking the Security tab (see Figure 12-7). This Security tab is not available from the Properties dialog box that appears when you select a folder in your site via IIS.

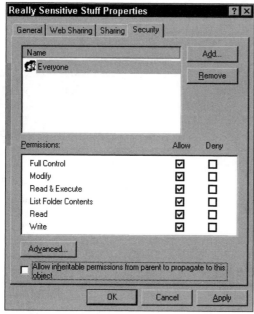

Figure 12-7:
Use NTFS permissions to keep browsers and FTPers from having free reign over the disks, data, and directories on your server.

✔ Use NTFS permissions to create the private areas of your Web or FTP site.

✔ Pay attention to the anonymous user account. Any access you grant to that account and any access that you grant to the group that has the anonymous user account as a member is applied to *any* visitor to your site. The exception to this rule is if you also are using one of the other authentication methods.

✔ Watch out for new folders! The Everyone group is assigned Full Control when a new folder is created with NTFS. Be sure to assign the correct permission when you create a new folder on the server where IIS is running.

Recording the Action on Your Site

The Web and FTP server software that ships with Windows 2000 have features that enable the servers to log all activity that occurs on the servers. Here are some of the details that the server can log:

- ✔ The IP address of the host that connected to your server
- ✔ The type of request the host makes to the server
- ✔ Unsuccessful logon attempts, including the time, date, and source IP address

The following is an excerpt from a log. The presentation isn't Web-site-pretty, but security isn't pretty.

```
#Software: Microsoft Internet Information Services 5.0
#Version: 1.0
#Date: 1999-09-12 18:18:15
#Fields: date time c-ip cs-username s-sitename s-
        computername s-ip s-port cs-method cs-uri-stem
        cs-uri-query sc-status sc-win32-status
1999-09-12 18:18:15 127.0.0.1 () W3SVC1 W2KDC1 127.0.0.1
        80 GET / - 401 5
1999-09-12 18:18:18 127.0.0.1 SEC4DUMMIES\theauthor
        W3SVC1 W2KDC1 127.0.0.1 80 GET /iisstart.asp -
        302 0
1999-09-12 18:18:21 127.0.0.1 SEC4DUMMIES\theauthor
        W3SVC1 W2KDC1 127.0.0.1 80 GET /localstart.asp -
        200 0
1999-09-12 18:18:21 127.0.0.1 SEC4DUMMIES\theauthor
        W3SVC1 W2KDC1 127.0.0.1 80 GET /win2000.gif -
        304 0
1999-09-12 18:18:21 127.0.0.1 () W3SVC1 W2KDC1 127.0.0.1
        80 GET /warning.gif - 401 5
1999-09-12 18:18:21 127.0.0.1 () W3SVC1 W2KDC1 127.0.0.1
        80 GET /mmc.gif - 401 5
1999-09-12 18:18:21 127.0.0.1 SEC4DUMMIES\theauthor
        W3SVC1 W2KDC1 127.0.0.1 80 GET /Web.gif - 304 0
1999-09-12 18:18:21 127.0.0.1 () W3SVC1 W2KDC1 127.0.0.1
        80 GET /help.gif - 401 5
```

You can also use the NTFS auditing feature, which lets you track the activity of Windows 2000 user accounts as they access folders, printers, files, the registry, and the like. Follow the advice in Chapter 11 for auditing user activity.

Here's more info on logging:

✔ Are you interested in figuring out the popularity of your site? Logging is an easy way to keep site statistics. Rather than buying or building something that tracks site activity, just use the site activity logging features that come with IIS.

✔ A new log can be started every day, every hour, every week, every month — it's up to you.

✔ You can use the same log file forever and ever. The log stands to become huge if you use this option, especially depending on the number and type of activities you choose to log.

✔ You can specify that a new log file be created when the current log reaches a certain size. You might want to consider maximum log file size that matches the capacity of some media you'd like to store the log on, like a 100-MB removable drive.

✔ Your server log can be stored in one of four formats:

• **Microsoft IIS Log File Format:** This is Microsoft's (noncustomizable) format. This log is comma-delimited, so it's a snap to load it into a spreadsheet program or database app for archiving or reporting.

• **ODBC Logging:** This format stores logged activity in an ODBC (open database connectivity) data source.

If you choose this option, you need to create an ODBC data source, as well as create a database that can store the logged data. An ODBC data source can be almost any database, such as a relational database, a spreadsheet, or even a text file, that is compatible with the ODBC standard. Many applications can read from an ODBC database, so you can use different applications to create reports with this option.

• **NCSA:** This is the National Computer Security Association (now ICSA) format, also not customizable.

• **W3C Extended Log File Format:** This is the format defined by the World Wide Web Consortium (W3C — get it now?). This format lets you choose the data you want to appear in the log. This is probably the best option because it provides the most information while being the easiest to customize.

Chapter 4 shows you how to set up auditing on NTFS drives. Follow these steps to setup logging on your FTP or web server.

1. **Open the Internet Services Manager tool and then click + next to the Windows 2000 server to see all the web and FTP servers.**

   The Internet Services Manager appears on the Administrative Tools menu, which you can find on the Programs menu.

2. **Right-click the site node for the server you want to log and then choose Properties from the menu.**

   The Properties dialog box for the server you selected appears.

3. **If you're working with a web server, click the Directory Security tab. If you're securing an FTP server, the FTP site tab should already be selected by default.**

   Depending on what kind of server you're working on, you should see a frame at the bottom of the dialog box labeled Enable Logging, as shown in Figure 12-8.

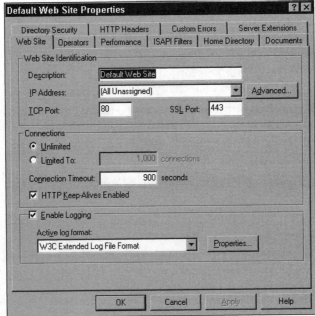

Figure 12-8: Regardless of whether you are working with an FTP or web server, you'll have the option to log all the activity that occurs on your site.

4. **Click the Enable Logging check box to turn the option on.**

   Select the format you want to use from the Active Log Format drop-down list.

5. Click the Properties button.

The Logging properties dialog box appears. Depending on the type of logging you chose, your dialog box might not look like the one shown in Figure 12-9, which reflects the W3C choice.

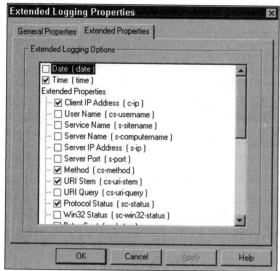

Figure 12-9:
The W3C log format gives you the opportunity to choose all kinds of events to log.

6. Continuing in the W3C, click the Extended Properties tab.

A list of about 22 items that you can track appears on the screen.

7. Choose the activities you want to track by clicking the check box beside each option.

Keep in mind, the more options you click, the larger your file will become.

8. Click the General Properties tab.

9. Choose how often, if at all, you want a new log file created.

You can do this by clicking the right option in the New Log Time period box.

Notice that when you click a time period option that the text at the bottom of the dialog box showing the name of the log file changes. For example, if you click monthly, the file name changes to exyymm.log. No, *exyymm.log* will not be the literal name of the file. When the log file is created, the current year will be substituted for *yy* and the current month for *mm*. For example, if the file is created in March 2002, the file-name will be ex0203.log. Yes, you noticed. Only two digits are reserved for the year. Table 12-4 shows you the prefixes for the different log file formats.

Table 12-4	IIS Log File Prefixes
Log File Prefix	*Format*
EX	W3C
IN	Microsoft IIS
NC	NCSA

10. **If you choose the When File Size Reaches option, the box where you can enter the size of the file lights up; enter the size.**

11. **Enter the location where you would like the log file to be stored in the Log File Directory box.**

    You may also click the Browse button to select the location using the lazy method.

12. **To have the changes take effect now, click Apply.**

Proving Your Point with Certificates

Your Web site might be the friendliest, prettiest, most-fun-to-browse-to stop on the entire Internet. Big deal! As much as your Web site puts on a happy face, browsing users will only trust your site so far. This means, for example, if your Web site asks for private information or if it provides sensitive data, a user probably will want your Web site to prove it is what it says it is. Certificates are the answer to this issue.

Here are a few more items of interest related to certificates with IIS:

- ✔ An organization that plans to do business on the Web and needs to prove its identity will obtain a certificate from a *certificate authority* (CA). A CA is a third-party, third to your web server and its browsers, that validates the identity of Web sites and users.

- ✔ A CA requests enough information from the organization requesting the certificate to verify their identity. Once the CA checks the information the requestor provides, it issues a certificate. This certificate isn't like a paper diploma. Rather, it is a piece of software that a web server installs. This certificate is used by the web server as proof of its identity. The amount of information the CA will need from your organization will depend on the strength and the use of the certificate you want to obtain. Figure 12-10 shows an example of a certificate.

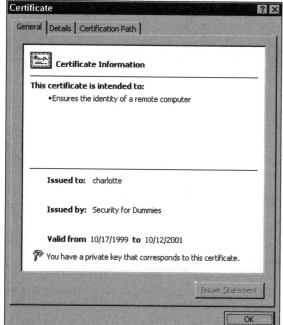

Figure 12-10:
A certificate
is really
nothing
more than
software.

✔ If all your users are internal to your organization, you can publish your own server certificate. After all, if you can't trust your employer, who can you trust? Windows 2000 comes with its own CA software that publishes certificates both for the enterprise and for users.

✔ Though Windows 2000 comes with its own CA, you should still request a certificate from a well-known CA. Don't take this the wrong way, but would you trust a company that, in effect, says to you, "Hey, you can trust me!"

✔ Individual users on the Internet also can acquire a certificate. This certificate is required if the users want to access Web content that requires one. *SSL*, which is a protocol used to secure Web servers, sometimes requires the browser to issue a certificate. Check out the section "Securing the Server-Browser Connection," later in this chapter for information on SSL. Also, refer to Chapter 13 for details on how a certificate is loaded into a user's browsers.

Obtaining a server certificate

You must obtain a certificate for your web server before you can graduate to secure connections. Also, you'll need a certificate to prove your site's identity. In fact, there are settings in Internet Explorer that prevent a browser from even accessing a site that doesn't have a valid site certificate, so it's worth the few minutes to complete these steps:

1. **Open the Internet Services Manager tool.**

   You can usually find the Internet Services Manager on the Administrative Tools menu, which you can find on the Programs menu.

2. **Click + next to the Windows 2000 server to see all the web and FTP servers.**

3. **Right-click the web server you want to work on and then choose Properties from the menu.**

   The Properties dialog box for the server you chose appears.

4. **Click the Directory Security tab and then click the Server Certificate button.**

   The Web Server Certificate Wizard starts.

5. **Click Next.**

   The wizard shows the Server Certificate screen with three options. The first option, Create A New Certificate, is applicable if you haven't requested or created a certificate on the server before.

6. **Be sure the Create A New Certificate option is selected and then click Next.**

   The Delayed or Immediate Request screen appears.

7. **Click the option to send the request immediately and then click Next.**

   The Name and Security Settings screen appears.

8. **Enter any name you like for the certificate, though accepting the default provided (the name of the web server) is a good idea.**

9. **If you plan to use 128-bit encryption to protect all or some content on your site (see the section "Securing the Server-Browser Connection," later in this chapter) and you expect some of the visitors to your site, if based in the U.S., to be unable to acquire the 128-bit version of a browser, click the SGC check box.**

   U.S. export law outlaws the export of browsers with 128-bit encryption to anywhere but Canada. If you expect visitors to your site to be in a location where they cannot acquire this version of a browser, this option allows 128-bit encrypted browsing without the need for the 128-bit browser.

   You can do your users a favor by providing on your Web site a link to another Web site where they can download the 128-bit version of their browser if they need it.

10. **Enter the name of your company and your department in the field provided; click Next.**

    If information already appears in the field, you can use what's there if it's accurate or enter your own.

    After you click Next, the Common Name screen appears.

11. **Accept the default name supplied by the wizard by clicking Next.**

12. **Supply the geographical information and then click Next.**

    The Choose a Certification Authority screen appears. The drop-down list shows all the CAs loaded on the server.

13. **Choose the CA you want to issue your certificate from the drop-down list; click next.**

14. **Review the information presented about your soon-to-be-published certificate and then click Next.**

    The CA you chose will create a new certificate for you.

15. **Click Finish.**

    You return to the Web site's Properties dialog box.

16. **Click View Certificate to view details about your certificate.**

Forcing browsers to show their ID

Turnabout is fair play. If your web server has to go through the effort to prove its identity with a certificate, why not ask users to do the same? You can set up your Web server to insist on receiving a client certificate, to ignore client certificates, or to accept them if they are offered. Keep in mind that you can apply the requirement for a certificate to any folder or page on your site. This way, you can lock down just certain elements of your site.

You don't have to force users to prove their identity via the provision of a personal certificate to access any of the content on your site. Keep in mind that you can secure just specific folders on your site with this option. The steps that follow show you how to force users to supply their certificate just on the content you specify.

1. **Open the Internet Services Manager tool.**

    You can usually find the Internet Services Manager on the Administrative Tools menu, which you can find on the Programs menu.

2. **Click + next to the Windows 2000 server to see all the web and FTP servers.**

3. **Right-click the web server you want to work on or the folder or page you want to secure and then choose Properties from the menu.**

    The Properties dialog box for the directory or page or file you chose appears.

4. **Click the Edit button in the Secure Communications section.**

    The Secure Communications screen appears, as shown in Figure 12-11.

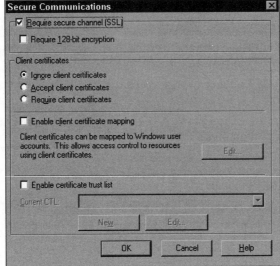

Figure 12-11:
You can demand, passively accept, or ignore certificates from browsing visitors.

5. To require a visitor to provide a certificate, click the <u>R</u>equire Secure Channel option.

6. Click the option you want in the Client Certificates section.

7. Click OK to return to the Properties dialog box.

8. Click OK again to return to the Internet Services Manager.

Securing the Server-Browser Connection

With the right tools and know-how, anyone can spy on network traffic, especially Internet traffic. This means it's possible for someone to actually see the content of a Web page as it passes from the server to the browser, as well as any information the browser sends to a server, like a request for a page or even data the user enters on a form. It's not really a big deal most of the time, because it's just as easy for someone, unless they have a lot of free time on their hands, to *look* at your Web site than to peek at the HTTP packets as they fly by.

What happens, though, when your Web site either provides or receives private information, such as a browser's credit card information, confidential data, financial information, and so on? If you're thinking of starting an Internet bank, it's time to pay attention. You probably would want to protect the connection between your server and a browser. This is an absolute requirement if your site will be involved in any kind of e-commerce activities.

Peeking under the SSL hood

A browser contacts a secure site by using the HTTPS protocol as part of the URL. The server responds by sending back to the client its certificate, which contains its public key, as well as the cryptography methods it is capable of using. After receipt of the message from the server, the client generates a master key that will be used to both encrypt and decrypt messages during the session. The client encrypts the master key with the server's public key, and this message is sent back to the server. The server receives the message, and by using its private key, the server can decrypt the message from the client and determine the cryptography method to use, as well as the master key. The server at this point has the option to check the identity of the client, provided the client has a personal certificate, using the same technique. Regardless, all messages between the client and server are encrypted with the master key. You might see this master key referred to as a *session* key.

The protocol that makes the secure connection possible is SSL for *secure sockets layer*. With SSL, the data exchange between the client and server is encrypted. The encryption applies to the URL the client requests, as well as the information on the pages, and any information entered onto forms, such as passwords, user ID, and personal information. You can configure IIS to provide an SSL connection to its clients.

Here are more must-know details on SSL:

✔ A Web site needs a certificate in order to provide an SSL connection.

✔ Any browser that will use a secure connection must be configured to use SSL.

✔ The user may need to acquire a personal certificate, if the server requires it. This can be provided by a CA (certificate authority) running on the Windows 2000 domain or by a third party, such as VeriSign.

✔ A user must substitute HTTPS for HTTP in a URL that accesses content that is secured with SSL.

✔ Because you can use certificates to secure your site on a folder-by-folder or a file-by-file basis, you'll need to select the folder or file you want to secure. If you select the entire site, then all content on your site will be certificate-secured.

✔ Apply SSL security to any folder or page that sends sensitive information or receives it. So, be sure to secure any page on your site where users enter private information, as well as any page that displays sensitive data for the user.

✔ All this encrypting and decrypting isn't free. Your users probably will notice (or, at least, they say they do) a downgrade in performance when they access encrypted content. Be sure to apply SSL to just the content that really needs it.

✔ The default encryption strength is 40-bit. Encryption strength indicates how tough it is to crack the code that protects the data. SSL can use either 40-bit or 128-bit encryption. 128-bit encryption is only available in the U.S. and Canada, so don't use 128-bit encryption if you expect your browsing users will be located elsewhere.

Follow these steps to configure your web server for a secure connection to its clients.

1. **Open the Internet Services Manager tool and then click + next to the Windows 2000 server to see all the web and FTP servers.**

   The Internet Services Manager appears on the Administrator tools menu, which you can find on the Programs menu.

2. **Open the web server you want to secure.**

3. **Right-click the folder you want to secure and then choose Properties from the menu.**

   The Properties dialog box for the server you selected appears.

4. **Click the directory Security tab and then click the Edit button in the Secure Communications group.**

   The Secure Communications dialog box appears.

5. **To require an SSL connection to the folder you selected, click the Require Secure Channel option.**

   When you turn this option on, the 128-bit encryption check box becomes active.

6. **Click the Require 128-bit encryption option if you know users connecting to your site can acquire a browser that supports 128-bit encryption; otherwise, keep this check box clear.**

7. **Click OK to return to the Properties dialog box and then click OK to return to the IIS snap-in.**

Chapter 13

Ensuring that Your Users Aren't Browsing into Trouble

• •

In This Chapter

▶ Wincing while you review browser risks

▶ Forcing Web sites to produce some ID

▶ Assessing whether cookies are a health food or a health risk

▶ Rezoning the Internet neighborhood

• •

*T*he Internet is like the Wild West. Like the Wild West, the Internet has been around a long time, but settling it and establishing order is going to take some time. Like the Wild West, the Internet has good guys and bad guys. Back in the days of the Wild West, everyone had a weapon, but there was not too much variety in those weapons. Same on the Internet. Everyone is packing a browser and TCP/IP. How you use your weapons determines whether you are a good guy or a bad guy. Do you use your knowledge of IP to understand how firewalls work, or do you use your knowledge to monitor and break into IP traffic?

The cowboys that seem to get into the most gunfights in today's virtual West are browsers. While the Internet is not the safest place for e-mail, and sometimes using FTP can get you thrown out of the saloon headfirst, the Internet presents the greatest set of threats for browsers.

This chapter explains the risks posed by browsing the Internet and how these risks can harm your network. The chapter doesn't leave you hanging, though. There's a new sheriff in town, and its name is Internet Explorer (IE). Its deputies are certificates, security zones, Authenticode, and common sense. You find out how these features in Internet Explorer can minimize those risks, if not completely eliminate them.

Browser Warts: Assessing Web Browser Security Risks

The web browser has become arguably the most important piece of software on today's corporate computer. The flexibility it offers in obtaining information and the access a browser gives you, though, doesn't come without a price. The price of access and flexibility is security. Just think, if the mouth of the pipe is so wide that so much data can get into it, it's also wide enough that lots of data can get out, too. Here's a look at the security risks you must deal with while users in your organization are browsing:

✔ **Downloadable browser content:**. To make your web browsing experience a little more exciting, some sites insist on downloading a small piece of software to your user's workstation. This software is in addition to the Web page and picture that normally get sent along the wire to your browser. Figure 13-1 shows you an example of a site requesting to drop off some software on your browser.

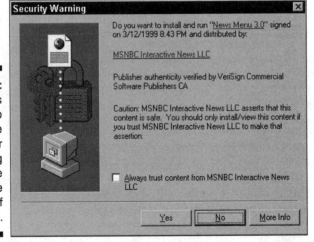

Figure 13-1:
Some sites try to enhance your browsing experience with some code of their own.

This is downloadable browser content. This kind of content is usually never a full application, only a component or feature of one. The larger application in the case of active content is the Web page in general. Active content provides some feature or component of the page. Have you ever gone to the computer store to buy a *Print Preview* application? Probably not. You don't see too many *make-the-stock-ticker-crawl-on-the-bottom-of-your-screen* suites advertised in magazines. These examples, plus others like mortgage calculators, animated celery sticks that tell jokes, browser-based spreadsheets, and live scoreboards, though, are real examples of downloadable content. Now that you know what active content is, you're probably interested in the risk. Here's how active content can be harmful:

- **Downloaded content may not be what it seems.** Just because the description on the Web site says the downloaded control or script will tell you the day of the week on January 13, 2009, it does not mean the program will not format your hard drive instead. Bad people do bad things.

- **Downloaded content may include a virus.** Not everyone practices safe computing. As much as the intentions of the content developer programmer were good, there's no guarantee that a nasty virus hasn't found its way onto the control or script.

- **Downloaded content can break something on your users' workstations that's not already broken.** Some of the content that can be downloaded might require a short installation program to be run, which, potentially, could overwrite existing important files. It may very well be, also, that your users' workstations just aren't compatible with the program being downloaded.

- **You can't trust everyone.** Certain software developers are reliable. Some are not. A risk in downloading content from the Web is that you just don't know whom you are getting content from.

✔ **Internet snoops:** Remember that the Internet is nothing more than a huge network of mismatched computers, both workstations and servers, all connected by the TCP/IP protocol. Messages, Web pages, and other information are passed from computer to computer over the Internet until the correct destination is reached. Though not easy, it is possible for nefarious persons to look in on the data being passed between computers on the Internet. It may not seem like a big deal for someone to snoop in on the stock quotes you download, but what about slightly more important information, such as a credit card number, password, or social security number?

✔ **Browser timesavers:** IE remembers where you have been on the Web and what you did there. You can see this feature in action when you type a URL into IE's address box, and the browser uncannily finishes entering the URL for you. Gee, what a timesaver. Gee, what a security gap! All it takes for someone to see what sites you have browsed to is to use your browser — and there's a chance that a password you may have supplied to access one of the sites may be cached, giving that someone the same access to the site! Hey, browser timesaver, thanks for nothing!

✔ **Web sites that impersonate other Web sites:** One of the greatest problems with the Web is the anonymity factor it places on most of your work and play. You generally never get to see the person or the server on the other end of the wire. A cost is associated with the anonymity of the Web, and that cost is *trust*. You really can't trust someone or something that you can't see or find out about, which is usually the case on the Web. As much as Web commerce is growing at an incredible rate, most users still hesitate just for a moment when they need to provide personal information on the Web. Web sites can impersonate other Web sites. This chance of impersonation poses a risk to your provision of personal information to the Web, as well as to the general acceptance of Web commerce.

This impersonation game can be played in a number of ways. Here's one of the most popular: A Web site appears on the Internet with a name very similar to a usually popular other site. For example, say that a Web site named `www.freecashfortheasking.com` made available no-obligation-no-repay-no-questions-asked loans. This would probably be a popular site. What if another site on the Web was named `www.freecashforthasking.com`? You would bet it would get a lot of hits as persons mistyped the name of the place where they really expected to get no-repay loans.

The Best Defense is a Good . . . Defense!

IE provides a handful of features to help ensure secure browsing. A firewall in many cases can accomplish much that the features in IE do, but not every organization can afford a firewall, much less hire the talent to maintain it. If you are unclear of the role a firewall plays in Internet security, be sure to refer to Chapter 17. Here's a list of the features IE uses to protect itself:

✔ Web content zones

✔ Prebuilt and customizable security levels

✔ Alphabet soup acronyms for secure server connections

✔ Big-bitted browsers

✔ Cookie management

✔ Certificate safety

Setting Up Web Content Zones

Web content zones are a feature in IE that allow you to predefine those Web sites you trust and those Web sites you don't. In addition, Web content zones help you specify what behavior is allowed for those occasions when the browser walks on the wild side and visits those untrusted sites, as well as what is appropriate for those visits to trusted sites. It may seem like a daunting task to categorize all the sites on the Internet into zones and then figure out what your users can and can't do per zone, and it probably is. When you complete these tasks, though, your only effort going forward is to respond by either tightening or loosening the security screws for certain sites.

Understanding Web content zones

This scenario demonstrates how the Web content zone feature of IE is so cool and saves you so much work. Here's a two-part example. Say that you assign your company's intranet to the Local intranet zone, which is one of the four predefined zones that come up with IE. Say that the Local intranet zone has a security level of Low, which is one of four predefined security settings that come with IE. This means that the browser will allow content to be downloaded without warning or confirmation whenever you browse through the intranet. Hold on, here's part two. Say that you like to browse your competitor's Web site, but as part of corporate policy, you're not allowed to accept downloaded content. Your competitor's Web site would probably be part of the Restricted Sites zone (another of the four zones), and that zone probably would be assigned the High Security level (another of the four security levels). With this configuration, you could browse that site as you please, but content would never be downloaded to the computer. If you jumped from the competitor's site directly to your intranet, the browser would automatically accept downloaded content without the need to reconfigure any browser options.

Adding sites to zones

IE makes you think of four categories of places your users' browsing can take them. These categories are known as zones. You can't add to the list of zones, so you should get comfortable with the zones provided:

- ✔ **Local intranet:** Your intranet.

- ✔ **Restricted sites:** This zone includes Web sites you do not want users to visit, period. An example of such a site may be `www.incrediblyfilthyadultobjectionablecontent.ugh`.

- ✔ **The Internet:** This zone includes any site on the Internet that you haven't assigned to one of the other zones.

- ✔ **Trusted sites:** The Trusted sites zone includes sites you don't mind your users visiting, such as `www.idgbooks.com`.

To take advantage of zones, you must assign a zone to teach Web site that you're interested in restricting access to or to which you're allowing access to one of the zones. You're probably wondering how you could possibly assign every Web site on the Internet to a zone. Not to worry. The Internet zone has been reserved as the home for any Web sites not assigned to another zone. Table 13-1 shows you how the four Internet zones are used, as well as the default security level assigned to each zone. As you refer to the table, think of the different sites you and your users frequent and decide which zone would be appropriate.

Table 13-1	Internet Zones
This Zone	*Is Used for These Types of Sites*
Local intranet	Sites in the Local intranet zone most likely are those maintained on this side of the firewall. Because you may not be sure who has access to your intranet, including who may have the rights to post content to the site, this zone has a default security level of medium-low.
The Internet zone	This zone is the easiest zone to maintain. Why? Because you don't have to do anything to maintain it! Yeh! This zone automatically includes any sites not added to either the list of Trusted sites or Restricted sites. Browsing to any new site is governed by the rules applied to the Internet zone. If you find a site you believe is safe, you can add it to the Trusted sites zone. If you browse to the bad part of town, you can add it to the list of sites in the Restricted sites zone. The default security level for this zone is medium.
Trusted sites zone	Sites you add to this zone are those you trust implicitly. Sites added here might be those companies you do business with, or extremely trustworthy/reliable sites. The default security level for this zone is low.
Restricted sites zone	This site is the badlands. The sites you add to this zone are those you know you or your users browse to that you don't trust. The sites you add to this zone might be those that have posted malicious, harmful, or just ridiculous content. Naturally, the default security level for this zone is high.

Now armed with an understanding of zones, you're ready to add sites to specific zones. Follow these steps to add any Web or intranet site to one of the four Internet zones:

1. **Start IE.**

   You don't need to connect to any specific Web site, or even be online for that matter.

2. **Select Tools⇨Internet Options.**

   The Internet Options dialog box appears.

3. **Select the Security tab.**

   The Security sheet appears. The sheet displays the controls where you define zones and security levels, as shown in Figure 13-2.

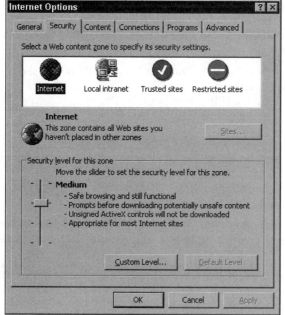

Figure 13-2:
You define
most
aspects of
browser
security
from one
tab in IE.

4. **Select the icon for the zone you want to assign a site to.**

   After you select a zone, the security level gauge, shown at the bottom of the dialog box, changes to reflect the level already assigned to the zone.

5. **Click the Sites button.**

   The Sites button will not be available if Internet Zone is selected. Keep in mind that the Internet Zone automatically includes all sites not explicitly added to the Local Intranet, Trusted Sites, or Restricted Sites zones.

   If you chose Local Intranet, you must configure three options before choosing sites. If you didn't choose Local Intranet, hop to Step 7.

6. **In the Local Intranet dialog box, select the options that are appropriate to how you want to define your Local Intranet zone and then click the Advanced button.**

   This list explains the relevance of each of the options for customizing your Local Intranet zone:

   - The first option to Include All Local (Intranet) Sites Not Included In Other Zones is used to add all other intranet sites on your network to the Local Intranet zone. Naturally, with this option selected, these other intranet sites will not be added to the Local Intranet zone if they are already added to one of the other zones.

- The option to Include All Sites That Bypass The Proxy Server is used to include in the Local Intranet sites that do not use the proxy server connection to the Internet. This option is useless if a proxy server is not used to protect your network.

- The third option to Include All Network Paths is used to include locations on the network to which the local intranet is attached and to which a URL might point to. For example, this URL points to a folder and path off of the intranet:

```
http://Myintranet/thisdirectory/thisfile.txt.
```

Check this option to include the `thisdirectory` folder in the Local Intranet zone.

The Local Intranet dialog box appears.

7. **In the Local Intranet zone dialog box shown in Figure 13-3, enter the name of the site you want to add to the zone; then click A̲dd.**

When you type any character into the box, a drop-down list appears listing the URLs of pages you have visited. This gives you the option to select the site from a list rather than typing in a URL. Either way, when the URL appears in the box, select Add.

Depending on the security level set for the zone you're adding sites to, you may be forced to enter a site with a secure server. Sites with a secure server require the use of the HTTPS protocol. For example, if the author's Web site used a secure web server, you would enter `https://www.paulsanna.com` as the URL. To specify that only sites requiring HTTPS belong to this zone, select the Require S̲erver Verification option. For more information on the topic of secure servers, refer to the "Securing Loose Connections with SSL, TLS, and PCT," section later in this chapter.

8. **Repeat Step 7 for every Web site you need to add to the zone.**

9. **When you have entered all the sites, click OK two more times in the next two dialog boxes you see (three OKs in three dialog boxes if Local intranet zone) to return to the browser window.**

Assigning security to zones

You can specify any level of security you feel is appropriate to each of your four Internet zones. IE ships with default settings for each of the three levels that seem to make sense, but you're an adult and can make your own decisions (with Bill Gates' help). You can use one of the four predefined levels (Low, Medium-Low, Medium, High), or you can create your own level (Custom Level).

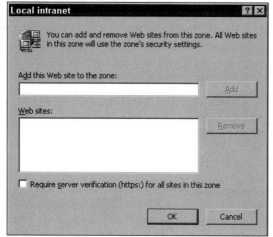

Figure 13-3:
Populate the
zone by
typing or
picking sites
from a list.

The High security level provides you the greatest degree of security, denying almost all active content access to your system, while the Low security level provides the least protection. As an example, the High security level restricts any download and use of ActiveX controls, while the Low security level allows ActiveX controls to be downloaded and run, without confirmation by you. So how do you decide what security level to use? Decisions, decisions, decisions.

The following list shows the various security features and functions that can be enabled, disabled, or whose actions prompt first, that you can control by specifying a security level. (See the sidebar "I have no idea what you're talking about" if you're unfamiliar with some of these terms.)

- ✔ Download signed ActiveX controls
- ✔ Download unsigned ActiveX controls
- ✔ Script ActiveX controls not marked safe
- ✔ Script ActiveX controls marked safe
- ✔ Run ActiveX controls
- ✔ Allow download and storage of cookies
- ✔ Allow use of cookie but not download and store
- ✔ File download
- ✔ Font download
- ✔ Access data sources in other domains
- ✔ Copy and Paste file (drag and drop, too)
- ✔ Install desktop icons

    ✔ Launch programs and open documents from IFRAME

    ✔ Navigate in subframes that link to points outside of user's domain

    ✔ Use Active Channels

    ✔ Submit unencrypted data entered into forms

    ✔ User data kept persistent

    ✔ Allow scripting in browser

    ✔ Allow copy and paste operations in browser

    ✔ Allow script with Java applications

To either check or change these settings:

1. **In IE, select Tools⇨Internet Options.**

   The Internet Options dialog box appears.

2. **Click the Security tab.**

   The Security sheet appears.

3. **Click the zone you're interested in and then select Custom Level.**

   The Security Settings dialog box appears.

4. **Scroll through the list of security options and click the security options you want to configure for the zone; when you're done, click OK.**

I have no idea what you're talking about

The list of security features and functions includes some terms with which you may be unfamiliar, such as signed, nonencrypted, and channels. A *signed control* is one that includes a digital signature. A digital signature always and forever associates the control with the company that built it. This way, you know someone isn't masquerading as another company and distributing nasty content. You can find more information on signed software later in this chapter in the "Getting a certificate for downloaded software" section.

Encrypted means that data, such as the information you enter on an order form on a Web page, is scrambled before it is sent to the Web page asking for it. Encryption is usually more sophisticated than pig Latin. This way, someone intercepting a retail order placed over the Internet will not be able to determine a dress size, favorite color, American Express number, anything. You can find details on encryption in Chapter 1.

Lastly, *channels* are a vehicle developed by Microsoft to deliver Web pages filled with exactly the content you're interested in to your desktop automatically. Channels, naturally, must be secured like any other content delivered to the computer.

You may be tempted to experiment with the security levels assigned to the four zones. To reset the security level for a zone back to the level to which Microsoft thinks it should be set, click the zone and then select the Default Level button. If the button is not available, then the level currently selected for the zone is the Microsoft-set default.

Securing Loose Connections with SSL, TLS, and PCT

You probably want to know how to protect that stream of data running to and from your client browser, especially when that stream contains personal information, like your credit card number, birth date, and social security number. Every day the number of persons buying, selling, trading, investing, and reporting on the Web for the first time grows, so the security of these online sessions also grows in significance. Just in time to save the day, IE supports three protocols that you can use for secure data exchange with a browser.

These protocols are known as *SSL (Secure Sockets Layer)*, *TLS (Transport Layer Security)*, and *PCT (Private Communication Technology)*. Use of these protocols creates a secure connection between a client and a server on the Internet. You can use this secure channel to exchange sensitive information with little chance of detection, interruption, decryption, or consumption by someone other than the sender or receiver. With SSL and PCT, the data exchange between the client and server is encrypted. The encryption applies to the URL the client requests, as well as the information on the pages, and any information entered onto forms, such as passwords, user ID, and personal information.

Using these protocols involves two components:

✔ Any browser that will use a secure connection must be configured to use SSL, TLS, and/or PCT. Configuring IE for SSL and/or PCT is nothing more complicated than playing Minesweeper.

✔ Web sites that will request and process data from clients using a secure channel also must be configured to use SSL and PCT. This is slightly more complicated than simply throwing a switch, but definitely less work than reformatting your hard drive and installing all server hardware from scratch. You can find information about configuring Web sites with SSL and PCT in Chapter 12.

Connecting to an SSL secure server

Desperate times call for desperate measures. With that in mind, connecting to a secure server requires a secure connection. To achieve this, you need to use a slightly different syntax in your URL. To connect to a secure server, the first part of the URL must change from `http` to `https`. Here is an example of a URL for a very secure server:

```
https://www.billgatesbankaccount.com
```

Configuring SSL, TLS, and PCT at the browser

It's really a no-brainer as to whether you should configure IE to work with SSL, TLS, and PCT. Without doing so, you cannot connect to secure servers.

1. **Start IE and then choose Tools⇨Internet Options.**

   The Internet Option dialog box appears.

2. **Click the Advanced tab.**

   The Advanced sheet appears.

3. **Scroll down the list of options until you see the Security group; once you reach the list of Security options, select the PCT 1.0, SSL 2.0, TLS 1.0, and the SSL 3.0 options, as shown in Figure 13-4.**

4. **Click OK to finish.**

128 bits of high-end encryption

The goal of this chapter is to show you how to use the bells and whistles in IE to make your users' browsing experiences secure ones. It may be the case, however, that the browsing your users do and the commerce users transact with their browser may require a higher grade of security than that provided by IE. Why would you need more security than provided by IE? Well, organizations look for the greatest security, naturally, when money is involved. Therefore, typical applications for top-notch browser security are finance related, such as online investments and transactions. The browser grade that most financial organizations have adopted is one with 128-bit encryption, and IE is available in a 128-bit version. This version represents an improvement over the standard version of IE, which uses 40-bit encryption.

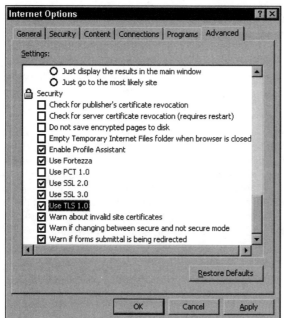

Figure 13-4:
Security by
acronym.

The difference between 40 bit and 128 bit isn't just 88 bits. Nor is 128 bit merely 320 percent better than 40 bit. A key tells the system using the data how to scramble the data so that no one without the key can use it, and the key (sometimes a different key) is used to tell the system receiving the data how to unscramble it. The number of bits indicates the size of the key. A 128-bit key is much larger and harder to break than a 40-bit key. Microsoft claims it would take "more than the age of the universe" in time to decipher 128-bit security, while hackers today are having some success deciphering 40-bit keys.

Choosing to use 128-bit encryption is not like waking up and deciding to stop smoking or to start exercising. A little entity you may have heard of, named the United States Federal Government, has imposed some restrictions. The government will only allow the use of 128-bit encryption in the U.S. and Canada. Use of it anywhere else is against the law, and the penalty for committing a federal offense is usually more severe than cleaning up trash on the shoulder of an interstate highway.

Under the secure connection hood

SSL and PCT work very similarly. Here is a rundown of what happens under-the-hood from a generic standpoint when you use one of these protocols.

A browser contacts a secure site by using the HTTPS protocol as part of the URL. The server responds by sending back to the client its certificate, which contains its public key, as well as the cryptography methods it is capable of using. After receipt of the message from the server, the client generates a master key that will be used to both encrypt and decrypt messages during the session. The client encrypts the master key with the server's public key, and this message is sent back to the server. The server receives the message, and by using its private key, the server can decrypt the message from the client and determine the cryptography method to use, as well as the master key. The server at this point has the option to check the identity of the client, provided the client has a personal certificate, using the same technique. Regardless, all messages between the client and server are encrypted with the master key.

Lastly, a Web site will not typically protect its entire site with SSL because of the overhead involved in exchanging information using SSL. Instead, SSL is used on a page-by-page basis, which means the folks running the Web server must specify exactly which pages on their Web would be protected by SSL.

Certifying Internet Safety with Certificates

Certificates help address the issue of trust on the Web. If you're unfamiliar with certificates, take a peek at Chapter 1. Specifically, certificates help with three practical tasks when it comes to browser security and trust:

- ✔ Certificates attest to the identity of a Web site that the browser connects to.

- ✔ Certificates prove the identity of individual users. Certain Web sites might require an individual to submit a certificate proving his or her identity.

- ✔ Certificates prove that software downloaded from the Internet really comes from the organization you're downloading it from, and certificates also assure you that the software has not been tampered with or altered.

You configure IE to work with these three certificate applications slightly differently. The next three sections explain each of these three applications.

Knowing who you are hyperlinking to

While the Web nicely accommodates the anonymity people like you and your users want to maintain as you hop from site to site, there may be times when you want to know who you are dealing with. You may want to know for sure that the server you're connected and exchanging information with is really the one shown in the URL in the Address bar at the top of IE. Knowing with confidence the identity of a Web site is important for two reasons:

- ✔ Users sometimes enter personal information to the site. Wouldn't your users like to know for sure that they are providing their social security number and credit card number to a real, honest-to-goodness vendor rather than a new organized crime Web site?

- ✔ A site may require a secure connection, which requires the server to authenticate itself successfully to the browser. Keep in mind that secure connections are not the default on the Internet, but when the server that the browser is connected to insists on secure connection, who are you to argue? In these cases, a server must absolutely identify itself to the browser.

Web sites prove their identity by providing a server certificate to those clients asking for one, like IE. Certificates come in a variety of shapes and sizes, and servers must use a specific type of certificate to handle this chore. These types of certificates contain the following information:

- ✔ The name of the organization represented by the certificate (for example, `www.goodbooksfromsanna.com`)

- ✔ Information about the company (for example, IP address, street address)

- ✔ The public key of the organization

- ✔ The name of the CA who issued the certificate

- ✔ A serial number

A server certificate for a Web site is issued by a CA, but you probably know that by this time. In turn, the browser is loaded with certificates for any CA that the person configuring the browser trusts. Certificates for CAs are known as *root certificates*. There can be as many root certificates from different CAs loaded on a computer as needed. These root certificates contain a CA's public key, as well as other goodies. You manage the list of root certificates in IE.

The root certificate plays an important role in this system because it actually does the work of attesting to the validity of an organization's certificate to the browser. You let the CA do the trusting of the site. Trusting the CA is all you must worry about. Here's how:

Who's running the prison?

You might run across a certificate presented by a company, which also happens to be the CA that authenticated the certificate. Huh? As an example, the certificate for Joe's Web site might have been provided by Joe the CA. While this may seem like the inmates running the asylum situation, there is good reason for this. Using software like Microsoft's Certificate Server, a company may act as its own certificate authority, publishing its own set of certificates, typically for use on the company's intranet. Companies in this situation typically use a third-party CA to vouch for their identity outside of their intranet.

When the browser runs across a site with a certificate, that certificate is provided to the browser. The certificate is encrypted with the CA's private key. Remember that when you install a root certificate for a CA, the CA's public key is installed on the browser. Hence, IE can decrypt the certificate because it has the CA's public key. Upon decryption, the browser inspects the certificate and verifies the site that you are connected to against the information contained in the certificate. Naturally, these should match. If they don't, IE lets you know about it. If any further decryption is required now with the Web site, the browser has access to the company's public key via the certificate.

Becoming the authority on the list of certificate authorities

IE automatically installs a number of root certificates on the computer where the browser is installed when the browser is installed. You can manage the list of CAs installed on any computer. For example, you can add new root certificates to a machine for the browser to use, and you can also disable root certificates already installed at the browser. You may also delete a CA's root certificate from a PC, forcing you to import a new version of the root certificate if you later find you must trust sites that the CA has certified.

Many CAs provide a range of services, such as providing certificates to servers, as well as to software publishers with which to sign downloadable content. IE allows you to trust CAs based on the service they provide. For example, you might trust ATT Certificate Services for network server authentication and network client authentication, but not for secure e-mail or software publishing. In addition, CAs provide different classes of certificates. You may disable a certain root certificate for one specific class for a CA but maintain the root certificate for another class. For example, you might have seven VeriSign root certificates installed, but only the Class 1 IDs are active.

To review and maintain the list of certificates, follow these steps:

1. **Start IE.**

   You don't need to connect to any specific Web site, or even to be online for that matter.

2. **Select Tools⇨Internet Options.**

   The Internet Option dialog box appears with a bunch of tabs.

3. **Click the Content tab.**

   The Content sheet appears.

4. **Click the Certificates button.**

   A list of certificate authorities appears. To see authorities of a specific type, such as only those that issue client certificates, choose the appropriate type from the Intended Purpose drop-down list.

   Click the appropriate tab to see certain types of certificate, such as ones issued for the user's personal use or for personal use by a person other than the user, or ones issued by certificate authorities or by intermediate issuers.

   You may notice that some CAs are listed multiple times. This may be the case if the CA offers different classes of digital certificates. Be sure that you select/deselect the proper class of certificate for your CA.

5. **To no longer trust a CA, select it and then click Remove; then answer Yes to the confirmation to delete the root certificate if this is something you really want to do.**

6. **To actually see information contained in a root certificate, select the certificate and then View.**

   Keep in mind that you won't see anything too exciting, just a bunch of information.

7. **To modify the certification services a certificate will provide for you, click the certificate and then click the Advanced button. When the Advanced Options dialog box appears, clear or check the service you want or don't want from the list of Certificate purposes. When you're done, click OK.**

   Certificates can provide you with services, such as client authentication, signing software, IP Security authentication, and more.

8. **When you're done looking at the certificate information, click Close.**

   You return to the Internet Options dialog box,

9. **Click OK to return to the main IE window.**

Adding a root certificate

There may be a CA whose certificates you want to trust but who is not listed in IE. After all, unlike the personal computer software market, more than just one CA may actually be in the certificate market! You can use IE to add this CA's root certificate, enabling you to trust organizations and companies certified by the new CA. To acquire and then install a new root certificate, stop by the Web site of the CA whose root certificate you want to add. You can find information as to how to download the certificate at the Web site. As soon as IE realizes you're downloading a root certificate, a dialog box appears asking you to confirm that you want to do so. Answer OK, specify which of the four types of uses (server authentication, client authentication, personal authentication, software signing) you want for the server, and then use the instructions in the last section to verify that the new certificate was properly installed.

Certifying yourself so that the Web knows you're safe

Web security issues place a great emphasis on the capability of Web sites to prove their identity. Turnabout, though, is certainly fair play. The growing number of Web sites and Web services that require individual clients to prove their identity demonstrates this. The most reliable method for users to prove their identity on the Web is the same one used by Web servers and Web software providers: using a digital certificate. You can approach the same CA used by the organizations and companies on the Web for personal digital certificates. These certificates can range from simple certifications that simply lock the certificate to your password and e-mail address, or they can reliably verify a user against your organization.

An example of a situation in which you may be asked to prove your identity would be if your company entered into a joint venture with another company. As a way to authenticate one another before exchanging corproate information over the Internet, a personal certificate may be used. In this situation, either a certificate server at your organization must provide the certificate to all of the users, or the users must acquire one from a CA.

If your users will obtain their own personal digital certificates, there probably will be little handholding needed. Acquiring a personal certificate is not difficult. The process usually involves stopping by the Web site of the CA you want to be certified by and then following the instructions you find there. Naturally, the CA service in Windows 2000 can provide a personal certificate as well.

Multiple certified personalities

There is nothing to stop you from acquiring multiple personal certificates. In fact, you may be asked to use a certificate from a particular CA in order to be authenticated against a site you work with on the Web, while using a different certificate simply to sign e-mail.

The process CAs use to issue the certificate varies. Regardless of the CA, though, before issuing a certificate, each CA has the responsibility of accurately determining you are who you say you are. Depending on the class of certificate, you may be asked simply to provide some personal information, or you may be asked to send or fax a copy of your driver's license or passport. Other classes of certificates may have to check with the employer of the person requesting the certificate.

When the CA has determined your rightful identity and has accepted your application, the CA will issue you your certificate. This process may be manual, in which you must download the certificate, perhaps after supplying a PIN sent to you via e-mail. Or the process may be automated where the CA does all the work involved in loading the certificate into IE. Again, regardless of the process, the CA's first responsibility will be to ensure that your certificate is sent to you. Check with the CA in which you are interested for the relevant rules of the road. Your mileage may vary.

Ensuring that Download Content Doesn't Cause Downtime for Your Network

Dangerous downloaded content is probably the most serious threat to a healthy browser, the computer it sits on, and the network that the computer is connected to. Downloaded content is nothing more than a small program downloaded to a computer from a Web site. The program is used to either execute some required function for the Web page (meaning it does some job), or it enhances the Web page (makes it look pretty). Because you can't be sure whether the content you download is a trick or a treat, IE lets you control the download of content to your computer.

There are two main types of downloaded content and, certainly not surprisingly, a specific software company champions each of the flavors.

- **Java programs from Sun Microsystems, including JavaScript, Jscript, Java Beans, and everything that reminds you of coffee.** Many sites produce content using the Java programming language from Sun Microsystems. Java is both compelling and popular because most Java code can run unchanged on any platform. Java content can be in the form of larger Java programs or small Java applets.

- **ActiveX Controls from Microsoft.** Downloadable content can also be produced using standards and tools developed by Microsoft. The programs are known as ActiveX controls. Smaller, very high-level programs known as scripts can support these Active X controls, like Java applets. These scripts are also downloaded to the computer, and they handle some of the work for the downloaded program, such as figuring out what browser you are running, or the resolution of your monitor.

So how do you and your users determine what software is good and what software is malicious? Well, the trial-and-error approach just isn't practical. Just imagine the next staff meeting. "Hey, did you hear about Marvin in accounting? He downloaded what he thought was a cool screen saver, but it ended up deleting the entire general ledger! Boy, let's not download that screensaver again!"

You need to arm yourself with the resources required to permit download and use of good content and to deny what you suspect to be bad content. For those applications your users choose to download, you need strong control to be sure that the applications do only what they should.

IE provides a gaggle of gifts and gadgets to help you manage active content. IE uses Internet zones and related security levels to help you browse through the web in a carefree manner. IE also helps you manage tricky Java security, as well as use certificates to check downloaded software.

Ensuring decaffeinated Java downloads

Do you like coffee? Well, it seems as if the general population of the Web does, too. Java applets are more prevalent on the Web than any other form of downloadable content. Winning the popularity contest, though, means more work for you, the security-minded network administrator. A Java application, like an ActiveX control, potentially has access to every nook and cranny on the browser machine. Unlike ActiveX controls, though, a Java applet must explicitly ask for permission to access a certain component of the machine, as well as to execute a particular task. Here is a list — not complete, mind you — of the tasks a Java applet must first be granted permission before being allowed to execute:

✔ Print

✔ See information about the computer from Windows system information

✔ Run other applications

✔ See network addresses

The fact that the application must ask for permission may not seem like a big deal considering the old saying, "You don't ask, you don't get." But at the same time, the flexibility inherent in Java security means that there are more settings to tune and more settings to pay attention to. Relax. This doesn't mean you must hire a full-time Java security dude. Fortunately, Java security is integrated in to the security zone/level model described in the previous section. This gives you the following options:

✔ **Least Amount of Work:** Use the predetermined Java safety levels set for the three built-in security levels, and you can utilize this option by following the instructions in the "Assigning security to zones" section, earlier in this chapter.

✔ **Medium Amount of Work:** Use the custom security level to choose which Java Safety level — High, Medium, Low — you want for the Security zone you're working on. You can set this option by following the instructions earlier in the chapter in the "Assigning security to zones" section.

✔ **Most Amount of Work:** Use the Custom Java Safety level to choose which Java permissions to allow and which to disallow for the Security zone you're working on. You must use the custom security level in order to use a Custom Java Safety Level. Don't let me hear you say that IE isn't flexible!

If you didn't get a chance to review the material related to Security zones and Levels, you may want to do so now before configuring Java. If you're ready, though, here is how to configure Java-specific security in IE:

1. **Start IE and then select Tools⇨Internet Options.**

   The Internet Options dialog box appears.

2. **Click the Security tab.**

   The Security sheet appears.

3. **Select the Web content zone whose Java permissions you want to customize.**

4. **Select the Custom Level option at the bottom of the dialog box and then scroll down the list to the Microsoft VM – Java Permissions section.**

In the Java section, you find five options. The options basically reflect three choices:

- To completely disable Java applets for the Web content zone, select the Disable Java option and then click OK. You return to the Internet Options dialog box.

- To choose one of the predetermined Java safety levels, choose High safety, Medium safety, or Low safety, and then click OK. You return to the Internet Options dialog box.

- To customize or view the Java safety permissions, choose Custom. The Java Custom Settings button appears. Select that button. The dialog box shown in Figure 13-5 appears on your screen.

5. **Choose the option in the Java section.**

   Java permissions are generally grouped into the three sets shown on the screen.

6. **Click any + symbol to expand the list until you see the value for the permission.**

   The value will be either OK or Not permitted.

7. **To change any of the permission values, click the Edit Permissions tab.**

   The Edit Permissions sheet appears, as shown in Figure 13-6.

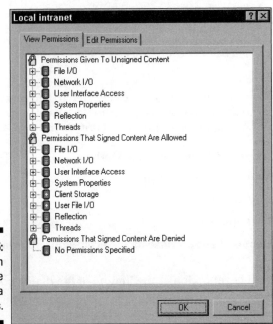

Figure 13-5:
You can
fine-tune
the Java
permissions.

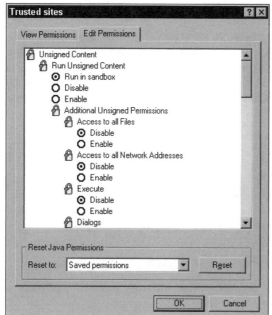

Figure 13-6:
The Edit
Permissions
sheet.

8. **Click either Enable or Disable for the permissions you want to change. If you want a head start and would like to use a predefined Java safety as a baseline, select the level from the drop-down list at the bottom of the dialog box and then click R̲eset.**

   In most cases, you're asked to allow (enable), disallow (disable), or be asked first (prompt) before the Java task is executed on the computer.

9. **Click OK, and you return to the Security Settings dialog box.**

10. **Click OK again to return to the Internet Options dialog box.**

11. **Click OK to return to the IE window, or you can stay in the Internet Options dialog box and continue work.**

Getting a certificate for downloaded software

One of the most important settings in the security levels is the option to allow the download of unsigned code. This option has nothing to do with the software that includes an image of a smiling Bill Gates and his signature. Rather, it relates to software that has been signed by the software publisher and whose signature has been verified by a certificate authority.

Why is signed software important? The digital signature on a piece of software verifies that the code has come from the publisher that appears on the certificate. This way, you can be assured of downloading that nice inspirational thought-of-the-day generator, say as opposed to a program that causes your mouse to catch fire. Software whose digital signature has been verified also can be counted on not to have been altered or mishandled between the time when it was baked by the software publisher and the time when it arrives at the browser.

You can configure IE to automatically accept software from publishers and from certificate authorities that verify software. This way, you don't have to explicitly say, "I trust you" each time you download software from a friendly force. With IE, you maintain a list of those publishers and certificate authorities that you automatically trust.

To add a publisher or certificate authority to the list of those you trust, follow these steps. You can also use these steps to review the list or to remove a publisher or CA.

1. **Find a piece of downloadable software from the software publisher you want to add to the list.**

   The easiest way to do this is to browse the publisher's Web site. It shouldn't be long before you run across a piece of code that the Web site would just love to download to your workstation PC. Otherwise, look for a Download link.

2. **When the dialog box appears warning you about downloading software, check the option to Always Trust Software From The Source.**

   Keep in mind that if the security level in place for the Web site specifies that software can be downloaded with verification, you need to change the setting in order for the confirmation dialog box to appear.

3. **Continue the download.**

4. **To verify the software publisher was added to the list of those you trust, choose Tools⇨Internet Options from IE.**

5. **Choose the Content tab and the click the Publishers button.**

   A dialog box appears on the screen similar to the one in Figure 13-7. You should see the name of the publisher in the list. You may also view the list all software publishers the browser trusts at this time.

6. **To remove a publisher from the list, select the publisher and then click Remove.**

Who's in charge? Trusted publishers or security levels?

Keep in mind that a security zone and security level setting will overrule any publisher or certificate authority that you add to your trusted list. This means that if you visit a Web site that is included in a zone whose security level calls for confirmation before signed controls are downloaded, you will be asked to confirm download even if the publisher of the software is one whose certificate you have previously installed.

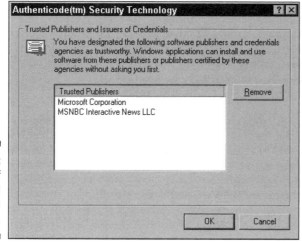

Figure 13-7: Your list of trusted software publishers.

Cookies: A Sweet Treat or Sour Candy for Security?

Web sites want visitors to be happy, and if their happiness is enhanced by a visit to the site, all the better! If visitors are happy, they might buy services or products from the site.

Characteristics of a user-friendly site (to some) include easy navigation and a recollection of who you are, if you have visited the site before, what type of information you like to look at, and any information it collected from you previously. Doing so usually means that you do not have to enter the same information every time you access the Web site. The vehicle that makes it possible for sites to remember this information is the *cookie.* A cookie is a small file placed on the browsing computer by a site that you visit. The cookie can contain any information the site wants to store in it. Again, the primary purpose for a cookie is to store information so you needn't re-supply the information every time you return to the site.

A cookie doesn't necessarily contain information you, any other program, or any other Web site can use. In fact, cookies can be coded so that only the Web site that baked the cookie can know the cookie exists and can make sense of the information in it. Not every cookie is coded, though, and some cookies contain fairly plain and easy-to-grasp information. The number of cookies that may be already downloaded to your computer right now may surprise you! Cookies are stored on an account-by-account basis in a sub-folder in the Documents and Settings folder. To see the cookies stored on your computer, as well as to see the inside of a cookie, use the Windows 2000 Search option on the Start menu to locate a file or folder named "cookies." Double-click any file the search function finds.

NTFS, which is the preferred file system (preferred by Microsoft), can be used to make sure that cookies are never created on a particular folder. Follow these steps to ensure cookies are no longer created on a workstation via Internet Explorer.

1. **Identify the folder where cookies are stored on a computer.**

2. **Display the folder using either My Computer or Windows 2000 Explorer.**

3. **Right-click the folder name and choose the Security tab.**

   The Security sheet appears.

4. **Click the Add button.**

   The Select Objects dialog box appears.

5. **Find Everyone in the list and then double-click it.**

   The Everyone group will appear in the bottom list in the Select Objects dialog box.

6. **Click OK.**

   You return to the Properties dialog box.

7. **With Everyone selected in the list, click the Deny check box for the Modify permission.**

8. **Click OK to close the dialog box.**

The ugly technical side of authenticode

This short sidebar puts the *T* in technical, so be ready! When an organization wants to make software available for download on the Internet, and that organization also wants to demonstrate its veracity, it first must acquire a certificate from a CA. This certificate is another of those special types, this one used specifically to sign software. Also, if the software is built and will be distributed using Microsoft tools, then the certificate must be one that supports Authenticode technology. Authenticode technology is Microsoft's brand of signing and verifying downloadable code. After the CA verifies that the software publisher is legit, the CA issues a certificate to the software publisher. The certificate contains, among other items, the software publisher's public key.

When the software publisher has completed the program, the publisher runs through a process that signs the software. Part of this process is to create a hash of the software developed. The hash is then encrypted with the publisher's private key. The hash, the code, the name of the algorithm used to create the hash, and the software publisher's certificate, which includes its public key, are compiled into the package of software that is distributed on the Internet.

When IE comes across downloadable code, the first thing the browser does is verify the credentials of the publisher. It does so by using the public key of the certificate authority already installed on the browser to decrypt the certificate of the publisher include in the software package. If this verification holds water, the next step is to check whether the software has been changed. The browser next decrypts the hash using the publisher's public key, which arrived at the client browser with the publisher's certificate. The client then creates a new hash against the delivered code (it knows which hashing algorithm to use because the name of the algorithm is part of the delivered code). If the new hash created matches the now decrypted code, the browser knows the software has not been tampered with.

You may be wondering about the location of the buttons, lists, and prompts that control this process. Don't bother looking. All of this happens under the hood. Phew.

Chapter 14

Keeping an Eye on IP Security

● ●

In This Chapter

▶ Becoming the first on your block to know IP Security

▶ Creating a console for IP Security work

▶ Creating an IP Security policy

▶ Defining IP Security rules

● ●

*I*f you're someone who buys the latest gadget, reads the newest book, and wears the newest style in clothes (if you truly are a computer professional, skip that last one), then IP Security is for you. IP Security is a new set of security tools you can use in Windows 2000. IP Security doesn't care about the software running on your computers or what kind of devices are connected to your network — IP Security does its work under the hood.

Finding Out about IP Security

IP Security is a new approach for securing and encrypting IP traffic. IP Security takes advantage of industry standard protocols, techniques, and so on to provide encrypted exchange between computers, routers, and just about any other devices running TCP/IP. IP Security is a full-featured security framework, not a set of tools that replaces any set of features in Windows 2000. Rather, IP Security represents another tool in the toolbox.

Disclosing the secret of IP Security

IP Security does its work at the IP layer of TCP/IP. The IP layer of TCP/IP is responsible for sending TCP/IP packets on their way and making sure that they know where they're going. Now, if you know TCP/IP, you know it's the protocol of the Internet. More importantly, TCP/IP is a protocol that enables different types of computers and operating systems to communicate with one another. Windows 2000 is one of those operating systems that makes use of TCP/IP. What all of this means is that IP Security does its work all the way down at the protocol level. You don't need to configure the applications your users use with IP Security. Your users just go about their normal business. When IP Security detects an exchange between a computer it has secured and another host, IP Security wakes up and applies the rules you have configured.

Knowing the basics about IP Security

You need to know three basic things about IP Security:

- ✔ **You've got it.** You don't need to download an "IP Security Pack" (as if one existed) from Microsoft's site on the Internet or ask your buddy for the diskette. IP Security comes along with Windows 2000, both the Server and Professional versions. Also, IP Security works with TCP/IP protocol, which you're sure to be using.

- ✔ **You make policy to control it.** IP Security is implemented through group policy. You create as many IP Security policies as you need to accommodate the different uses of hosts in your network, as well as to accommodate the different hosts outside of your network trying to access hosts inside your network.

Remember, a computer running TCP/IP with its own IP address is known as a *host*. Also, if you want to read about how group policy is applied to things in your network, take a look at Chapter 7.

- ✔ **You don't have to congratulate Bill.** Everyone loves Microsoft, but you can't give it full credit for IP Security. IP Security is being developed by the Internet Engineering Task Force (IETF). The IETF is one of the groups working toward standard ways of doing things on the Internet.

Knowing how IP Security works

You define IP Security policies to control how, when, and on whom IP Security works. An individual IP Security policy defines a number of rules, including what IP addresses to be on the lookout for, what to do if one of the packets flying through the network is either heading to or heading from one of those IP addresses, how to encrypt packets, and more. An IP Security policy will have as many rules as it needs to accommodate different scenarios, such as intra-network exchanges, or incoming packets governed by ICMP.

ICMP is the protocol used at the IP layer to report errors and deliver information to the hosts.

The most important part of the rule is the filters. The filters take a look at all the IP traffic passing through the object on which the IP Security policy is applied, such as a domain, organizational unit, domain controller, local machine, router, Internet appliance, whatever. If the packet matches any of the attributes of the filter, IP Security begins to pay attention to it. These are the filters to watch for:

- ✔ IP address of the target (where the packet is heading)
- ✔ IP address of the destination (where the packet came from)
- ✔ The IP protocol in use by the packet
- ✔ The target and destination port

IP Security filters are like parents being sure that their children don't run with the wrong crowd. Here's how: When an IP Security filter becomes interested in a packet, it will try to set up a secure environment for the packet to travel in. IP Security uses something called ISAKMP to start setting up this environment. ISAKMP stands for Internet Security Association and Key Management Protocol.

The ISAKMP protocol is used by two computers to determine how they'll communicate privately. Believe it or not, this discussion about encryption occurs publicly. ISAKMP uses Oakley to help figure out what private keys will be used to encrypt the packets that travel between the two hosts. Oakley is another protocol that specializes in figuring out private keys to use.

Oakley does not work alone. Oakley counts on Diffie-Hellman for help in determining the private key for IP Security traffic. Diffie-Hellman makes it possible for two hosts that previously knew nothing of one another to cooperatively develop their own private keys to use to encrypt packets.

The benefit of Diffie-Hellman is that the private key is never exchanged. Instead, both parties generate a random number based on a prime number each also generates. Both parties exchange this data publicly. The Diffie-Hellman protocol generates the same private key based on the random values exchanged.

In addition to the development of private keys, the negotiation between the two hosts also yields the follow decisions:

- ✔ What encryption algorithm to use (DES, 3DES, 40-bit DES, or none). If you would like more on encryption, including various encryption techniques, head back to Chapter 1.
- ✔ What integrity algorithm to use (MD5 or SHA).
- ✔ What authentication method to use (Public Key Certificate, pre-shared key, or Kerberos V5 (the Windows 2000 default).
- ✔ How complicated the key must be.

Once all the details are sorted, something called an SA is developed. *SA* stands for security association. An SA contains all the agreed upon rules for the IP Sec-controlled relationship between the hosts.

Mastering the elements of an IP Security policy rule

An IP Security policy rule is comprised of a handful of attributes. These attributes determine what IP packets the rule applies to, how the host where the policy is located communicates with the host on the other end of the packet, and more.

Authentication with IP security

Every rule in every IP Security policy has three choices for authentication:

- **Kerberos V5:** This method uses the Kerberos authentication scheme. This method makes sense if both the parties are validated on a Windows 2000 domain.

- **Public Key Certificate:** You can use a public key scheme for IP Sec authentication. You'll be asked to choose the CA you want to use to hold the public key half of the key pair.

- **Pre-Shared Key:** You won't find this method on the list of most technologically elegant solutions. Both parties decide on a string and both parties configure IP Security to use the preshared key method and the string they decide on. The string could be anything: "Mary had a Little Lamb," "How many authors does it take to change a light bulb," anything.

When you create a rule, you specify which authentication methods are valid. You can specify that all three are valid, or just one or two. You also define which methods should be attempted first, which second, and so on.

IP Security tunneling settings

IP Security supports tunneling. Tunneling involves packaging an IP packet into a new packet. The new packet contains the destination information for the packet. The most prominent application of tunneling is in virtual private networks in which network traffic uses the Internet to get from point to point.

You specify one of the following tunneling options for every IP Security rule.

- Disable tunneling for connections affected by the rule.

- Allow tunneling to an endpoint (the computer receiving the packet as opposed to the one doing the sending) defined by a DNS name. This option assumes the endpoint can be identified by a DNS name. If you select this option, you must supply the DNS name of the endpoint.

✔ Allow tunneling to the endpoint (the computer receiving the packet as opposed to the one doing the sending) identified by the IP address you supply.

IP filter list

The IP Filter list defines what IP traffic your policy will watch for. This is commonly known as packet sniffing! Congratulations, you're now doing something hackers have been doing for years! You can filter IP traffic by any of these attributes:

✔ Source address, including an IP address, a DNS name, or a subnet

✔ Destination address, including an IP address, a DNS name, or a subnet

✔ The protocol type

✔ The port number

IP filter action

The Filter Action properties of the IP Security policy rule determine what IP Security should do when a packet matches one of the filters defined in the rule. Here are your choices:

✔ Negotiate security per normal

✔ Block the passage of the packet

✔ Permit the passage of the packet

Connection type

An element of an IP Security policy rule is the connection type that the rule applies to. There are three choices.

✔ All

✔ LAN

✔ Remote

Creating an IP Security Console

If you plan to implement IPSec, you need the tools to help you build policies, filters, and more. A handy snap-in is available for you to work with IPSec. Follow these steps to create your own IP Security console:

1. **Click the Start menu, choose Run, enter MMC and then press Enter.**

   A new console window appears.

2. **Choose Console⇨Add/Remove Snap-in from the menu and then click Add when the Add/Remove Snap-in dialog box appears.**

3. **Scroll down the list of snap-ins and find IP Security Policy Management in the list; click once on it and then click Add.**

   The Select Computer dialog box appears, as shown in Figure 14-1.

4. **Click the option indicating where you want the new IP Security policy created and then click Finish.**

   To create the IP Security policy for the local computer, make sure that the Local Computer option is selected.

   To create the IP Security policy for the domain where you are logged on, click the Manage Domain Policy For This Computer's Domain option.

   To create the IP Security policy for another domain, click the Manage Domain Policy For Another Domain and then enter the name of the domain.

   Lastly, to create the IP Security policy for another computer, click the Another Computer option and then supply the name of the computer in the box provided.

5. **Click Close in the Add Standalone Snap-in dialog box and then click OK in the Add/Remove Snap-in dialog box.**

   Your console should look very similar to the one shown in Figure 14-2.

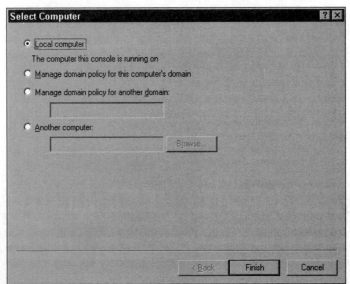

Figure 14-1:
The Select
Computer
dialog box.

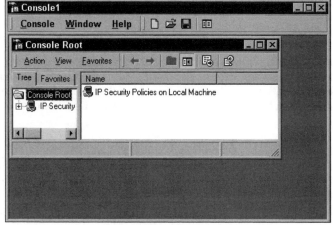

Figure 14-2:
A console
with the
IP Security
snap-in
loaded.

6. **Choose Console⇨Save As from the menu.**

   The Save As dialog box appears.

7. **Enter a name for the console, such as My Local Computer's IP Security Policy, in the File name edit box and then click the Save button.**

   Be sure that the Administrative Tools folder is selected as the target folder. By saving the console in the Administrative Tools subfolder, you can open the IP Security Policy console easily by just clicking on it on the Administrative Tools menu.

Creating a New IP Security Policy

Windows 2000 ships with a few basic IP Security policies. These policies cover fairly generic scenarios (an unsecured client, a moderately secured server, a locked-down tight server), so it's likely you'll want to create some new policies to configure IP Security just the way you like it.

Follow these steps to create brand new IP Security policy:

1. **Open a console that provides you access to IP Security policies.**

2. **Right-click anywhere in the details pane and choose Create IP Security Policy from the menu.**

   The IP Security Policy Wizard welcome screen appears.

3. **Click Next.**

   The IP Security Policy Name dialog box appears.

4. **Enter a name for your new IP Security policy.**

5. **Enter a description for the policy in the Description box.**

   If you named your IP Security policy something vague, like IPSEC1-2, then you probably should add some sort of description for the policy.

6. **If you want the hosts for which you're creating the policy to respond to requests for security from remote computers with a default rule when you either have not created any other rules or none of them apply, check the Activate The Default Response Rule option.**

7. **Click Next.**

   If you checked the option to use a default rule, you next have an option to define this rule; if you didn't, skip to Step 11. The Default Response Rule Authentication Method dialog box should be on the screen, as shown in Figure 14-3.

8. **Click the authentication method you want to use as a default.**

   If you choose the second option, Use a certificate from this certificate authority, you must select the CA you want to use. Click the browse button and then select the certificate from the CA you want to use. Then click OK.

   If you choose the third option, enter the string that you and the other party using IP Security have agreed on.

9. **Click Next.**

   The Completing the IP Security Policy Wizard dialog box appears.

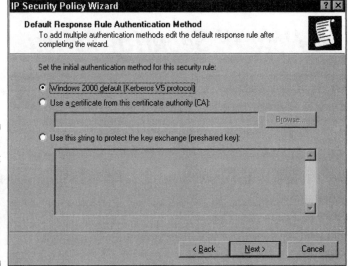

Figure 14-3:
The Default
Response
Rule
Authen-
tication
Method
dialog box.

10. **If you want to add rules for the new policy, be sure the Edit properties option is checked; if you want to take a break and define rules for the policy later, clear the check box.**

    This way, you can create rules for the policy right away.

11. **Click Finish.**

    If you checked the Edit properties option, the Properties dialog box for the policy you just created appears on the screen. You can find help defining the options for the policy in the next section of the chapter.

Changing the Rules of an IP Security Policy

Even in IP Security the rules can change. Follow these steps to add to or modify the rule of a policy.

1. **Open a console that provides you access to IP Security Policies.**

2. **Right-click the policy you want to edit and then choose Properties from the menu.**

    The Properties dialog box appears, as shown in Figure 14-4.

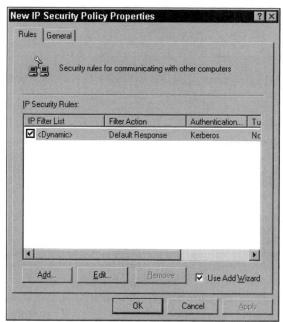

Figure 14-4:
The IP
Security
Policy
Properties
dialog box.

3. **To disable any of the rules in the list, clear the check box next to the name of the rule.**

4. **To edit a rule in the list, click the rule and then click the Edit button.**

   The Edit Rule Properties dialog box appears. The Security Methods tab should be active, as shown in Figure 14-5.

   You can capture security options into something call methods. You change the order of methods the IP Security rule uses to attempt to negotiate with.

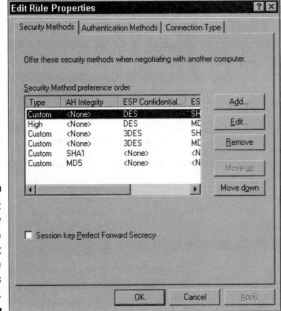

Figure 14-5:
The Security
Methods tab
of the Edit
Rule
Properties
dialog box.

5. **Click the method and then click Move Up or Move Down.**

   You can change the settings for a method by clicking the Edit button, and you can create a new method by clicking the Add button.

6. **Click the Authentication Methods tab to specify what authentication methods are attempted and in what order.**

7. **Click the Connection Type tab to specify the type of connection that the rule should be applied to.**

8. **Click OK to save the changes to the rule.**

   You should be at the Properties dialog box for the policy.

9. **To add a new rule, click the Add button.**

You may want to clear the Use Add Wizard check box to follow the next few steps.

You must define an IP filter for a rule.

10. **Click the IP Filter tab and select one of the existing tabs by clicking in the option circle or click the Add button to create a new IP filter.**

    Be sure that you select the filter after you create it.

    You must select an action to match the filter you just created.

11. **Click the Filter Action tab to select what you need IP Security to do once it captures a connection that matches your filter; click the existing actions or create a new one by clicking the Add button.**

    If you do not want help from the wizard in creating a new filter, be sure to clear the Use Add Wizard check box.

12. **If this rule will allow tunneling, click the Tunnel Setting tab and then specify the endpoint IP address of the tunnel.**

13. **If you want to use an authentication method other than Kerberos, click the Authentication Methods tab; add another authentication method by clicking the Add button.**

    You can also change the order in which IP Security attempts to authenticate the other host by clicking the Move Up and Move Down button.

14. **If you want the rule to apply only to LAN connections or only to Remote access connections, click the Connection Type tab and choose the appropriate option.**

15. **Click Close when you have completed configuring the new rule.**

16. **Click Close.**

Assigning the Policy

IP Security policy won't work until you assign it. This means that after all the work you put into creating a new policy, you won't reap its benefits until you click your mouse button two more times.

Follow these steps to assign a policy:

1. **Open a console that provides you access to IP Security Policies.**

2. **Right-click the policy and then choose Assign from the menu.**

    You'll notice that the Policy Assigned field in the Details pane of the IP Security console you're using changes to Yes.

Part V

The Part of Tens

The 5th Wave   By Rich Tennant

"If it works, it works. I've just never seen network cabling connected with Chinese handcuffs before!"

In this part . . .

The old saying is that too much of anything is no good. Well, as long as you don't think that ten is too much, then start turning pages! You find snips, nuggets, plans, and procedures on four (six less than the recommended dosage) cool topics.

Do folks in your organization travel? Woops! Do they travel for business and take portable computers with them? If so, have I got a ten for you!

Do you want your organization to make the top ten list of most technologically sophisticated companies when it comes to security? Then the ten steps provided to help set up smart cards is recommended reading.

Do you think dealing with security is important? Popular opinion says the answer is yes, so the chapter on the ten elements to a good corporate security in this part is worth looking at.

Chapter 15

Ten Intelligent Steps for Setting Up Smart Cards

In This Chapter
▶ Discovering why smart cards are the coolest new things
▶ Mastering the steps for rolling out smart cards

Smart cards aren't just a great option for Windows 2000 network authentication; they also look cool, and users look cool using them. It's likely that your organization will experience high turnover after you roll out smart cards as many of your employees leave your company for positions as paid extras in high-tech spy movies!

You can increase your overall network security, as well as the impression other persons have of your network, by moving to a smart card architecture. Of course, looking good isn't important (kind of), being secure is. This chapter takes you through the smart card rollout steps.

Step 1: Find Out about Smart Cards

Smart cards are the newest and easily the most impressive components to come down the Windows 2000 security highway in a long time. Using a card no larger than a credit card, users can authenticate themselves on Windows 2000 networks simply by entering their card into a reader and supplying a PIN number. Here's why everyone (especially me) is so excited about smart cards.

✔ Face it; user IDs and passwords are a weak combination for authenticating users. A user ID and password are pieces of information; a smart card is a real thing that you can touch, hold, and protect (and lose; that's why PIN numbers are used, too). If someone can figure out your user ID and password, they're in! It's a lot harder to get someone's smart card.

✔ Users don't *know* when they have *lost* their user ID and password. This means it's not obvious to a user when someone else has discovered (or obtained) her user ID and password. This could be an extremely damaging scenario as a person who has obtained another's user ID and password can masquerade as that user as long as he likes or until he is caught. This contrasts with smart cards, with which a user knows right away when she has lost her source of authentication.

✔ Password exchange is weaker than the private/public key scheme used by smart cards and digital certificates. If you need to know more about private and public key schemes, refer to Chapter 1.

✔ While smart cards in Windows 2000 contain a certificate that authenticates them on Windows 2000 networks today, there's no telling what the cards will store tomorrow. For example, a user's credit card information might be stored on the card, enabling her to use the card for personal transactions, as well as for network authentication. In addition, the card might store other personal information about the bearer, such as information HR normally maintains.

Step 2: Choose and Buy Smart Card Readers

You're going to need the devices that users actually insert their smart cards into. You're going to need one smart card reader for every user you want to arm with smart cards, as well as one reader for each computer that will make smart cards.

Keep in mind that readers available will be different for laptop computers than for desktop computers. Be sure that you get an accurate count of the readers you'll need of each type.

Table 15-1 shows some of the smart card readers supported by Windows 2000, but certainly more and more manufacturers make compatible smart card readers all the time.

Table 15-1	Smart Card Readers	
Manufacturer	*Model Name*	*Interface*
Bull CP8	Smart TLP3	RS-232
Gemplus	GCR410P	RS-232
Gemplus	GPR400	PCMCIA

Manufacturer	Model Name	Interface
Litronic	220P	RS-232
Rainbow Technologies	3531	RS-232
SCM Microsystems	SwapSmart	RS-232
SCM Microsystems	SwapSmart	PCMCIA

A few more notes about buying smart card readers:

✔ Check the Hardware Compatibility List (HCL) that ships with Windows 2000. This list shows every single device that is compatible with Windows 2000. You can find the list on the CD that ships with Windows 2000, as well as on Microsoft's Web site (www.microsoft.com). If the smart card reader you want to buy is not on the list, you should check with the manufacturer whose device you're interested in to see whether it's supported.

✔ More and more PCs are being shipped with smart card support. Be sure that there are no compatibility issues between the support provided by the PC and the readers you plan to buy.

Step 3: Choose and Buy Smart Cards

You need to buy the actual smart cards that users will use. Two types of smart cards are supported automatically by Windows 2000:

✔ Gemplus GemSAFE

✔ Schlumberger Cryptoflex

In addition, other manufacturers can make cards available by providing the required drivers for their cards. Before acquiring cards from someplace other than these two sources, check with the manufacturer to be sure that the software for Windows 2000 is available.

Step 4: Install Your Smart Card Readers

The smart card devices Windows 2000 supports are Plug and Play compliant. This means that you should shut down the computer where you're installing the reader, install the reader according to the manufacturer's instruction, and then power that computer back up. Windows 2000 should automatically detect the device, know what the device is, and then automatically load the software for the device.

✔ You may need to insert the CD or diskette provided by the manufacturer, so pay attention to messages that may appear on the screen.

✔ Windows 2000 may start the Add/Remove Hardware wizard if it cannot figure out that the device you attached is a smart card reader.

✔ You may need to manually start the Add/Remove Hardware wizard to install the driver if Windows 2000 does not detect the smart card reader at all.

Step 5: Prepare Your Certificate Authority to Issue the Smart Card Certificates

You need to create a certificate template for smart cards. This way, your certificate authority (CA) can issue certificates for use on smart cards when a smart card needs to be created. If you haven't configured a CA yet for your domain, you need to do so. If you would like some advice on setting up a CA in your domain, refer to Chapter 10. In addition, part of the preparation of your CA to issue smart card certificates is to enable your CA to issue the certificate necessary for the administrators to, in turn, request certificates on the part of smart card users.

Here is how to prepare your CA to issue smart card certificates:

1. **Open a console that gives you access to the Certificates Authority snap-in.**

2. **Open the certificate authority item and then open the CA that you want to use to issue certificates for smart cards.**

   To do so, click the + button next to the name of the CA.

3. **Right-click the Policy Settings item and then choose New➪ Certificate to Issue from the menu.**

   The Select Certificate Template dialog box appears, as shown in Figure 15-1. The dialog box shows the different certificate templates your certificate authority can issue.

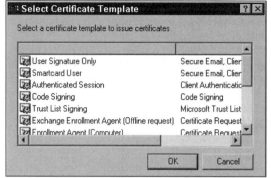

4. Click Smartcard Logon in the list and then click OK.

These steps don't result in the creation of a certificate, rather a template for a certificate used when a certificate of the Smartcard logon type is requested.

You can also choose Smartcard user as a certificate template. This enables the smart card to be used for e-mail signing, as well.

This next step doesn't necessarily prepare your certificate authority to issue smart card certificates as the heading of this section suggests. Rather, it prepares the CA to issue certificates to users who will, in turn, issue smart cards.

5. Right-click the Policy Settings item and then choose New⇨ Certificate to Issue from the menu.

The Select Certificate Template dialog box appears again.

6. Click Enrollment Agent in the list and then click OK.

You're done. You can close the console by choosing Console⇨Exit.

Step 6: Setting up a Smart Card Issuing Station

Unless you want complete network access anarchy, you should probably control the generation of smart cards. Generating smart cards shouldn't be handled at one of those self-service stations. Rather, this should be a very controlled, secured process. With that in mind, an important step in rolling out smart cards is to prepare the station where smart cards will be issued.

This station can be nothing more than a computer with someone manning it at certain times when users can get a new smart card or where someone from HR can acquire a smart card for a new hire.

You'll probably use one or two computers to issue smart cards. You can call these machines *smart card issuing stations*. Actually, you can call these computers anything you like, but I needed a name for the heading of this step. You can use a dedicated computer to issue smart cards, or you can use a machine that is being used for some other task in your organization, like a file server or the administrator's desktop machine.

Considering how busy this machine will be, from issuing smart cards when you roll them out for the first time to responding to requests for new cards for new employees and from users who lose theirs, you should consider a dedicated machine or two for this job.

1. **Install a smart card reader on the computer you plan to use as a smart card issuing station.**

2. **Log on to the computer with the account that will be used to issue smart cards.**

   Keep in mind the relative significance of this account. The user who has the rights to issue smart cards has basically the tools necessary to access your network from any workstation.

3. **Open a console that provides you access to the Certificates - Current user snap-in.**

4. **Open Certificates - Current User\Personal.**

   You can open these items by clicking the + button next to the item.

5. **Right-click Certificates and then choose Request New Certificate from the menu.**

   The Certificate Request Wizard starts.

6. **Click Next to advance past the welcome screen.**

   The Certificate Template dialog box appears.

7. **Click Enrollment Agent in the list and then click Next.**

   The Certificate Friendly Name and Description dialog box appears.

8. **Enter a name for the certificate in the Friendly Name edit box.**

   It's your choice as to the name for your certificate. You will probably want to use a name that is descriptive of what the certificate does.

9. **Review the information that will be used to create the certificate and click Finish if the information is correct.**

   A dialog box appears with three buttons: Install Certificate, Cancel, and View Certificate.

10. Click the Install Certificate Wizard button.

The Confirmation dialog box appears.

11. Click OK.

Step 7: Burn and Issue Smart Cards

Okay. This is the step you've been waiting for! Here's how to actually create a smart card. Don't worry, you won't have to wear one of those protective space suits worn by persons working in clean rooms where computer chips are developed, nor will the users you're burning the cards for have to recite a pledge or oath (unless you play a trick on them and force them to recite some idiotic pledge). To create a smart card for logon and client authentication, you just need

✔ A real Windows 2000 account for the user who will be assigned the card.

✔ Access to the machine where the smart card will be burned.

✔ Successful completion of Steps 1 through 6 in this chapter.

Here's how to burn and issue a smart card for logon and client authentication:

1. Log on to the domain where the CA and the user account to receive the smart card are located.

2. Start Internet Explorer and access the Certification Services Web page.

This page normally has the following URL:

www.*name_of_web_server*.com/Certsrv

where name_of_web_server is the web server running on the domain. The page should look like the one shown in Figure 15-2.

3. Click the Request A Certificate option and then click Next.

The page appears in which you select whether to issue a request for a User Certificate or whether to make an advanced request.

4. Click the Advanced request option and then click Next.

The page appears where you select the type of advanced certificate request you want to make.

5. Click the option Request a Certificate For A Smart Card On Behalf Of Another User Using The Smart Card Enrollment Station and then click Next.

Figure 15-2:
You request
enrollment
certificates
from a web
server
running on
your domain
(and from
a pretty
boring Web
page).

6. **Select Smartcard Logon from the Certificate Template drop-down list.**

   This tells the CA what kind of certificate you need to issue.

7. **Select the CA from which the certificates will be generated from the Certification Authority drop-down list.**

   No surprise here. This is the CA you have been using to create the enrollment certificate template, as well as the smart card logon certificate template.

8. **Select the type of smart card you are creating from the Cryptographic Service Provider drop-down list.**

9. **Click the Select Certificate button.**

   The Select Certificate dialog box appears.

10. **Select the Enrollment Agent certificate that will sign the smart card certificate and then click OK.**

    The user name associated with the certificate you choose appears in the Administrator Signing Certificate box.

11. **Click the Select User button.**

    Not surprisingly, the Select User dialog box appears.

12. **Select the user account for which the smart card will be produced from the list and then click OK.**

    The Select User dialog disappears, and the user you selected appears in the User to Enroll box.

13. **Click Enroll.**

14. **Follow the instructions to insert a smart card into the reader and also to enter a PIN number.**

    If the card has already been used, you will be prompted whether to replace the certificate on the card with the certificate you just created. Also, the prompt that appears to enter the PIN will vary based on the Cryptographic Service Provider.

15. **Test the card!**

    Don't wait for the user to report a problem with the card. First, take the card out of the reader. Then, log off of the computer where you created the card (you don't have to shut it down). When the Windows 2000 logon screen appears, slide the card into the reader and enter the PIN when you're asked. The logon process should start for the user.

Step 8: Set the Option to Require Smart Cards (Where Appropriate)

You might not allow certain users to log on to your network without smart cards. This might be a good solution for contractors who work at your office for a short amount of time. You might issue a smart card (as well as create a user account) to a contractor when they start an assignment for you and hold payment until they return the smart card!

You can find the option to require smart card authentication on the Properties sheet for the user account. Follow these steps to set this option:

1. **Log on to a domain controller using an account with sufficient rights to administer users.**

2. **Open the Active Directory Users and Computers snap-in.**

To start the Active Directory Users and Computers snap-in, click the Start menu and then choose Programs⇨Administrative Tools⇨ Active Directory Users and Computers.

3. **Open the domain where the user account is located.**

   To open the domain, click the + button next to the name of the domain.

4. **Open the Users items and locate the account.**

5. **Right-click the account when you find it and then choose Properties from the menu.**

   The account's Properties dialog box appears.

6. **Click the Account tab.**

   The Account properties sheet appears.

7. **Scroll down the list of items in the Account options list until you see the Smart card is required for interactive logon option; check that option and then click OK.**

Exception time! Certain tasks cannot be performed by users who log on with smartcards:

✔ Join a computer to a domain.

✔ Domain and domain controller maintenance, such as promoting a computer to an Active Directory domain controller.

Be sure that this option to only allow authentication of certain users with their smart cards is not set for users who perform these tasks, such as members of the Administrators or DomainAdmins group.

Step 9: Show Your Users How to Log On with a Smart Card

The easiest step in the entire process of rolling out smart cards is showing users how to use them. A user simply inserts his card into his reader and enters his PIN when prompted. That's it. You might also provide the users with guidelines as to their use:

✔ Tell them what to do if they lose their cards.

✔ Remind them not to write down their PINs.

Step 10: Protect the Certificate Template

If your organization is taking the time and expense to roll out smart cards to beef up authentication, you should probably be sure that the entire process and infrastructure around smart cards in your organization is secure, too. One element of this is to be sure that only the administrators or the group you designate have the rights to generate certificates for smart cards.

1. **Log on to a domain controller using an account with sufficient rights to administer users.**

2. **Open the Active Directory Sites and Services snap-in.**

   You can find the Active Directory Sites and Services snap-in on the Administrative Tools menu, which hangs from the Programs menu.

3. **If you do not see the Services item in the tree, choose View⇨ Show Services Node from the menu.**

   The Services tree appears.

4. **Open Services\Public Key Services and then click Certificate Templates.**

   You screen should look something like the one shown in Figure 15-3.

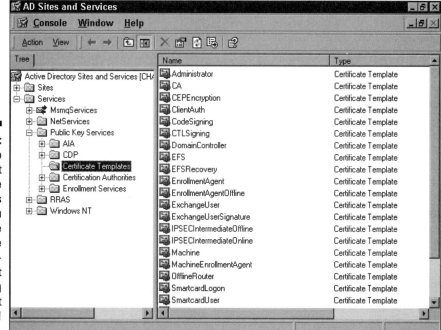

Figure 15-3: Be sure to select Certificate Templates so that you can be sure that the entire organization isn't distributing smart cards!

5. **Find SmartcardUser in the list of certificate templates, right-click it, and then choose Properties from the menu.**

   The Properties sheet for the certificate template appears.

6. **Click the Security tab.**

   The security sheet appears.

7. **Inspect the permissions.**

   Be sure that only the appropriate users have the Enroll permission selected. It would make sense that only members of the Administrators and DomainAdmins group would have this right. Also, be sure that the Allow inheritable permissions option at the bottom of the dialog box is cleared. This way, the permissions for this template would not change should the permissions for the Certificate template container be mistakenly changed by someone.

Chapter 16

Ten (Or so) Pieces of Advice for the Secure Road Warrior

● ●

In This Chapter

▶ Discovering the art of trust on the road

▶ Checking great gadgets to help secure your laptop

▶ Avoiding the security-stop laptop-grab scheme

▶ Securing hard drives

▶ Shopping for a new computer bag

● ●

*A*ll rules seem to fly out the window when corporate travelers travel. Besides eating all the wrong foods and not exercising, corporate travelers are tough to reach on the road, they don't sleep well, they don't have their typical access to the corporate network (for some), and their office transforms into a virtual location defined by wherever they're working. The one element of a corporate person's life that shouldn't change on the road is the attitude about security and protecting corporate computer assets.

In fact, not only should the same security-minded practices be maintained, but the security antennae should be even more sensitive. Why? Well, you kind of know the persons in your organization — heck, someone had to hire them. But you have no idea who you'll meet on the road.

If you've got a company-full, an office-full, a department-full, or just one or two folks who travel, pass these tips their way. Doing so might save your company some insurance dollars — and, most importantly, save potentially sensitive company information from falling into the hands of the wrong persons.

What about airborne bio-breaks (and I have to submit my budget when I land)?

Say that you're slaving away on your budget on your laptop computer flying from city A to city B. And say that you'd like to take a break. What do you do with the laptop? If you don't want to carry your laptop with you to the airplane lavatory, do the next best thing. Power down, remove the hard drive (most laptops allow you to pop out the hard drive), and bring it with you. There's a chance you'll lose the laptop, but there's no chance of losing the data.

Trust No One

Most travelers think that fellow travelers are the most honest persons around. Travelers always lean over to the person standing or sitting next to them and say, "Hey, can you keep on eye on this?" Unfortunately for road warriors, *this* is sometimes a laptop computer, and the person they have entrusted their *this* with they have known (if sitting next to someone qualifies as knowing someone) less than a few minutes. This doesn't seem too great an idea. Say that the person you have decided to trust really can be trusted. What happens if that person becomes distracted? Yeah, it's too bad, but trust is a valuable commodity on the road, and you should spend it very wisely.

Guard that Screen

If you travel alone, then it's a safe bet you won't know the person sitting next to you. If you're not careful, though, that person will get to know you very quickly by peeking over your shoulder as you work at your laptop. Consider purchasing a screen guard that permits only the operator of the PC to see what's on the screen. You can find guards that act like glare filters, or you can find devices that look like hoods, preventing everyone but Superman the ability to see what you're working on. Be sure that you find a guard that matches your screen size.

Don't Delay at X-Ray

When you travel with your laptop, stay alert at those airport x-ray machines. There are countless stories of travelers losing their laptops to well orchestrated schemes when their laptops are passed through the airport x-ray machines. No, the laptops do not magically disappear or change into elephants like at a magic show.

Here's how the scheme works: There are usually two persons working together to separate you from your laptop. Somehow, you are identified as a target, probably because you are obviously carrying a laptop computer in some sort of travel bag. As you near the x-ray machine, predator No. 1 passes through the security booth before you. As soon as you place your laptop on the conveyor belt, predator No. 2 slides through the x-ray machine *just in front of you,* but does so with something in his or her pocket that is bound to set off the alarm. As you wait for the security guards to check out predator No. 2, predator No. 1 grabs your laptop from the other side of the x-ray machine.

Sounds like a smooth scheme. Here's how to avoid it. Refuse to place your laptop on the belt until there is less traffic around the conveyor belt. Wave people past you until the coast is clear. If you are late for a flight or the line to pass through security is long, ask one of the guards to catch the bag as it comes through.

Protect It Like You're Going to Lose It

Face it. A laptop has a much greater chance of disappearing than a desktop computer. I know desktop footprints are getting smaller, but I can't remember the last desktop monster that could fit in my briefcase or knapsack. With that in mind, prepare as if someone is going to grab your laptop. Here are some tips:

- ✔ **Install software that password-protects the laptop at startup.** This way, even if your laptop does get stolen, the stealers will have to get past the password-prompt to use the PC. Many times, a password feature is built into the BIOS of a computer. If you're not sure whether this feature is available, either check the documentation shipped with the computer, or watch the messages that appear on the screen as your computer boots. You should see instructions on how to start the setup program for the BIOS. Start the setup program and see whether you can locate a password feature.

- ✔ **Backup before you leave.** If you think you're going to lose your data, be sure that you have a backup copy.

- ✔ **Record serial numbers and other details.** If your machine does disappear, at least you'll have all the details available for your conversation with the police and insurance company.

Secure Those Removable Hard Drives

Most laptop computers let you remove the hard drive. What happens, though, if that hard drive falls into the wrong hands? Laptop hard drives are small enough these days that they can be yanked out of a computer and dropped into a shirt pocket in seconds.

Now, if the assumption is made that the operating system on the drive is secure — meaning you must log on to Windows 2000 to access the drive and that the drive is formatted with NTFS — then the only way the thief can see the contents of the drive is to access it from a computer booted with another drive. Many laptop computers allow you to load two hard drives at once. To keep the data on your drive secret even when it is accessed from another drive, use the encrypting file system (EFS) features. The EFS secures files and folders on your drive, and only the account that secured the data in the first place can decrypt them. While using the EFS is a good idea for any computer user, it's a great idea for anyone traveling with their data.

If you're interested in more information on EFS, refer to Chapter 5.

Avoid the Cube of Risk

Practice safe computing wherever you go, even if the place you go is one of your company's local offices (not local to you). You'll most likely be dropped into a cube, which means no door, no privacy, no nothing. You might feel at home because you're in one of your company's buildings, but you're still kind of a visitor in a strange land. Be sure to use a password-protected screen-saver, protect your laptop if you're away from it for a while, and so on, while you're visiting remote offices.

Dump the Fancy Computer Bag

You might get advice out there that says always pack your laptop in a strong sturdy bag that is designed to house and protect your laptop. Well, nothing sends the "I HAVE AN EXPENSIVE LAPTOP" message louder than a full-featured, no-frills-missing, super-Gore-Tex-lunar-padded-duro-leather-aero-cushioned laptop bag. If the laptop is small enough, consider carting it around in a regular briefcase. This way, it's a bit less obvious that you're carrying a laptop. This solution doesn't necessarily eliminate you as a target; you just become a less attractive target.

Go Shopping for Gadgets

Every day more and more cool security gadgets for laptops show up for sale. One of the most interesting types of gadgets is a two-piece alarm system. One unit is kept in your computer bag, the other component in your pocket. As long as the two components stay within 50 feet of each other, everything is okay. The moment the two are separated by more than 50 feet, a screeching alarm sounds from the component in your computer world.

Go Shopping for More Gadgets

Once you have reached your destination, you can ensure that your laptop stays at that destination using a locking gadget for your laptop. These gadgets attach one end of an indestructible cable to your laptop, usually with glue or to existing screw holes on your PC. The other end of the cable has a loop and lock that lets you attach it to anything, like a chair or table.

Pack one of these into your travel bag and use it in your hotel room when you leave your laptop there. Though it makes sense to hide your laptop in a drawer, if you must leave your laptop out, secure it to a table or the bed. The person who cleans your room might be a bit inconvenienced, but not as badly as you'll be if your laptop is stolen.

Another cool class of gadgets is those that protect your floppy or CD-ROM drives. These key-lock devices attach to the actual slot where you insert your disk. Without the key, the CD or floppy drive is unusable.

You can find dozens of examples of these gadgets on the Internet:

✔ www.kensington.com
✔ www.secure-it.com
✔ www.laptopguardian.com
✔ www.isecure.com
✔ www.pcguardian.com

Know that Event Logs and Audits Aren't Just for Administrators

Be sure that you use the same great security practices on the road and with your laptop as you do at the office and on your desktop machine. One of these practices should be to do a regular survey of the event viewer in Windows 2000.

- ✔ Create a folder structure where you keep your work files. Then, apply auditing to those folders. This way, you can focus your auditing activities on just a small portion of your hard drive, rather than the entire hard drive.

- ✔ Audit all the typical security events, such as:
    - logon
    - logoff
    - system startup
    - failed logon

For lots of information about event auditing, refer to Chapter 11.

Chapter 17

Ten Questions You Might Ask about Firewalls

*T*he Internet world is filled with *FAQs* (frequently asked questions). A FAQ is usually a list of questions (and answers) about a topic that the author either finds interesting or has been assigned to write about. The idea of a FAQ is to provide a foundation of information for the reader about the topic. It is not clear whether the questions answered here have been asked frequently, so this chapter might not be a FAQ. Regardless, you can still get a baseline of information about firewalls in this chapter. If your organization or users have a presence on the Internet, you should consider how to protect yourself from the Internet threat with a firewall.

What Is a Firewall?

An attempt to define a *firewall* usually attracts analogies the way food attracts ants at a picnic. Here are some of the most popular analogies for a firewall:

- ✔ A firewall is the security checkpoint of your network.
- ✔ A firewall is like a dam at a hydroelectric water plant.
- ✔ A firewall is like the border control for a country.
- ✔ A firewall is like the security guard in the lobby of your building.

> ✔ A firewall is like a special kind of wall in a structure that keeps a fire from spreading to other parts of the structure. Woops! That's the real definition of a firewall, though not in the context of computers — sorry!

Okay. Enough with the analogies.

A firewall ultimately is a piece of software. The software monitors traffic into and out of your network to and from the Internet. Based on rules set up by someone important in your organization, certain data is allowed in, and certain data is allowed out. A good firewall also will keep a record of the comings and goings so that you can review who's been in and out of your network, as well as who tried to get out and wasn't allowed and who tried to come in and had the door slammed in his face.

Some of the better firewalls will do your work for you. Yeah! For example, a firewall might actively watch the traffic on your network for suspicious activity. If it detects something peculiar, it might record some information and then pull the plug.

How Are Firewalls Used in Real Life?

Here are a few examples of how organizations use firewalls. These are real examples. The names have been changed to protect the vigilant.

> ✔ Restrict users' access to outlawed Internet sites.
>
> ✔ Deny inbound e-mail from unknown Internet hosts. (Your organization can create procedures that register external suites to allow inbound e-mail from partners and so on.)
>
> ✔ Deny FTP connections to your network.
>
> ✔ Deny FTP connections.
>
> ✔ Deny inbound connections of any type from unknown hosts.
>
> ✔ Allow or deny specific TCP/IP services or applications, such as FTP, Telnet, HTTP, X Windows, and so on.

How Do I Know whether I Need a Firewall?

Good question. The first thing to do to find out whether you really need a firewall is to first determine that you definitely do not need a firewall. This should be quick:

✔ If you're not running the TCP/IP protocol on your network, you can skip the rest of this chapter. Actually, you can probably skip the rest of this book.

✔ If the Internet isn't a part of your organization, then you probably won't be too concerned about your threat from the Internet. Do not pass Go, do not collect $200.

So, now that it's been established that you might need a firewall, consider these questions to help you make your decision.

✔ What would happen if someone were able to sneak onto your network? What is the value of your electronic assets? Perhaps first, figure out what *are* your electronic assets. What does your organization store online, such as on an intranet site, and how attractive is it to persons outside of your organization?

✔ Do you think you're at risk? Just because you're a nonprofit organization, for example, does not mean that you're not at risk. Sometimes, the attraction in breaking into your network is in the challenge, not the result. How would your organization react if your Web site were defaced?

✔ What would the impact be if your network were down for a few hours, or a few days? A firewall can help be sure that your network is not susceptible to denial-of-service attacks, which could bring down your network. If you would like to read about types of threats, check out Chapter 1.

✔ What does your organization think of its persons browsing the Internet? Does your organization mind if users browse to find out your or another company's stock price? How about online job search sites? How about sites that some employees might consider objectionable? A firewall can help shoot down access to these sites.

How Long Does It Take to Set Up a Firewall?

The initial setup time for a firewall, which includes the time to take it out of the box (if it came in one), can vary based on a few things.

✔ Naturally, you probably want to take time to test your firewall. Heck, you might even put together a project plan to manage the entire process of acquiring, setting up, testing, and deploying your firewall!

✔ What kind of firewall are you putting up? If the firewall is software based, then you could have the system up and running in as little as one hour. If your new firewall involves using a new computer, then you need to consider the time to acquire the equipment, install the network cards, install the operating system, and so on.

Considering all this, you might reserve about one week's worth of man-hours to simply get the firewall up and running. Consider as much time as you need to then test it, tweak it, develop policy about it, and inform your users about it.

Does Using a Firewall Mean That I Do Not Have to Worry about Network Security?

Nope. In fact, definitely nope. A firewall addresses just one component of your security. You need to think of a firewall as part of your entire security picture, not just one color or one stroke.

✔ A firewall won't protect your network from infection by a computer virus. If a virus attached to a message hits your network from an approved site, there's not much you can do about it (except hope your antivirus software is working).

✔ There's an old expression that goes like this: "If the barn door is never closed, don't bother making keys for the cows." Perhaps you've heard that expression. This means that you need to be sure that remote users practice safe computing from their remote connections. If users forget to log off from your network when they wander from their laptop, or if your users allow snoops to observe them as they log on, then the best firewall will do you no good. Be sure to give the firewall a chance to work by locking down every type of remote access to your network.

✔ Lastly, any security risk that exists inside your network walls won't be addressed by a firewall. If you have lapses in your NTFS permissions, weak password policies, and the like, your network will be compromised from the inside, not just from the outside.

Are There Different Kinds of Firewalls?

Yes, most industry smarty-pants would probably agree that there are five different types of firewalls.

✔ **Packet filter:** Data on TCP/IP travels in packets. A bunch of data sent along TCP/IP, such as a message or a Web page, is broken into packets. Each packet contains a destination address, a source address, and a port. The source address says where the data came from, the destination address says where it's going, and the port says what service will be using the data. A *packet filtering firewall* can look at the address of a packet headed for your network and reject it, such as if it's coming from a restricted Internet site, such as one of the spicier cyber-locales. A packet filtering firewall also can inspect the destination address of data heading out of your network and stop it, such as if it were headed to one your competitors' Internet sites. This kind of firewall also can discard any kind of packet headed for a particular service.

A packet filter firewall might also be capable of redirection. For example, all incoming IP traffic, regardless of the destination address, might be routed to a special e-mail server set up where you can inspect messages that arrive. The workstation might be quarantined.

✔ **Proxy server:** A *proxy server* is your network's emissary to the Internet. As hosts on your network head out to the Internet, the proxy server first inspects the request, and if the request is appropriate, the proxy server makes the request for the host. This way, the Internet isn't able to see details about your network by inspecting the individual host's request.

Certain proxy servers can do more for your network than just provide security. For example, a proxy server can save the content of a particular Web site visited by someone on your network. The proxy server then sends the cached version of the content to subsequent visitors to the site from your network. The result? Great speed for all browsers except for the first one to a site.

✔ **Application gateway:** The name of this firewall is descriptive of how it does its job. A firewall might be in the form of an application that serves as the gateway between your network and the Internet. An *application gateway firewall* works both sides of the fence. It receives data from your network and the Internet, gives the data the once-over, and then sends the data on its way as if it came from the application. This solution provides great control in that the application can inspect the entire request, whether it be an e-mail message, Web page, or something else, not just the IP addresses and the port.

The complaint that you'll hear most often about application gateways is about their performance. Considering the work an application gateway performs, your network performance will take a hit.

One last point. Keep in mind that the application gateway you put up must be able to support every application you want to support through your firewall. For example, say that you want your users to be able to hit FTP sites on the Internet. Be sure that the firewall you get supports FTP.

✔ **Circuit-level gateway:** This type of firewall inspects data at the TCP level as it flies by. TCP is one component of . . . that's right, TCP/IP. Any application that works TCP to TCP, such as TELNET, would be approved. Because the applications operate only at the TCP level, the data exchange can proceed securely. Any application that attempts to work outside of TCP is dropped.

✔ **Stateful inspection:** The stateful inspection firewall uses a long memory to allow and deny connection to the Internet. This type of firewall remembers characteristics of hosts on the Internet your network users try to connect to. When the response comes back from the Internet, if those characteristics do not match what the firewall already knows about the host, the connection is dropped.

The best characteristic about stateful inspection is speed. But, faster is not always better. The cost of the speed is the inspection of the data as it passes through the firewall. You might consider matching a stateful inspection firewall with a small solution that handles packet filtering, too.

Is a Firewall Really Just a Computer?

Yes and no. In most cases, a firewall is nothing more than a PC with firewall software installed. To be honest, machines running operating system other than Windows 2000 certainly exist, especially running firewall applications, but I suspect your interest is in Windows 2000.

Routers can also perform firewall functions, so, depending on your definition of computer, the answer to the question of this section might be no. Not sure about routers? A *router* is a kind of network black box that sends network data packets along to their correct target location.

Firewall appliances are beginning to show up on the market, too. A firewall appliance is not something that protects your network and makes ice. Rather, a firewall appliance is a ready-to-go, turnkey machine that does the firewall work for you.

Can a Firewall Be Beat?

Did man walk on the moon? Did someone break Roger Maris' single-season home run record? Did we find out who shot J.R.? Anything is possible, including breaking through a firewall; the issue really is how much work one is willing to put into the breakthrough before they pursue another way in.

What's the No. 1 Complaint about Firewalls?

Firewalls are the big bully of the network, but you can't ask an older brother (unless he's a network administrator) to protect you from a firewall. And that's the problem with firewalls. They bully your users.

If the firewall on your network keeps your users from browsing to sites with off-limit content, your users might not be able to get to sites that might use words or phrases typically used in off-limit sites, though in an acceptable context. For example, say that your organization has determined that computer firewalls is an illegal, offensive, and outlawed type of content, and that your firewall prevents users from browsing to sites with content about computer firewalls. It's likely that your users will not be able to view content about firewalls of any type, such as those used to protect structures from fires.

Here's a bonus. The No. 2 complaint you might hear from users is about performance. Depending on the firewall you choose, the number, and complexity of rules you create, users might notice slower performance connecting to the Internet at the office than at home with their DSL or cable modem connection. Be ready for users to complain about speed. Your response to these complaints should be to suggest to users that they spend the time lost waiting to connect to the Internet in contemplation about ways to make the office a more tolerable and loving place to work.

Is There Anything Else I Should Think about Once I Get This Crazy Firewall Up?

You feel good. You've installed your firewall. You probably tested it. Life is good! Hold on, speedy! Here are a few things you might have forgotten.

- ✔ Who in your organization is responsible for responding to the alarms your firewall might sound?
- ✔ Who is in charge of setting the policy on which the firewall rules are based?
- ✔ How often are the firewall logs reviewed?
- ✔ How will your organization react when users complain that the firewall unreasonably, they claim, denies them access to some spot on the Internet?

Chapter 18

Ten Things to Add to Your Corporate Security Policy

*W*hat? You don't have a corporate computer policy? You wouldn't build a house without a blueprint, would you (though the author's builder did)? There's no way to really know if you're secure, or at least know if you are meeting your own accepted level of security, if you don't have a policy to check against. This chapter provides you with a starting point for building that policy. You won't find every possible element here (hey, the publisher said I could only write ten or so things), but you'll get a greater head start in writing your policy by reading this chapter than if you started with just a blank piece of paper.

Who Is in Charge around Here?

It's not a project without a plan, and every plan needs an owner. Consider placing someone in charge of security. Call this person the Chief Security Officer (CSO), raise their pay, give them the best parking spot, whatever. Just be sure that at least one person is thinking about security at all times. Without a central focal point, you'll experience too many scenarios of one administrator in your organization thinking the other administrator was looking out for some risk or checking some audit log, and vice versa. Better yet, hire the CSO, hand them this chapter, and then let them write the corporate security policy.

Who's Watching for Viruses?

Virus protection shouldn't be an afterthought. Don't think that virus issues aren't related to security: A particularly malicious virus can do more damage than a mean-spirited hacker in a fraction of the time. Also, don't leave the responsibility to the users to ask for and then install on their own virus protection software. Instead, install a virus protection program on each network computer via group policy and update the definitions as often as possible.

The two leading companies providing virus protection are Symantec at www.symantec.com and McAfee at www.mcafee.com.

Here's where the policy comes into play.

✔ Is your organization (administrators and users) educated on the threat posed by viruses and the things they can do to prevent spreading them throughout the organization?

✔ Who is responsible for acquiring the latest virus definitions?

✔ What should users do when their virus protection software sounds an alarm? Do the users know the answer?

✔ Do you have a policy regarding bringing floppy disks into the office?

✔ Do you allow e-mail messages with attachments to reach users' machines, or are they dumped at a holding PC?

Password Policies

By using Windows 2000's support for complicated passwords, you can be sure that users do not enter 1 2 3 4 as their password. Also, you can legislate how often users change their password. At the same time, there's no easy way to be sure that users aren't taking the easy road when they create their passwords. Here are some sample rules to add to the policy. Be sure that your user community sees these rules and abides by them:

✔ Intersperse (that means mix) capital and lowercase letters and letters and numbers (1ToughPaSsWord9).

✔ Do not use names of family members.

✔ Do not use birthdays or phone numbers.

✔ Do not use a sequence of numbers or letters (for example, ABCDE, 123456).

✔ Do not use a repeating sequence of characters (for example, 111111).

✔ Do not pick words out of the dictionary (hackers can easily use a data-base of dictionary words to attack a logon).

✔ Do not use names of favorite anythings (foods, friends, cars, and Australian Rules football teams).

✔ Do not write passwords down.

Physical Security and Asset Protection

Security isn't just about software. You need to consider the physical security protecting your building and your servers.

✔ Does your corporate security policy concern itself with access to the server rooms?

✔ Do you have a policy about visitors? A small company might skimp on these details, but a small company with a great idea has as much to lose as a large company.

✔ How about backups? How often should they be run? Where should the media that the backups were created on be stored? Who can get the media if need be? Who is their backup?

✔ How about fault tolerance? Is your building grounded? Are UPSs (unin-terrupted power supplies) in use in your organization? Have you thought about the use of RAID (redundant arrays of inexpensive disks) systems to protect against disk failure as a result of attack or otherwise?

✔ Have you checked out the cleaning crews and/or the security guards?

True story from the security files

One weekend day a few years ago, I stopped by the offices of the company that employed me in the mid-1990s to finish up some work. I noticed the security guard who was on duty at the front desk (and who had signed me in) walk past my office. About 15 minutes later, I got up to take a break. When I walked past the cube of our department's administrative assistant, I discovered the guard at the PC in the cube! I asked him what he was doing. He reported he was brows-ing the Web for cheap travel reservations. I suggested he head back to his post downstairs. Now, consider the problems. The administrative assistant had left her computer running. The account was in an active, logged-on state on the network. What if the security guard was up to no good? At the minimum, knowing nothing of the location of sensitive information, this fellow had full access to the company's Intranet. What if he were doing some snooping for a competi-tor? Incredible!

What's Secret, What's Not

When it comes to data, someone must figure out what needs to be secured and what doesn't need to be. While it's rare for one person, like a new Chief Security Officer, to know the relative security value of a software design specification versus an earnings announcement prerelease draft, there should be some process so that users can know how to properly secure their data.

Test Planning

Before you go to bed at night, do you check the doors and windows? Do you give a quick twist to every doorknob leading to the outside? Do you take a quick peek outside? Now the hard question: Who is doing the same type of things for your network, and what are those things?

Third-party companies would love to spend some of your organization's money if you hire them to audit the security at your organization. You can save yourself some money with the purchase of a port scanner to check services running on your TCP/IP ports. How about a war dialer? What better way to check the stability of your remote access protection than by trying to break in on your own?

A *war dialer* is a software program that is used to dial a large list of phone numbers quickly, noting the response from the number being called, and usually watching specifically for the tones sounded by a modem. The war dialer is used to determine phone numbers a hacker might target, now knowing the modem, a possible breach point, sits at the other end of the number.

You Installed What?

Do users in your organization run to the software store at lunch to buy the latest shoot-em-up game? Do users typically install versions of software other than the corporate standard? What does your organization think about users installing software without your approval on their computers? While most software installed by users is harmless and is more a function of personal preference, your policy should account for all software. How can you be sure that users don't install a piece of malicious software, thinking that it was a game given to them by cousin Harold? Consider all the protection you place at your network walls with firewalls, encryption, and authentication. Consider how useless all of that protection is when Ralph in Receiving installs something nasty on his computer.

What, When, and Who to Audit

Windows 2000 provides pretty good tools for auditing access to all kinds of things on the network. There's not much value in the software, though, if you don't use it.

- ✔ What events do you audit?

- ✔ If you audit everything, the logs become huge and impossible to inspect on a regular basis. If you don't audit enough, you might miss an intrusion attempt.

- ✔ Who reviews the logs?

- ✔ Where are logs archived?

The Authentication and Encryption Assessment

So now that you have Windows 2000, what are you going to do with it? This book presents options and advice; now you have to figure out what's right for your organization, especially regarding authentication:

- ✔ Does Kerberos sound good to you? (For more on Kerberos, see Chapter 1.)

- ✔ Should you significantly upgrade your authentication efforts with smart cards?

- ✔ Does your business require even stronger authentication schemes, such as the use of bio-tech devices (for example, fingerprint scanners)?

- ✔ Are digital certificates/public key-support efforts worth the return? Don't forget, it's a bit more work to maintain a Windows 2000 CA or to interface with a third party like VeriSign.

How about encryption?

- ✔ What encryption do you use?

- ✔ Are there pre-Windows 2000 clients out there who may not be capable of the most challenging encryption?

- ✔ How about your partners? How secure are the businesses you do business with?

- ✔ Are some of your users in locations where they cannot legally obtain the encryption tools that you can?

What-If Scenarios

An important part of any corporate security policy is contingency planning. Has anyone thought about what you'd do if you found your Web site had been disfigured? Does anyone know how to shut down the web server? What if you found out you'd been hacked? Then what?

Checking the Insiders

The number you see most often for the percent of Windows NT violations by insiders is anywhere from 60 to 80! With that in mind, does your security policy consider the following?

- ✔ Background checks for new hires
- ✔ Rules concerning your employees' rights to discuss your organization when they participate in newsgroups after hours (are they mistakenly giving away secrets?)
- ✔ Limited network access for some new hires
- ✔ More robust auditing for new hires during a probationary period
- ✔ Timing of surprise audits of existing hires' event logs

Appendix

About the CD

• •

*O*n the CD-ROM, you'll find Proxy Server, Microsoft's firewall and web cache application.

System Requirements

Make sure that your computer meets the following minimum system requirements listed. If your computer doesn't match up to most of these requirements, you may have problems using the contents of the CD.

- ✔ A PC with a Pentium 90 MHz or faster processor.
- ✔ Microsoft Windows 2000 or Windows NT 4.0 with Microsoft Internet Explorer 5 or later
- ✔ At least 32MB of total RAM installed on your computer (64 MB recommended).
- ✔ At least 230MB of hard drive space available to install all the software from this CD. (You need less space if you don't install every program.)
- ✔ A CD-ROM drive — quad-speed or faster.
- ✔ A monitor capable of displaying at least 256 colors or grayscale.
- ✔ Either a working connection to the Internet and/or connection to the LAN/WAN, depending on the purpose of the application.

Using the CD with Microsoft Windows

To install the items from the CD to your hard drive, follow these steps.

1. **Insert the CD into your computer's CD-ROM drive.**
2. **Click Start⇨Run.**
3. **In the Run dialog box that appears, type** D:\SETUP.EXE.

   Replace *D* with the proper drive letter if your CD-ROM drive uses a different letter. (If you don't know the letter, see how your CD-ROM drive is listed under My Computer.)

4. **Click OK.**

   A license agreement window appears.

5. **Read through the license agreement, nod your head, and then click the Accept button if you want to use the CD — after you click Accept, you'll never be bothered by the License Agreement window again.**

   The CD interface Welcome screen appears. The interface is a little program that shows you what's on the CD and coordinates installing the programs and running the demos. The interface basically enables you to click a button or two to make things happen.

6. **Click anywhere on the Welcome screen to enter the interface.**

   Now you are getting to the action. This next screen lists categories for the software on the CD.

7. **To view the items within a category, just click the category's name.**

   A list of programs in the category appears.

8. **For more information about a program, click the program's name.**

   Be sure to read the information that appears. Sometimes a program has its own system requirements or requires you to do a few tricks on your computer before you can install or run the program, and this screen tells you what you might need to do, if necessary.

9. **If you don't want to install the program, click the Back button to return to the previous screen.**

   You can always return to the previous screen by clicking the Back button. This feature allows you to browse the different categories and products as well as decide what you want to install.

10. **To install a program, click the appropriate Install button.**

    The CD interface drops to the background while the CD installs the program you chose.

11. **To install other items, repeat Steps 7 through 10.**

12. **When you've finished installing programs, click the Quit button to close the interface.**

    You can eject the CD now. Carefully place it back in the plastic jacket of the book for safekeeping.

In order to run some of the programs on the *Windows 2000 Server Security For Dummies* CD-ROM, you may need to keep the CD inside your CD-ROM drive. This is a Good Thing. Otherwise, the installed program would have required you to install a very large chunk of the program to your hard drive, which may have kept you from installing other software.

What You'll Find

Here's a list of the software you'll find on the CD. Please take note of the version of the software provided. Some versions will not work after the trial-period is over. Some ask that you pay the vendor if you decide to keep the software.

✔ **Interceptor 1.0:** Tired of dealing with junk e-mail? Interceptor 1.0 from Grok Developments, Ltd. works with a POP3 e-mail program, like Outlook, to filter unwanted e-mail. The version provided on the CD is good for a 30-day evaluation. You can find more information about interceptor 1.0 at www.grok.co.uk.

✔ **ISS Internet Scanner:** Internet Scanner, from Internet Security Systems (www.iss.net) is a great product for evaluating your network's security configuration. The product interrogates, analyzes, and then reports on your network's relative vulnerability.

✔ **Profile Maker 2000 v3.03:** This product, from Automated Profile Management, LLC (www.autoprof.com), helps you manage users' access to its e-mail from any workstation on the network. The application works with Microsoft Exchange server, which means your clients will be using Microsoft Outlook.

During installation, Windows asks you if you want to associate .PRF files with Profile Maker 2000. Doing so doesn't affect the performance of Windows 2000 or other programs, so go ahead and click Yes.

✔ **Emergency Undelete for Windows NT:** This product helps you undelete files mistakenly deleted from network drives or local workstations. The version on the CD is provided with a 30-day trial from Executive Software International, Inc (www.execsoft.com).

This product is designed for use with Windows NT 4.0 only, and the Windows 2000 version was unavailable at the time of publication. If you want to use this product under Windows 2000, please check the preceding Web site for updates.

✔ **Cookie Pal:** Cookie Pal helps users manage the requests to store cookies on their workstation as they browse the Web. Cookies are small files that Web sites like to store on users' computers, making it easy for sites to know whether a visitor is a repeat visitor, as well as where they browsed to the last time they visited. Cookie Pal is provided on the CD as shareware by Kookaburra Software (www.kburra.com).

✔ **Synchronicity 2:** Synchronicity helps you manage users' passwords by synchronizing their Windows NT4 or Windows 2000 passwords with passwords they use for Lotus Notes and Novell Netware. In addition, the product alerts you when someone changes a user's password. This product is provided as a 30-day trial version from NetVision Inc. (www.netvision.com).

This product requires the Novell NetWare Client Version 4.0 for NT, and higher to run.

✔ **SpamKiller:** This product, provided on the CD as shareware, helps you intercept electronic advertisements, known as SPAM, as they head toward your inbox. You can use this product with either POP3 or MAPI e-mail clients. You can filter incoming e-mail by sender, country code, message subject, message text, and more. SpamKiller is published by Novasoft.

✔ **SmartFilter for MS Proxy Server v2.1:** Installing this product is a two-step process. Ensure that you follow the numbered steps in the CD interface. This product is an add-on to Microsoft Proxy Server 2.0, which is also provided on the CD. SmartFilter, from Secure Computing Corporation (www.securecomputing.com), helps network administrators manage users' access to sites on the Web. The product filters URLs, allowing or denying users access to URLs specified by the administrator. The product provides prebuilt lists of URLs and also lets the administrator customize the messages that appear when users attempt to access an outlawed site. The version of the CD is provided as an evaluation version.

✔ **FREEping v1.0:** Want to know when there's trouble with one of your servers? FREEping from Simac Software Products (www.tools4nt.com) will ping all of your servers and send you a pop-up message when one doesn't respond. FREEping is on the CD.

✔ **MS Proxy Server 2.0:** The CD includes an evaluation copy of Microsoft (www.microsoft.com) Proxy Server product. Proxy Server lets you manage the traffic in and out of your network. In addition, the product provides Web cache capabilities, which manage the access to resources on the Web for users on the network.

✔ **Internet Explorer 5.0:** Windows 2000 ships with Microsoft Internet Explorer 5.0, but Windows NT 4.0 may need an upgrade to IE5 before other software can work with it. Also, you may need to reinstall IE5 or some of its components onto Windows 2000 sometime in the future.

If You've Got Problems (Of the CD Kind)

I tried my best to compile programs that work on most computers with the minimum system requirements. Alas, your computer may differ, and some programs may not work properly for some reason.

The most likely problems are that you don't have sufficient rights to install the software, you don't have enough memory (RAM) for the programs you want to use, or you have other programs running that are affecting installation or running of a program. If you get error messages like insufficient privilges or Not enough memory or Setup cannot continue, try one or more of these methods and then try using the software again:

- ✔ **Logon with sufficient privileges.** The installation programs may require you to be logged on with administrator-level rights. If you can log on with these rights, do so. Otherwise, you will have to get help from someone with those rights.

- ✔ **Close all running programs.** The more programs you're running, the less memory is available to other programs. Installers also typically update files and programs; if you keep other programs running, installation may not work properly.

- ✔ **In Windows, close the CD interface and run demos or installations directly from Windows Explorer.** The interface itself can tie up system memory, or even conflict with certain kinds of interactive demos. Use Windows Explorer to browse the files on the CD and launch installers or demos.

If you still have trouble installing the items from the CD, please call the IDG Books Worldwide Customer Service phone number: 800-762-2974 (outside the U.S.: 317-596-5430).

Index

• *R* •

● *X* ●

● *Z* ●

IDG Books Worldwide, Inc., End-User License Agreement

READ THIS. You should carefully read these terms and conditions before opening the software packet(s) included with this book ("Book"). This is a license agreement ("Agreement") between you and IDG Books Worldwide, Inc. ("IDGB"). By opening the accompanying software packet(s), you acknowledge that you have read and accept the following terms and conditions. If you do not agree and do not want to be bound by such terms and conditions, promptly return the Book and the unopened software packet(s) to the place you obtained them for a full refund.

1. **License Grant.** IDGB grants to you (either an individual or entity) a nonexclusive license to use one copy of the enclosed software program(s) (collectively, the "Software") solely for your own personal or business purposes on a single computer (whether a standard computer or a workstation component of a multiuser network). The Software is in use on a computer when it is loaded into temporary memory (RAM) or installed into permanent memory (hard disk, CD-ROM, or other storage device). IDGB reserves all rights not expressly granted herein.

2. **Ownership.** IDGB is the owner of all right, title, and interest, including copyright, in and to the compilation of the Software recorded on the disk(s) or CD-ROM ("Software Media"). Copyright to the individual programs recorded on the Software Media is owned by the author or other authorized copyright owner of each program. Ownership of the Software and all proprietary rights relating thereto remain with IDGB and its licensers.

3. **Restrictions on Use and Transfer.**

   (a) You may only (i) make one copy of the Software for backup or archival purposes, or (ii) transfer the Software to a single hard disk, provided that you keep the original for backup or archival purposes. You may not (i) rent or lease the Software, (ii) copy or reproduce the Software through a LAN or other network system or through any computer subscriber system or bulletin-board system, or (iii) modify, adapt, or create derivative works based on the Software.

   (b) You may not reverse engineer, decompile, or disassemble the Software. You may transfer the Software and user documentation on a permanent basis, provided that the transferee agrees to accept the terms and conditions of this Agreement and you retain no copies. If the Software is an update or has been updated, any transfer must include the most recent update and all prior versions.

4. **Restrictions on Use of Individual Programs.** You must follow the individual requirements and restrictions detailed for each individual program in the Appendix of this Book. These limitations are also contained in the individual license agreements recorded on the Software Media. These limitations may include a requirement that after using the program for a specified period of time, the user must pay a registration fee or discontinue use. By opening the Software packet(s), you will be agreeing to abide by the licenses and restrictions for these individual programs that are detailed in the Appendix and on the Software Media. None of the material on this Software Media or listed in this Book may ever be redistributed, in original or modified form, for commercial purposes.

5. **Limited Warranty.**

   (a) IDGB warrants that the Software and Software Media are free from defects in materials and workmanship under normal use for a period of sixty (60) days from the date of purchase of this Book. If IDGB receives notification within the warranty period of defects in materials or workmanship, IDGB will replace the defective Software Media.

   (b) IDGB AND THE AUTHOR OF THE BOOK DISCLAIM ALL OTHER WARRANTIES, EXPRESS OR IMPLIED, INCLUDING WITHOUT LIMITATION IMPLIED WARRANTIES OF MERCHANTABILITY AND FITNESS FOR A PARTICULAR PURPOSE, WITH RESPECT TO THE SOFTWARE, THE PROGRAMS, THE SOURCE CODE CONTAINED THEREIN, AND/OR THE TECHNIQUES DESCRIBED IN THIS BOOK. IDGB DOES NOT WARRANT THAT THE FUNCTIONS CONTAINED IN THE SOFTWARE WILL MEET YOUR REQUIREMENTS OR THAT THE OPERATION OF THE SOFTWARE WILL BE ERROR FREE.

   (c) This limited warranty gives you specific legal rights, and you may have other rights that vary from jurisdiction to jurisdiction.

6. **Remedies.**

   (a) IDGB's entire liability and your exclusive remedy for defects in materials and workmanship shall be limited to replacement of the Software Media, which may be returned to IDGB with a copy of your receipt at the following address: Software Media Fulfillment Department, Attn.: *Windows 2000 Server Security For Dummies*, IDG Books Worldwide, Inc., 7260 Shadeland Station, Ste. 100, Indianapolis, IN 46256, or call 800-762-2974. Please allow three to four weeks for delivery. This Limited Warranty is void if failure of the Software Media has resulted from accident, abuse, or misapplication. Any replacement Software Media will be warranted for the remainder of the original warranty period or thirty (30) days, whichever is longer.

   (b) In no event shall IDGB or the author be liable for any damages whatsoever (including without limitation damages for loss of business profits, business interruption, loss of business information, or any other pecuniary loss) arising from the use of or inability to use the Book or the Software, even if IDGB has been advised of the possibility of such damages.

   (c) Because some jurisdictions do not allow the exclusion or limitation of liability for consequential or incidental damages, the above limitation or exclusion may not apply to you.

7. **U.S. Government Restricted Rights.** Use, duplication, or disclosure of the Software by the U.S. Government is subject to restrictions stated in paragraph (c)(1)(ii) of the Rights in Technical Data and Computer Software clause of DFARS 252.227-7013, and in subparagraphs (a) through (d) of the Commercial Computer–Restricted Rights clause at FAR 52.227-19, and in similar clauses in the NASA FAR supplement, when applicable.

8. **General.** This Agreement constitutes the entire understanding of the parties and revokes and supersedes all prior agreements, oral or written, between them and may not be modified or amended except in a writing signed by both parties hereto that specifically refers to this Agreement. This Agreement shall take precedence over any other documents that may be in conflict herewith. If any one or more provisions contained in this Agreement are held by any court or tribunal to be invalid, illegal, or otherwise unenforceable, each and every other provision shall remain in full force and effect.

Installation Instructions

To install the items from the CD to your hard drive, follow these steps.

1. **Insert the CD into your computer's CD-ROM drive.**

2. **Click Start⇨Run**

3. **In the dialog box, type** D:\SETUP.EXE.

4. **Click OK.**

5. **Read through the license agreement, nod your head, and then click the Accept button if you want to use the CD — after you click Accept, you'll never be bothered by the License Agreement window again.**

6. **Click anywhere on the Welcome screen to enter the interface.**

7. **To view the items within a category, just click the category's name.**

8. **For more information about a program, click the program's name.**

9. **If you don't want to install the program, click the Back button to return to the previous screen.**

10. **To install a program, click the appropriate Install button.**

11. **To install other items, repeat Steps 6 – 9.**

12. **When you've finished installing programs, click the Quit button to close the interface.**

In order to run some of the programs on the *Windows 2000 Server Security For Dummies* CD-ROM, you may need to keep the CD inside your CD-ROM drive. This is a Good Thing. Otherwise, the installed program would have required you to install a very large chunk of the program to your hard drive, which may have kept you from installing other software.

IDG BOOKS WORLDWIDE
BOOK REGISTRATION

We want to hear from you!

Visit **http://my2cents.dummies.com** to register this book and tell us how you liked it!

- Get entered in our monthly prize giveaway.

- Give us feedback about this book — tell us what you like best, what you like least, or maybe what you'd like to ask the author and us to change!

- Let us know any other *...For Dummies*® topics that interest you.

Your feedback helps us determine what books to publish, tells us what coverage to add as we revise our books, and lets us know whether we're meeting your needs as a *...For Dummies* reader. You're our most valuable resource, and what you have to say is important to us!

Not on the Web yet? It's easy to get started with *Dummies 101*®: *The Internet For Windows*® *98* or *The Internet For Dummies*, 6th Edition, at local retailers everywhere.

Or let us know what you think by sending us a letter at the following address:

...For Dummies Book Registration
Dummies Press
7260 Shadeland Station, Suite 100
Indianapolis, IN 46256-3917
Fax 317-596-5498

BESTSELLING
BOOK SERIES